D0535588

PROPHETS OF WAR

ALSO BY WILLIAM D. HARTUNG

Lessons from Iraq: Avoiding the Next War
(co-edited with Miriam Pemberton)

How Much Are You Making on the War, Daddy?
A Quick and Dirty Guide to War Profiteering in the
George W. Bush Administration

And Weapons for All

PROPHETS OF WAR

Lockheed Martin AND THE Making OF THE Military-Industrial Complex

WILLIAM D. HARTUNG

NATION
BOOKS
New York

Published by Nation Books,
A Member of the Perseus Books Group
116 East 16th Street, 8th Floor
New York, NY 10003

Nation Books is a co-publishing venture of the Nation Institute
and the Perseus Books Group.

Books published by Nation Books are available at special discounts for
bulk purchases in the United States by corporations, institutions, and other
organizations. For more information, please contact the Special Markets
Department at the Perseus Books Group, 2300 Chestnut Street, Suite 200,
Philadelphia, PA 19103, or call (800) 810-4145, ext. 5000, or e-mail
special.markets@perseusbooks.com.

Designed by Brent Wilcox

Library of Congress Cataloging-in-Publication Data
Hartung, William D.
    Prophets of war : Lockheed Martin and the making of the military-
industrial complex / William D. Hartung.
        p.   cm.
    Includes bibliographical references and index.
    ISBN 978-1-56858-420-1 (alk. paper)
    1. Lockheed Corporation.   2. Lockheed Martin.   3. Aircraft
industry—Corrupt practices.   4. Military-industrial complex—United
States.   5. Defense contracts—United States.   I. Title.
    HD9711.U64L635 2011
    338.7'62910973—dc22
                                                                2010039571

10 9 8 7 6 5 4 3 2

To Ruth F. Hartung
(1920–1997)

Contents

1 THE RISE AND FALL OF THE RAPTOR   1

2 FROM LOUGHEAD TO LOCKHEED   31

3 FROM WAR TO COLD WAR   51

4 THE C-5A SCANDAL   69

5 BAILOUT: TOO BIG TO FAIL?   95

6 BRIBERY   115

7 REAGAN TO THE RESCUE   133

8 SAINT AUGUSTINE'S LAWS   163

9 THE ADVOCATE   191

10 GLOBAL DOMINATION   215

Acknowledgments   251
Notes   253
Index   279

Chapter 1

THE RISE AND FALL OF THE RAPTOR

It is a striking ad. An intimidating combat aircraft soars in the background, with the slogan up front in all capital letters: 300 MILLION PROTECTED, 95,000 EMPLOYED. The ad—for Lockheed Martin's F-22 Raptor fighter plane—was part of the company's last-gasp effort to save one of its most profitable weapons from being "terminated," as they say in standard budget parlance. The pro–F-22 ad ran scores of times, in print, on political websites, and even in Washington's Metro. One writer at the *Washington Post* joked that at a time when many companies had been cutting back on their advertising budgets, Lockheed Martin's barrage of full-page ads in February and March 2009 was the main thing keeping the paper afloat.

When an arms company starts bragging about how many jobs its pet project creates, hold on to your wallet. It often means that the company wants billions of dollars' worth of your tax money for a weapon that costs too much, does too little, and may not have been needed in the first place. So it is with the Raptor, which at $350 million per plane is the most expensive combat aircraft ever built.[1] Secretary of Defense Robert Gates has suggested that the F-22 needs to be cut because even with wars raging in Iraq and Afghanistan, it has never been used in combat. In fact, in its first "mission"—flying to Japan for deployment at a U.S. air base there—the plane had technical difficulties and had to land in Hawaii, far short of its final destination.

But Lockheed Martin insists that the Raptor's unique capabilities more than justify its huge price tag. For example, did you know that it is the "first and only 24/7/365 All-Weather Stealth Fighter"? That it has a radar signature "approximately the size of a bumblebee"? Or that it provides "first-look, first-shot, first-kill air dominance capability"? Lockheed Martin has a lot to say, and it is serious about selling you its most profitable plane. How else to explain the statement from the F-22 Raptor web page that, "when we meet the enemy, we want to win 100–0, not 51–49"?[2] It is hard to take this claim seriously. The Raptor has never seen combat—and it may never do so given that it was designed to counter a Soviet plane that was never built—so at best the score is zero to zero. But the statement has a grain of truth—it describes Lockheed Martin's lobbying efforts a whole lot more accurately than its fighter plane's mission success rate.

The company never reached its goal of 100–0 support in the Senate, but not for lack of trying. As soon as there was even a whisper of a possibility that the F-22 program would be stopped at "only" 187 planes—about what the Pentagon wanted, but only half of what the Air Force and Lockheed Martin were striving for—the company started racking up big numbers on its side. By early 2009, months in advance of President Barack Obama's first detailed budget submission to Congress—which would decide the fate of the F-22—Lockheed Martin and its partners in the F-22 project (Pratt & Whitney and Boeing) had lined up forty-four senators and two hundred members of the House of Representatives to sign on to a "save the Raptor" letter. A similar letter was sent by twelve governors—including prominent Democrats like David Paterson of New York and Ted Strickland of Ohio. R. Thomas Buffenbarger, the president of the International Association of Machinists and Aerospace Workers (IAM), also weighed in.[3] The governors' letter reads as if it was drafted by Lockheed Martin, which it probably was. "We urge you," it begins, "to sustain 95,000 jobs by certifying continued production of the F-22 Raptor—a defense program that is critical to our defense industrial base." After describing it as "the world's only operational 5th Generation fighter" (a popular Lockheed Martin description of the Raptor), the letter returns to the jobs argument, asking the President to "consider carefully the economic impact of your decision."[4]

At the heart of the lobbying campaign was the mantra of "jobs, jobs, jobs"—jobs in forty-four states, or so the company claimed. Lockheed Martin's PR barely bothered to mention that the F-22 is needed to defend the country; that argument was there in the background, but it wasn't the driving force. Lockheed's ads for the plane got more and more specific as time went on, with a series showing people at work on components of the plane with legends like 2,205 F-22 JOBS IN CONNECTICUT; 125 SKILLED MACHINISTS IN HELENA, MONTANA; 50 TITANIUM MANUFACTURING JOBS IN NILES, OHIO; and 30 HYDRAULIC SYSTEMS SPECIALISTS IN MISSISSIPPI. All that was missing were ads for 132 LOBBYISTS, WASHINGTON, D.C.

There was only one problem with this impressive flurry of job claims: They were grossly exaggerated. Utilizing standard techniques that estimate the numbers of jobs generated by different kinds of economic activities, the $4 billion or so per year that the federal government was spending on the F-22 would create less than half as many jobs as Lockheed was claiming. The estimating method—known as input-output analysis—covers all the bases. It measures every job involved, from directly working on the plane, to working in plants supplying components, to working in the restaurant across the street from the plant where workers spend their wages, and so on.[5]

As for those assertions about where the F-22 jobs were located, when pressed the company refused to back them up. When a *USA Today* reporter asked for details on the locations of F-22 supplier plants, the company claimed that such information was proprietary and refused to provide it.[6] Never mind that Lockheed Martin gets almost all of its revenues and profits from the federal government—when it's time to come clean about how it is using our tax money, it's none of our business.[7]

But whatever the exact number is, a job is a job is a job. And unlike many government programs whose impact is more dispersed, a military contract generates jobs in large, identifiable locations that can be directly linked to decisions made by the President and the Congress.

Add to that the money and lobbying muscle of a company like Lockheed Martin and it's a tough combination to beat. Members of Congress don't want to have someone say that they voted against jobs in their state or district—or didn't do enough to keep jobs there. And when a factory scales back or empties out, it's hard to miss. The irony is that almost any other form of spending, from education to health care to mass transit to weatherizing buildings—even a tax cut—creates more jobs than military spending.[8] For example, if the F-22 gets funding and spending on other public investments goes down accordingly, there will be a net *loss* of jobs nationwide. But most of these other jobs are less visible and more widely dispersed, and most importantly, their advocates lack the well-oiled lobbying machine that a firm like Lockheed Martin can bring to bear.

This wasn't the first time the future of the F-22 had been threatened. Back in 1999, the odd couple of the late Representative John "Jack" Murtha (D-PA) and Representative Jerry Lewis (R-CA) teamed up to withhold production funding from the F-22 in protest over the program's huge cost overruns. There was no immediate question of ending the program, just a pause to get the company's—and the Air Force's—attention.[9] But to make sure that the pause didn't become more than a pause, Lockheed Martin pulled out all the stops, deploying Republican ex-Senator Matt Mattingly of Georgia and former House members like Democrats "Buddy" Darden of Georgia and G. V. "Sonny" Montgomery of Mississippi as paid lobbyists. From a luxury box at a Baltimore Orioles game to the steam room of the House gymnasium—fair game to ex-members like Montgomery and Darden—the urgent message went out that allowing funding to slip for even a few months might strike a devastating blow to our security and our economy. Representative James Moran (D-VA) was taken aback when Sonny Montgomery confronted him in the House steam room: "We sat on the sauna naked together and talked about the F-22. . . . That's the advantage former members have."[10]

Lockheed Martin even went so far as to send its then-CEO, Vance Coffman, to visit Lewis and Murtha face to face. Coffman complained bitterly to Lewis that "you went around our back, you didn't give us a heads-up." Coffman also showed up at Murtha's office.

Murtha—an ex-Marine who embodied the word "gruff"—had heard about Coffman's meeting with Lewis. He was furious, telling Coffman, "Don't ever [mess] with my chairman again." Murtha then said, "I think you better leave," only to relent and grudgingly let Coffman make his case.[11]

Despite the chilly reception from Lewis and Murtha, Lockheed wasn't about to give up. Former Senator Dale Bumpers (D-AR) described its efforts as "one of the most massive lobbying efforts I've ever witnessed."[12] The Lockheed Martin campaign included a push by the 570,000-member IAM to lobby key senators. The IAM's Washington lobbyist held out hope for this approach because jobs "are the one thing they [members of Congress] understand."[13]

Meanwhile, the Air Force wasn't exactly sitting on its hands. Although technically prohibited from lobbying Congress, the Air Force formed a "Raptor Recovery Team," which, according to General Claude Bolton, put on "a full court press to tell our senior leadership in Congress . . . that we believe the Air Force and the country need this." The Air Force called its pressure tactics an "informational" activity and therefore got away with them despite the restrictions on lobbying members of Congress.[14]

✳ ✳ ✳

In the meantime, Lockheed's arguments on the military need for the plane prompted sharp responses even among those who thought the plane was a "technological marvel," as one company spokesperson put it. Williamson Murray of the Army War College was one such critic: "The F-22 is the best fighter in the world, no doubt about it. But there ain't any opposition out there. It's sort of like holding a boxing tournament for a high school and bringing Mike Tyson in."[15]

The F-22's growing cost caused its own concerns. It was so expensive that it threatened to crowd out spending on other combat aircraft.[16] It was a question of blowing billions now on a plane with no clear mission or saving up some money to buy the planes of the future.

At this point the plan was to buy 339 planes for a projected cost of over $62 billion—up from an initial proposal to buy 750 planes for a total price of $25 billion. That's more than half as many planes for well over twice the price. How could this happen? Unfortunately, all too easily. First, Lockheed Martin put in a low bid, knowing full well that the planes would cost far more than its initial estimates. This approach, known in the business as "buying in," allows a company to get the contract first and then jack up the price later. Then the Air Force engaged in what is known as "gold-plating"—setting new and ever more difficult performance requirements after the plane was already in development. Last but not least, Lockheed Martin simply screwed up certain aspects of the plane's production, even as it gouged the Pentagon on costs for overhead and spare parts. As we will see later, this is a time-tested approach that virtually guarantees massive cost overruns.

All of this didn't sit well with Lewis and Murtha. The two congressmen argued that the funds allocated for the Raptor would be better spent on pilot training, aerial refueling planes, surveillance aircraft, and upgraded F-15 fighter planes (the generation of combat aircraft that came prior to the F-22). The Army quietly but firmly agreed. Army officials had noted that the service could equip a whole division—as many as fifteen thousand soldiers—for the cost of one F-22.[17] The Army/Air Force split over the F-22 was an example of "interservice rivalry"—the competition among the Army, Navy, Air Force, and Marines for the largest possible share of the Pentagon budget pie. These battles generally occur behind the scenes, but the details occasionally leak out, as in the case of the F-22. It's one of the complexities of the military-industrial complex: The military part of the complex is often divided against itself, not about how much to spend on the Pentagon, but about what to spend it on.

The future of the F-22 was finally decided in October 1999, and Lockheed Martin won in a split decision. The final deal gave the company $2.5 billion—less than the amount originally budgeted by the Clinton administration but more than the reduced level sought by Lewis and Murtha. In addition, the funding package called for more testing before the program could go full speed ahead.

* * *

The lesson for Lewis, Murtha, and the other congressional critics of the F-22 seemed to be "don't mess with Lockheed Martin." But they took solace in having at least succeeded in imposing a requirement for further testing. As for Lockheed, it learned that its lobbying machine could get the job done, although a number of observers suggested that it needed to revamp its approach to avoid being caught off guard in the future.

Cost concerns over the F-22 lingered into the early months of the George W. Bush administration, with some of his advisers suggesting that it might be necessary to kill or dramatically cut back the program to make room for other systems. But as it turned out, a second rescue of the Raptor wasn't necessary. The tragic terrorist attacks of September 11, 2001, radically changed the character of the military budget debate. A massive increase in Pentagon spending and a new attitude toward security combined to save the F-22 and other threatened projects from potential cuts. To give a sense of the magnitude of the shift, the *increase* in military spending from 2001 through 2003 was more than the *entire military budget* of most countries, including major powers like the United Kingdom and China.[18] In this new climate, no major weapon system was likely to be cut, no matter how irrelevant it may have been to fighting Al Qaeda. As Harry Stonechipher, then Vice President of Lockheed Martin's chief rival Boeing, put it in an interview with the *Wall Street Journal*, "the purse is now open," and "any member of Congress who doesn't vote for the funds we need to defend this country will be looking for a new job after next November."[19]

In light of political precedent, anyone looking at the situation when the Obama administration came into the White House would have concluded that the F-22 would inevitably survive any potential budgetary threat, just as it had during the Clinton and Bush years. Despite the pledge of Obama administration Defense Secretary Robert Gates to cut outmoded systems from the military budget, the popular wisdom was that the F-22 would be spared, owing to Lockheed's lobbying clout.

But the conventional wisdom was wrong. Not only did Gates eliminate funding for additional F-22s, but he also made it clear that doing so was among the easier decisions he had to make.

At an April 6, 2009, press conference, Gates cited the need to "rebalance this department's programs" to enable it to "fight the wars we are in today and the scenarios we are most likely to face in the years ahead." In what appeared to be a rhetorical preemptive strike against opponents of particular cuts, Gates put his decisions in a strategic perspective: "Every defense dollar spent to over insure against a remote or diminishing risk, or in effect to run up the score in a capability where the United States is already dominant, is a dollar not available to take care of our people . . . [and to help] win the wars we are in and improve capabilities where we are underinvested and potentially vulnerable."[20] In keeping with that perspective, Gates announced a $13 billion increase in spending on military personnel, for everything from salaries for new troops to military health care to child care, housing, and education. Gates also added $2 billion for "drones" like the Predator, an unmanned aircraft that was to cause such controversy when it launched missile strikes in the border areas of Pakistan as part of the Obama administration's stepped-up war in the region. He also proposed a 5 percent increase in funding for the Special Forces, the leading edge of any counterinsurgency effort.

The Defense Secretary also announced a series of *increases* in weapons spending, including an additional $4 billion for the F-35 Joint Strike Fighter (JSF), which, like the F-22, is a Lockheed Martin product. Referring to his strategic mix of cuts and increases—akin to what Representatives Jerry Lewis and Jack Murtha had tried to do in their fight to slow the F-22 program a decade earlier—Gates bragged that his decisions had done "a pretty good job, I think, of taking care of the industrial base."[21]

It was in this context that Gates revealed that he was ending the F-22 program at 187 aircraft: the 183 that had already been purchased and four more that were included in the fiscal year 2009 emergency appropriations for Iraq and Afghanistan. Given that Gates had repeatedly stressed that the F-22 had never been used in Iraq or Afghanistan, putting the four planes in the emergency appropriation for the wars was essentially a going-away present to Lockheed Martin that would extend production of the F-22 from late 2011 into mid-2012. Three more years of production was hardly the emergency the company and its allies had intimated in its lobbying materials and newspaper ads, which made it sound like ninety-five thousand jobs would disappear overnight if Congress failed to fund more F-22s.

The Gates decision sparked a minor uproar, as members of Congress such as Senator Saxby Chambliss (R-GA), Senator Joseph Lieberman (I-CT), and Senator Christopher Dodd (D-CT) cried foul and pledged to put up to twenty of the planes back into the fiscal year 2010 budget (compared to the twenty-four that would have been purchased if Gates had agreed to continue the program at prevailing rates). Chambliss promised to fight "as hard as I can" to save the program. Representative Phil Gingrey (R-GA), whose district contains the F-22 assembly plant, searched frantically for somewhere to get the money to keep the F-22 going. He went so far as to issue a bizarre statement to the effect that the plane should be funded in lieu of "wasting money" on developing a vaccine for swine flu. Another Georgia representative, Republican Tom Price, excoriated the President for the F-22 decision: "It's outrageous that President Obama is willing to bury the country under a mountain of debt with his reckless domestic agenda but refuses to fund programs critical to our national defense."[22]

F-22 supporters outside of Congress were even harsher. Retired Lieutenant General Michael Dunn of the Air Force Association—a powerful lobby representing tens of thousands of ex–Air Force personnel—argued that Gates's decisions "may cost us lives and reduce our strategic options in a very dangerous world."[23]

Even as they geared up for a vigorous effort to save the F-22—a campaign described by one former congressional staffer as verging on "an ugly food fight"—Lockheed Martin supporters were caught short when the company itself appeared to withdraw from the field of battle. In an April 22 conference call with defense industry analysts—just over two weeks after Gates's announcement—Lockheed Martin's Chief Financial Officer (CFO), Bruce L. Tanner, announced that the company would put no more effort into restoring funding for the F-22. "We had our chance to lobby this matter," Tanner said. "We think we had a full hearing of that discussion. We are disappointed with these decisions, but we will accept those and go on."[24] The Lockheed Martin decision was no accident. An observer with inside knowledge of Robert Gates's efforts to terminate the F-22 program said that

Gates called Lockheed Martin CEO Robert Stevens into his office and essentially said, "If you oppose me on this, I'll eat your lunch." Given all the other business the company had with the Pentagon, Lockheed's top management decided to back off on lobbying for the F-22 for fear of alienating the company's biggest customer.

Congressional boosters of the F-22 like Saxby Chambliss and Joe Lieberman—whose state is home to Pratt & Whitney, the engine-builder for the F-22—vowed to carry on the fight for the plane, as did the machinists' union. Jeff Goen, the president of the IAM branch in Marietta, Georgia, continued to play the jobs card: "It doesn't make sense that the government is looking at trying to save or create jobs at the same time it's cutting something like this." The union's political director, Richard Michalski, pledged that its members would send thousands of messages to Congress urging them to restore Gates's proposed cuts when the budget came before them in June or July 2009. "It's going to be about jobs at the end of the day, but not in a selfish way," said Michalski.[25]

For all of his proposed cuts—the elimination or sharp reduction of eight programs—President Obama's proposed military budget still represented an increase over the last year of the Bush administration. The difference was in the distribution of the funds—spending more on personnel and partially shifting funds away from big-ticket items like the F-22 that were designed to address Cold War threats and into systems like the Predator that would be immediately put to use in current conflicts. Secretary Gates had achieved a shift in military spending, not a cut. But even this was no small achievement, given how rarely a major weapon system is eliminated.

Like a chess player looking two moves ahead, Gates had taken the jobs argument into account. While his official position regarding congressional opposition was to say, "My hope is that . . . the members of Congress will look past parochial interests and consider what is in the best interest of the country as a whole," Gates's package of cuts was clearly crafted with the jobs issue in mind. He maintained that the decision was all about the defense needs of the country, but Gates was quick to point out that the job increases resulting from the acceleration of the F-35 program would more than offset the job losses from ending the F-22 program. He indicated that while direct F-22 jobs would fall by eleven thousand—from twenty-four thousand to thirteen thousand—between 2009 and 2011, the F-35 program would gain forty-four thousand jobs over the same time period. Given that Lockheed Martin was also the prime contractor on the F-35, and that many of the same subcontractors involved in the F-22 worked on the F-35, Gates appeared to have trumped the jobs argument.[26]

But that didn't mean there wouldn't be a nasty "food fight" in Congress. The opposition to the cuts was bipartisan, pork-driven, and led by senators whose home states had the biggest stake in the program—Chambliss, whose home state of Georgia housed the F-22's assembly operations, and Dodd, whose state was home to Pratt & Whitney, the producer of the engine for the F-22.

The initial skirmish occurred in the Senate Armed Services Committee, which voted 13–11 to build another seven F-22s, a maneuver that would keep the production line up and running and open the door to the provision of even more funds the following year. The goal of program advocates was to get at least to the Air Force's prior goal of 243 planes, an additional 56 beyond what Gates was willing to buy. That would mean another $10 billion or so in taxpayer money that wouldn't be available for other purposes, military or domestic.

The Armed Services Committee vote reflected the domestic politics of F-22 production, with liberals like Massachusetts Democrats John Kerry and the late Ted Kennedy voting for the plane because they had F-22 work in their state. But the economic tie to Massachusetts was marginal at best. Raytheon, a major Massachusetts-based weapons maker, is responsible for key electronics systems on the plane, but the work is done mostly in California. In explaining his support, Ted Kennedy's office suggested that the senator hoped to see F-22s based at National Guard installations in his state. But even these fairly modest connections were enough to swing the votes of Kerry and Kennedy, perhaps out of the habit of voting for all things Raytheon.[27] Meanwhile, Senator John McCain (R-AZ), President Obama's opponent in the 2008 presidential elections, voted with committee chairman Senator Carl Levin (D-MI) to kill the plane. McCain was to be a key player as the fight moved to the Senate floor.

The vote in the House Armed Services Committee was far more dramatic, with lawmakers staying up until 2:30 in the morning before voting to support $369 million in long lead-time funding to help keep the project going. The vote was 31–30. Confirming the point that a little pork goes a long way, Utah Republican Rob Bishop had sponsored the amendment, even though no significant manufacturing work on the plane would be done in his state. His interest had to do with the fact that F-22s would probably be deployed at Hill Air Force Base in Utah as replacements for three squadrons of F-16s stationed there.[28]

Now that the Armed Services Committees had spoken, the real action moved to the Senate, where a vote would be held on the fate of the F-22 during consideration of the Pentagon budget as a whole. Senators Levin and McCain joined hands to promote an amendment that would strip the money for F-22s that had been added by the Senate Armed Services Committee. The lines were drawn. Given Lockheed Martin's claim that work on the plane was being done in forty-four states (represented by *eighty-eight* of the body's one hundred members), the company seemed to have the odds in its favor, even without putting on a major lobbying campaign in the wake of Gates's decision to cancel the program. But Levin and McCain were not alone. Gates had persuaded President Obama to threaten a veto of any defense bill that included the F-22, the first such veto threat he had made as president. Defense industry analyst David Berteau described the move as "virtually unprecedented," asserting that he "[hadn't] seen anything like it" in his decades in and around the Pentagon and the defense industry.[29]

But Obama did more than threaten a veto. He put the full power of his administration behind the threat, with intense lobbying by Robert Gates and Vice President Joe Biden and White House Chief of Staff Rahm Emanuel "whipping" the issue in the Senate (counting votes and pressuring undecided members to go the administration's way). A few weeks out from the mid-July 2009 vote, Senator Chambliss thought F-22 advocates would win by a comfortable margin, perhaps by as many as eighteen votes. But he didn't count on the effect of the White House's lobbying effort. Gates had told Obama that he couldn't get anything else done on defense budget reform if they lost on the F-22. Obama acted accordingly.

Critical support for the administration's efforts came from a network of arms control and good government organizations that included Women's Action for New Directions, Business Leaders for Sensible Priorities, Taxpayers for Common Sense, Common Cause, Peace Action, the Institute for Policy Studies, and the Project on Government Oversight.[30] Members of these groups generated phone calls, e-mails, and letters while simultaneously working the halls of Congress in support of the Levin-McCain amendment to kill the F-22.

But perhaps the most extraordinary development of all was a speech that Robert Gates gave to the Economic Club of Chicago less than a week before the Senate vote. Gates opened with a dig at the Washington elite, telling his Chicago audience that the District of Columbia was the true "Windy City," a nod to all the hot air expended there. He went on to give a frank assessment of what the administration was up against, noting that the F-22 cuts were meeting a "less than enthusiastic" response from "the Congress, among defense contractors, and within some quarters of the Pentagon itself." He made the "guns-versus-guns" argument, suggesting that the Pentagon was still buying weapons designed for the Cold War even after the 9/11 attacks and the wars in Iraq and Afghanistan had confirmed the need for a different kind of equipment. Rather than framing the debate as a jobs argument, Gates was putting it in the context of what troops in the field needed to be safe and effective. He noted the need to cancel weapon systems that were "grotesquely over budget" and "increasingly detached from real-world scenarios"—a veiled reference to the F-22, among other programs.[31]

As for the F-22 itself, Gates suggested that it could be supplanted by buying more F-35 Joint Strike Fighters, which carried "a superior suite of weapons" that would be better at destroying enemy air defense systems. He also suggested that unmanned aerial vehicles could carry out many of the bombing missions formerly reserved for piloted aircraft like the F-22. As for the issue of the "Chinese threat," Gates noted that by 2025, even without more F-22s, the United States would possess over 1,700 of the most advanced fighter aircraft "versus a handful of comparable aircraft for the Chinese."[32]

But Gates's harshest words were reserved for Congress. Noting that the Obama Pentagon budget was higher than the last budget submitted by George W. Bush, he asserted that, "by one estimate, our budget adds up to what the entire rest of the world spends combined on defense." Said Gates, "Only in the parallel universe that is Washington, D.C., could this be considered 'gutting' defense."[33]

Gates's speech set the tone for the July 21, 2009, debate in the Senate, which sealed the fate of the F-22.

The supporters of killing the plane rallied around the amendment sponsored by Carl Levin and John McCain. McCain wasn't against high military budgets, but he was a longtime opponent of pork barrel projects—weapon systems pushed by the Congress despite the fact that the Pentagon had never requested them. The amendment didn't call for a reduction in the military budget. Instead, it sought a shift of the $1.7 billion that had been added for unnecessary F-22s back into operations and maintenance spending for the Army, Navy, and Air Force. As had happened with the effort by Jack Murtha and Jerry Lewis a decade earlier, this helped insulate the F-22's opponents from charges of being "soft on defense." The amendment would also provide fuel, spare parts, and other support equipment needed to keep America's high-tech military functioning properly.

The arguments from Gates's Chicago speech formed the backbone of the case in favor of the McCain-Levin amendment. Levin started out by warning against buying F-22s for purely "parochial reasons" and then cited the calls from the Secretary of the Air Force, the Air Force Chief of Staff, Joint Chiefs of Staff Chairman Admiral Michael Mullen, and Secretary Gates himself to end the program. The thrust of Levin's argument was that the conflicts the United States will face in the decades to come are more likely to call for F-35 Joint Strike Fighters and unmanned aerial vehicles (UAVs), which are better suited to hitting terrorist sanctuaries and enemy air defense systems. In the much less likely case of an out-and-out air war with a country like China in which the United States would have to shoot down enemy fighter planes, he argued, the current F-22 "buy" of 187 planes would be more than adequate.

Levin cited a passage in Gates's Chicago speech that underscored the absurdity of some of the "new missions" suggested by the plane's supporters. These included "using F-22s to go after Somali pirates who in many cases are teenagers with AK-47s—a job we already know is better done at much lower cost by three Navy SEALS [elite Navy commandos]."[34] The net result of Levin's statement was to make the F-22 proponents look desperate. Coming up next, Saxby Chambliss did nothing to dispel this impression.

Chambliss tried to brush off the views of Gates, Mullen, and other high-ranking officials; they were all appointed by the President and as such could never be truly "independent."[35] Of course, by this logic no presidential decision would be considered valid. Chambliss did have two authorities to cite—the head of the Air Force's air combat branch and the head of the Air National Guard—but neither provided persuasive evidence of the need for F-22s. The heart of the pro–F-22 argument was not strategic but economic, and Chris Dodd was called on to make that case.

Dodd had three main arguments. First, he noted that the added funding for the F-22 was only "two-tenths of one percent of the [military] budget" and that it made no sense to put up to ninety-five thousand jobs at risk for such a "small" sum. Second, he argued that cutting a major program and the jobs associated with it was the wrong thing to do in the midst of a recession. And third, he suggested that it was essential to keep skilled workers engaged in the defense industry in case there was a need to increase production at some future date—an element of what is known as the "defense industrial base" argument.

While perhaps persuasive on the surface, Dodd ignored two key points. For starters, the Gates budget increased spending on the F-35 Joint Strike Fighter at the same time as it terminated the F-22, to the point that there might even be a net jobs *increase* as a result of the Pentagon's new priorities. But even before finishing his first round of arguments, Dodd managed to get in a dig at Levin by referring repeatedly to the tens of billions of dollars spent to bail out the auto industry, the largest employer in Levin's home state of Michigan: "We have provided $63 billion to Chrysler and General Motors to keep their production lines running . . . [and] I worked with my colleagues who represent those States to provide federal assistance."[36]

The implication was that it was time for Levin and others to do for the aerospace industry what they had done for the auto industry by providing financing for the F-22.

From then on, variations on the same arguments were made by each side, just by different speakers. In keeping with the "strange bedfellows" phenomenon generated by pork barrel interests, liberal Senators Barbara Boxer (D-CA) and Patty Murray (D-WA) spoke for the F-22, out of concern for jobs in their states. An interesting interlude was provided by Senator Daniel Inouye, the Hawaii Democrat who has spent two decades as a leading member of the Defense Appropriations Subcommittee of the Senate Appropriations Committee. Inouye was legendary for bringing home the bacon in the form of earmarks for unrequested defense projects. He was proud of this role, describing himself as "the #1 guy for earmarks" in a presentation to a Hawaii business group.[37] Inouye brought home over $206 million in 2009 alone, according to data compiled by the watchdog group Taxpayers for Common Sense. In return, Inouye had received over $117,000 in campaign contributions since January 2007 from companies that benefited from his earmarks, with over half coming from Lockheed Martin.[38]

It was in this context that Inouye made a strong call for the F-22 while lamenting virtually every weapons program termination of the prior twenty-five years. Apparently, Inouye never met a weapon system he didn't like.

Inouye tried to bolster the authority of his case not just by citing his long service on a relevant committee but by noting that "to my knowledge there isn't a single worker in the state of Hawaii whose job is dependent on continuing production of the F-22. . . . I believe that the program merits continued production." But Inouye was telling only half of the story. While there may or may not have been *F-22* jobs in Hawaii, there were significant numbers of *Lockheed Martin* jobs at several facilities in the state. Company activities in the state have included testing components of the Theater High-Altitude Area Defense (THAAD) antimissile system at the Pacific Missile Range Facility in Kauai; experimentation aimed toward the construction of an Ocean Thermal Energy Conversion (OTEC) facility; and the establishment of a 31,000-square-foot facility near the Hawaii airport to coordinate Lockheed Martin's operations across the islands.[39]

The clinching argument for ending the F-22 program came from President Obama's 2008 rival John McCain. For all of their battles during the campaign, this was one issue they could agree on. McCain opened by citing what was at stake:

> This amendment is probably the most impactful amendment I have seen in this body on almost any issue, much less the issue of defense. It boils down to whether we are going to continue the business as usual of once a weapons system gets into full production it never dies or whether we are going to take the necessary steps to reform the acquisition process in this country.

He reminded his fellow senators that a vote for the F-22 would distort defense budget priorities away from what was most needed for "equipping the men and women of the military." He further noted that "the earmarking and pork-barreling of billions of dollars . . . has bred corruption—we have former Members of the Congress residing in federal prison."[40]

McCain ended with a flourish, quoting two paragraphs from President Dwight D. Eisenhower's famous military-industrial complex speech about the "unwarranted influence" of the arms lobby and the need for "an alert and knowledgeable citizenry" to keep it in its rightful place. McCain suggested that the only addition he would make to the speech was to "replace military-industrial complex" with "military-industrial-congressional-complex" in recognition of the role of Congress in funding unnecessary weapon systems like the F-22.[41]

In the end, the McCain-Levin amendment to end F-22 funding won by a significantly larger margin than expected—58–40. Conservative Republicans like Jim DeMint of South Carolina—the man who had suggested that the Republicans could "break" Obama if they blocked his health care plan—as well as John Ensign of Nevada and Judd Gregg of New Hampshire, joined the anti–F-22 bandwagon. Democrats Barbara Boxer (D-CA), Diane Feinstein (D-CA), Patty

Murray (D-WA), and Jeanne Shaheen (D-NH) voted for the plane. All of them had significant F-22 production in their state.

Perhaps the most important lesson of the F-22 vote was that the jobs argument doesn't have to carry the day when it comes to decisions on what weapons to buy. The company's claim that the F-22 was made in forty-four states was exaggerated: Many of these states had only marginal F-22 involvement. Having the President, the Secretary of Defense, and the head of the Joint Chiefs of Staff on record against the plane was obviously a huge boost to F-22 opponents, as was President Obama's threat to veto any bill that included funds for the aircraft. And some Democrats, like Senator John Kerry, switched to the anti–F-22 side for the final vote in part because they felt that it was important for the President to have a "win" as he worked to enact other aspects of his agenda, including health care reform.

The most amazing thing about the F-22 affair was that Lockheed Martin was so large, and involved in so many weapons programs, that in the end, despite all of its alarmist rhetoric, the company may well have come out ahead of the game under the Gates budget package, owing in large part to the counterbalancing increases in the F-35 Joint Strike Fighter, designed to be the largest program in the history of military aviation.

Without the Joint Strike Fighter, the loss of the F-22 would have hit Lockheed Martin a lot harder. Instead, the company was able to preserve its role as the dominant player in the market for combat aircraft for the next generation and beyond.

Lockheed Martin's victory over Boeing in the JSF competition was announced in October 2001, shortly after the 9/11 attacks. Original plans called for the United States and the United Kingdom to buy over 3,000 planes, a huge number compared with the 187 F-22s that were ultimately produced for the U.S. Air Force.[42] The company was already on the upswing by mid-September, gaining $5 a share even as the Dow Jones industrial average dropped by seven hundred points.[43] The win on the JSF solidified Lockheed Martin's position as the most likely beneficiary of soaring Pentagon budgets in the post-9/11 period.

While each individual plane is slated to cost about one-third to one-half the cost of an F-22, the plan to buy up to three thousand of them—over fifteen times as many as the number of F-22s purchased by the Air Force—may make the JSF deal the largest in the history of combat aircraft. U.S. and U.K. customers for the plane include the U.S. Air Force, Navy, and Marines and the Royal Air Force and Royal Navy. Seven other partner nations—Italy, the Netherlands, Norway, Turkey, Canada, Australia, and Denmark—have invested about $4 billion in the JSF project up front in exchange for a role in designing the plane and preferred access to planes as they come off the production line. The bulk of production work will be carried out in the United States and the United Kingdom, including production of the front fuselage and wings—as well as final assembly—at Lockheed Martin's plant in Fort Worth, Texas. The center fuselage will be produced by Northrop Grumman at facilities in Palmdale and El Segundo, California. BAE Systems will produce the aft (rear) fuselage in the United Kingdom. Other partner countries have no guaranteed role but will instead be given work on a "best value" basis, according to the Pentagon's official F-35 website. This arrangement has already caused political friction among secondary partner countries vying for what they view as their fair share of F-35 development and production business.

However much work they receive, the partner countries are expected to buy another six to seven hundred planes beyond the U.S. and British purchases.[44] The sheer size and scope of the program spurred an outbreak of hyperbole. In a single interview, Lockheed Martin executive Micky Blackwell described it as "the Super Bowl," "the huge plum," and "the airplane program of the century."[45] The Pentagon's F-35 program manager later pointed to the complex network of partner nations involved to assert that "the sun never sets on the Joint Strike Fighter."[46] And Merrill Lynch analyst Byron Callan asserted that Lockheed Martin "owns the manned fighter business" as a result of the JSF victory.[47]

This huge initial market was meant to reduce the unit costs of the F-35, as were plans to set reasonable performance requirements that wouldn't push the price through the roof. The buzz phrase that came to dominate early discussions of the JSF was that it would be "a

Chevrolet, not a Porsche," or alternatively, "the Chevrolet of the skies."[48] By forgoing the gold-plating that had characterized the development of the F-22, the JSF designers hoped to create a highly capable aircraft without the performance glitches that plagued the Raptor and many prior combat aircraft programs.

The whole approach to the F-35 project was designed to head off what former Lockheed Martin CEO Norm Augustine has described— only partly in jest—as a situation in which, absent cost controls, the Pentagon budget would be able to afford only one fighter plane by 2054.[49] The aspiration of the Joint Strike Fighter program to be the first in the modern era to produce an aircraft cheaper than its predecessor is one of its most revolutionary aspects.

Winning the JSF contract was a protracted process. After some early research in the first part of the 1990s, the Air Force finally narrowed down the competition to two companies, Boeing and Lockheed Martin. The stakes in the JSF competition were so high that the third bidder, McDonnell Douglas, faced the prospect of being driven out of the fighter plane business altogether. Why? Because McDonnell Douglas's two most lucrative combat aircraft programs were going to be replaced by versions of the JSF. The company's F-15 fighter— heretofore the Air Force's top-of-the-line fighter plane—was now to be supplanted by a combination of the F-22 and the Joint Strike Fighter. And the company's F-18 fighter/attack jet, which operates from the deck of an aircraft carrier, would be replaced by the Navy version of the JSF.

The JSF decision set off a virtually unprecedented game of corporate musical chairs that changed the face of weapons contracting in both the United States and the United Kingdom.

Within a month of being dropped from the JSF competition, McDonnell Douglas agreed to be purchased by Boeing, creating a formidable rival for Lockheed Martin in the process.[50] Lockheed Martin itself was composed of parts of over a dozen different companies brought together under one roof during the defense merger boom of the 1990s (see chapter 8 for more details). So to some degree Boeing was just playing catchup when it swallowed McDonnell Douglas whole. It needed the McDonnell Douglas deal to stay competitive.

Although Boeing was able to beef up as a consequence of the Mc-Donnell Douglas loss in the F-22 sweepstakes, another side effect played in Lockheed Martin's favor. British Aerospace, which had been teamed with McDonnell Douglas for its JSF bid, came over to join the Lockheed Martin team. This gave Lockheed Martin a leg up in persuading Britain to weigh in on its behalf. It is one thing to have a given state or senator in one's corner. It is quite another to have a sovereign state and longtime U.S. ally like the United Kingdom ready to go to bat for you.

Lockheed Martin took one additional step that strengthened its hand politically. It offered Northrop Grumman—the third major defense behemoth left standing after the merger boom—a role as principal partner. Northrop Grumman would be responsible for at least 20 percent of the work on the plane. This agreement gave Lockheed Martin even greater pork barrel clout and created a vested interest in key districts and states where Northrop Grumman had operations.[51]

Once McDonnell Douglas was out of the way, Lockheed Martin and Boeing waged a five-year battle to produce a prototype that would win the hundreds of billions in contract revenue promised by the JSF program. In airplane hangars in the Mojave Desert, surrounded by high fences and armed guards, each company quietly worked away at its designs, code-named the X-32 (Boeing) and the X-35 (Lockheed Martin). On the highway between Los Angeles and the desert design facilities were billboards reminding people of just who was working on the secretive project: One said BOEING, THE BEST, JSF, and the other was simply a picture of the Lockheed Martin prototype with the word IMMINENT.

Ultimately, "Team Lockheed" carried the day, to the delight of its employees, hundreds of whom came to the company's Fort Worth, Texas, facility to celebrate the company's victory over Boeing.[52]

But the celebration was shadowed by concerns about how to actually produce an aircraft with all of the capabilities required of the Joint Strike Fighter. "The fun starts now," noted Lockheed Martin's JSF program manager Tom Burbage. "We've got a lot of work to do."[53] Industry analyst Jon Kutler put it in even more daunting terms: "This really should be considered a 40-year marathon, and we're nowhere near the finish line."[54]

Sure enough, the early years of the program were plagued by the kinds of political, technical, and cost problems that have become endemic in Pentagon contracting. The notion that "this one will be different"—owing to economies of scale, requirements that would favor the good over the perfect, and the unique, multi-nation partnership that was involved with the program from the outset—was proving not to be the case. The version of the plane being developed for the Marines and the British Royal Navy was already two thousand pounds overweight, and partner countries were bickering over how the work was being split up. Norway was threatening to pull out of the project if its companies didn't get more work, and Italy sent a special delegation to Washington to press not only for a greater share of funding but also for access to more of the critical technologies its engineers would need to carry out their part of the design work. Lockheed Martin was trying to hold firm against these demands, arguing that spreading the work thinner would push the JSF well above its then-target price of $40 million to $50 million per plane. As Tom Burbage of Lockheed Martin put it, "Everyone wants to have more work, but this is not a jobs program and should not be confused as a jobs program. Our overarching goal is to produce affordable air power for the future." Of course, this position was easy for Lockheed Martin to take, given that it already had the bulk of the money and the jobs involved in the project.[55]

At the June 2007 Paris Air Show the company was embarrassed when schedule slippage meant that only one JSF—a prototype—had been produced. In lieu of having planes to show—or to do stunts in the ever-popular flight exhibitions that form the backbone of the Paris meetings—Lockheed Martin commissioned paintings portraying imaginary F-35s flying over each partner nation, from gliding into Sydney Harbor in Australia to whizzing over the mountains of the Canadian Northwest. The art exhibit drew a decent turnout of the press, but hardly the level of attention that would have ensued if there had been actual planes there.[56]

The F-35 program's difficulties carried over into late 2009, even after Secretary of Defense Robert Gates had vouched for it as a worthy follow-on to the F-22. An internal Pentagon report leaked in late November, five months after Congress ended the F-22 program, suggested that the Joint Strike Fighter was so far behind schedule that it could cost an extra $16.6 billion over a five-year period. The rush to produce the planes without full testing raised the specter of expensive fixes after the aircraft had been produced and thus the retention of large, expensive engineering staffs much further into the life of the project than originally intended.[57] These potential problems had been foreshadowed in a Government Accountability Office (GAO) report that expressed concern about the fact that the first 360 F-35s were going to be produced *before* full testing had occurred. The maxim of "fly before you buy" had been violated in yet another program, with costly consequences for the budget as well as for the product's performance.[58]

The problems with the F-35 Joint Strike Fighter came to a head in early 2010, just six months after Secretary of Defense Gates had touted it as a capable, affordable alternative to building more F-22 Raptors. A report by the Pentagon's Office of Independent Testing found that Lockheed Martin had completed only *16* of 168 proposed test flights for 2009. And the multibillion-dollar cost overruns had brought the projected price to over $300 billion, making it the costliest weapons program in the history of Pentagon procurement. In response to these developments, Gates decided to cut the production run for the 2011–2015 time frame while shifting roughly $3 billion from production to development.[59] He also fired the Pentagon's F-35 program manager. And he denied Lockheed Martin $614 million in award fees as a way to make the company pay at least a small share of the cost overruns on the plane. In the public relations battle that ensued, Lockheed's efforts were supplemented by a piece written by Loren Thompson of the Lexington Institute. Thompson—who is often portrayed in press accounts as an objective analyst despite the fact that he does consulting work for Lockheed Martin—dismissed the cost concerns over the F-35 and made the astonishing claim that it would cost no more than a current-generation F-16 fighter. Lockheed Martin liked Thompson's analysis so much that it posted it on the front page of its website.[60]

But even given Lockheed Martin's troubles on the F-35 program, there was plenty of business to be had. As Loren Thompson told the *New York Times*: "The defense industry is pleased but bemused. It's been telling itself for years that when the Democrats got control it would be bad news for weapons programs. But the spending keeps going on."

It is ironic that the greatest rival of the Lockheed Martin F-22 is the company's own aircraft, the Joint Strike Fighter. Despite the mounting problems with the F-35, funding for the aircraft will still be substantial, in keeping with Gates's April 2009 pledge. So will funds for other Lockheed Martin programs, including building and/or upgrading its C-130J and C-5 transport aircraft, and for its Littoral combat ship program—involving combat vessels designed to operate close to shore in support of counterinsurgency efforts. And the company even stands to gain from plans to make the F-35 capable of dropping nuclear bombs. The bomb in question—an upgrade of an existing design known as the B-61—may be developed in part at Sandia National Laboratories, a $2 billion per year operation that is a subsidiary of Lockheed Martin.

Even Lockheed Martin's Marietta, Georgia, factory—the center of F-22 production—looks like it is going to do just fine. With significant work on not only the F-35 but also the C-130J and the C-5, even F-22 booster par excellence Saxby Chambliss acknowledged that, "irrespective of what happens on the F-22, there's going to be plenty of work in Marietta for those 2,000 folks. . . . Jobs [are] probably not going to be an issue."[61]

But advocates of the F-22 haven't given up yet. If the Pentagon won't buy more, maybe Japan, Australia, or Israel will. Even before the Senate vote that ended the F-22 program, Daniel Inouye had written to the Japanese Ambassador to the United States arguing that he could get the existing export ban on the plane lifted. The scaled-down versions offered under this scenario would be shorn of key classified components. But they could still cost over $250 million each. As of press time, the Air Force was opposed to lifting the export ban, but Inouye had succeeded in passing an amendment requiring it to at least study the idea of developing an export version of the F-22. Despite the obstacles, Inouye will doubtlessly continue to promote the export option on Lockheed Martin's behalf.[62]

Even without an export option, there is still a possibility that the F-22 could be revived. As defense contracting expert David Berteau has noted, if the problems with the F-35 program get much worse, "it's not too late to undo the decision."[63]

The F-22 wasn't the only budget battle Lockheed Martin had to fight during the first year of the Obama administration. Another major system—the VH-71 presidential helicopter—was also on the chopping block. In his July 2009 speech to the Economic Club of Chicago—the same address that helped drive the nail in the coffin of the F-22 program—Secretary of Defense Gates singled out the VH-71:

> We must also get control of what is called "requirements creep"—where more features and capabilities are added to a given piece of equipment, often to the point of absurdity. The most flamboyant example of this phenomenon is the new presidential helicopter. . . . Once the analysis and requirements were done, we ended up with a helicopter that cost nearly half a billion dollars each and enabled the President to, among other things, cook dinner while in flight under nuclear attack.[64]

Even prior to Gates's move to cancel the helicopter program, it had become a target of budget-cutting efforts. And like the F-22, it brought John McCain and Barack Obama together. At a February 2009 "fiscal responsibility summit" held at the White House, McCain didn't participate much. He sat through the meeting with what one reporter described as a "stern expression." Another observer noted that he "appeared irritable and close to losing his temper at one point." But when President Obama invited McCain's input near the end of the meeting, his former rival jumped to attention and spoke about the need to go after wasteful military spending. He used the presidential helicopter as his case in point: "Your helicopter is now going to cost more than Air Force One. I don't think there is any more graphic demonstration of how good ideas have cost taxpayers an enormous amount of money." Obama agreed; citing the VH-71 as "an example of the procurement process run amok," he pledged that "we're going to have to fix it."[65]

The fact that Lockheed Martin got the contract in the first place—in a competition that reached its high point in the run-up to the 2004 presidential election—was a surprise to many industry watchers. The Sikorsky Helicopter Company, a division of the Connecticut-based United Technologies Corporation, had built every presidential helicopter since President Dwight D. Eisenhower first requested one in the 1950s to facilitate trips back and forth from the White House to the Camp David retreat. To make up for its lack of experience with helicopters, Lockheed Martin had teamed up with the Anglo-Italian firm Augusta-Westland, with the idea of adapting an Italian-designed aircraft for use as the presidential helicopter. Although the partnership strengthened Lockheed Martin's technical case, it appeared to give Sikorsky a leg up in the game of pork barrel politics, since the latter could claim that its version would be 100 percent American and could argue that its rival would be shipping jobs to Europe at the expense of U.S. workers.

The battle for the contract got downright nasty, with Sikorsky Vice President Jeffrey Pino suggesting that "there is a visceral gut feeling that you don't want the president in a Mercedes or flying around in an Italian helicopter. We want the president in an American chopper." Firing back, Stephen Moss of Augusta-Westland asserted that "the real question is whether you want competition on a level playing field or a win based on jingoistic antiforeign sentiment in an election year."[66]

Lockheed Martin was able to counter the "anti-foreign" argument on several fronts. First the company tried to turn the European connection to its advantage. British Prime Minister Tony Blair, high on the list of those who could influence President George W. Bush owing to the United Kingdom's strong support for the U.S.-led war in Iraq, sent a note to the President touting the helicopter. And a delegation of Italian business executives and government officials did a lobbying blitz through Congress that claimed that the Augusta/Lockheed aircraft would create three thousand jobs in the United States. Most of those jobs would be at a Lockheed Martin facility in the town of Owego, New York, home state of Senator Hillary Rodham Clinton, who also worked aggressively on behalf of Lockheed's bid. Lockheed refused to give an inch on the jobs issue: Its brochures on the helicopter were headlined "American Jobs, American Pride."

For its part, Sikorsky's biggest advocates were its home-state officials from Connecticut, bolstered by executives from major firms like Northrop Grumman and General Electric that were to build parts of their version of the helicopter. In a move designed to embellish its "all-American" credentials, Sikorsky went so far as to cut potential subcontractors in Brazil, Japan, and China out of the deal. Pino of Sikorsky tried the ultimate scare tactic, suggesting that foreign suppliers couldn't be trusted because they might turn on America one day: "You just cannot bring in a spare part from anywhere overseas. How do you modify a part that's been built with an Italian design? What if Italy is not so friendly to us?"[67]

Anti-foreign appeals aside, the Augusta/Lockheed team won the contract. In describing it as "the last big undecided military competition on the horizon," aircraft industry analyst Richard Aboulafia suggested that it would have psychological as well as financial implications, for the winner and the loser alike.

Four years later, it was Lockheed Martin that endured the fallout from the VH-71 selection. But as with the F-22, proponents of the aircraft didn't give up. Representative Maurice Hinchey (D-NY), a well-respected liberal whose district included Lockheed Martin's Owego facility, argued strenuously that the government should *at least* finish building the five prototypes that were already in the works, given that $3 billion had already been invested in developing them. Hinchey's arguments were backed up by Jack Murtha, the powerful chair of the House Defense Appropriations Subcommittee and a master of pork barrel politics. Murtha's position seemed to be based on the merits of the case, but it probably didn't hurt that Lockheed had built a missile defense plant in his district. The company also went so far as to curry favor with him by giving a contribution to the Johnstown, Pennsylvania, symphony orchestra, of which Murtha's wife was the main patron. But the VH-71 was a smaller project than the F-22, so Hinchey was not able to mobilize the kind of national support that the Raptor had garnered—albeit in a losing battle. Gates held firm. In doing so, he addressed Hinchey's main argument directly, asserting that the helicopters did not meet requirements and "are estimated to have only a five-to-ten-year useful life."[68]

Hinchey's perseverance did yield a consolation prize of $100 million to continue R&D on the VH-71. But with no funds for production, it did little to stave off layoffs in his district.

Don't count Lockheed out yet. On April 19, 2010, the company announced that it would be teaming up with its former competitor Sikorsky to bid for the new version of the VH-71. The heated rhetoric from the first VH-71 competition was all but forgotten. This was business, and if dumping Augusta-Westland and teaming with Sikorsky gave Lockheed Martin a better chance at winning the contract, that's what the company would do. The new helicopter will be based on Sikorsky's design, with Lockheed Martin providing many of the basic components.

How much responsibility should Lockheed Martin itself be apportioned for the failure of the VH-71? Was the government just asking for too much, even as it kept changing what it wanted in ways that drove up costs dramatically? Defense industry analyst David Berteau has suggested that "requirements were a big part of the problem" and that what the U.S. government was asking for would have been "unexecutable on any platform."[69] A March 2009 Defense Science Board study argued that another major issue was "poor communications" among the White House, Navy, Marines, and the contractors. These in turn resulted in having to re-engineer "entire subsystems and structures."[70] As requirements grew, they came to include everything from operating in an arctic environment to surviving a nuclear, chemical, or biological attack. Berteau summarized the process by saying that although "the performance of the contractor left much to be desired . . . I'm not sure what other company could have done better."[71]

For the moment, Lockheed Martin may have lost the battle over the F-22 and the presidential helicopter. But so far it is still winning the war over increased military contracts. The company has proven to be far more resilient than it had represented itself to be in the early days of the F-22 campaign. It is the nation's top government contractor, with $36 billion in federal contracts in 2008 alone. That comes to roughly $260 per taxpaying household, an amount that can be thought of as "the Lockheed Martin tax."

Of course, Lockheed Martin is also the nation's leading weapons contractor, with over $29 billion of its $36 billion in government contracts coming from the Pentagon contracts. It is the number-one contractor not only for the Pentagon but also for the Department of Energy and the Department of Transportation. It ranks number two for the Department of State, number three for the National Aeronautics and Space Administration (NASA), and number four for the Departments of Justice and Housing and Urban Development.[72] Many of these activities go far beyond the normal range of the work one would expect from an arms manufacturer. As part of the growing trend of outsourcing the implementation of U.S. foreign policy to private companies, Lockheed Martin has done everything from supplying interrogators for U.S. military prisons at Guantanamo Bay, Cuba, to staffing a human rights monitoring mission in Darfur, to training police in Haiti, to running a postal service in the Democratic Republic of the Congo, to helping to write the Afghan constitution. On the home front, the company helps scan our mail, designs and runs the U.S. census, processes taxes for the Internal Revenue Service (IRS), provides state-of-the-art "biometric identification" devices to the Federal Bureau of Investigation (FBI), and plays a role in building billions of dollars' worth of new ships and communications equipment for the Coast Guard.

The F-22 loss notwithstanding, Lockheed Martin has more power and money to defend its turf than any other Pentagon contractor. It spent $15 million on lobbying and campaign contributions in 2009 alone. Add to that its 140,000 employees and its claim to have a presence in forty-six states, and the scale of its potential influence starts to become clear. And while its current political activities are perfectly legal, the company has also been known to break the rules: It ranks number one on the database on contractor misconduct maintained by the Washington-based watchdog group Project on Government

Oversight (POGO); according to POGO, Lockheed Martin has "50 instances of criminal, civil or administrative misconduct since 1995."

Recent troubles aside, Lockheed Martin is far too big and far too diversified to feel serious pain from the loss of one or two weapons programs. But that wasn't always the case. Today's mega-firm started out as the aerospace equivalent of a mom-and-pop store, running on the edge of bankruptcy from its first days of operation.

Chapter 2

FROM LOUGHEAD
TO LOCKHEED

Just a few years after Orville and Wilbur Wright launched the first successful flight in Kitty Hawk, North Carolina, another set of brothers, Allan and Malcolm Loughead (pronounced "Lockheed"), of Burbank, California, decided to get into the aviation business. After several years piloting and designing aircraft, the brothers formed their first company in 1916, the Loughead Aircraft Manufacturing Company. It would take them nearly two decades to change their names to Lockheed to avoid the inevitable mispronunciations that otherwise occurred. At the 1934 appearance in the Los Angeles Superior Court where he officially changed his name, Allan said he made the switch because "people keep calling me log head."[1] But in those early years, having their names mispronounced was the least of their troubles.

Journalist and aviation historian Wayne Biddle describes the Loughead brothers as "carnival performers who had become enmeshed in the birth of the aviation industry."[2] They were raised by a single mother, Flora Loughead, who had separated from the boys' father when they were still quite young. After their father moved to San Francisco to start a hardware store, Flora made money writing feature stories for the *San Francisco Chronicle* and moved the boys to a fruit ranch in the Santa Clara Valley.

Their education was limited. Allan didn't make it out of elementary school, although he received the equivalent of what later would be referred to as "homeschooling" from Flora. Both Malcolm (the older by two years) and Allan, encouraged by their older half-brother Victor, were devotees of John Montgomery, a builder of gliders who launched his contraptions in the skies above Santa Clara starting in 1905. Malcolm and Allan were eighteen and sixteen when they first saw one of Montgomery's machines.[3]

Victor was the first of the Lougheads (or in his case Lougheed, as he chose to spell the family name) to dip his toe into the world of aviation. An accomplished automobile engineer, he sought out Montgomery to ask him whether he thought propellers powered by gasoline engines could be mounted on a glider. In correspondence with Montgomery, Victor's enthusiasm grew to the point that he wrote his own book on the subject, entitled *Vehicles of the Air*. Montgomery was the hero of the piece, while the Wright Brothers drew little respect from Victor Lougheed, a man who had yet to attempt to build an airplane of any kind.[4]

Victor gave Allan his first crack at the aviation business, putting him in touch with a Chicago automobile distributor named James Plew who was interested in building powered aircraft based on Montgomery's gliders. Before moving to Chicago to take up the task, Allan assured his friends that airplanes would soon become a cheap, reliable, and safe mode of transportation—an assertion that seemed fantastic at the time.

Allan failed in his mission to build a powered aircraft based on a glider design, but he did learn to fly a Curtiss biplane. After he came back to California in 1911 a pilot, he demonstrated the planes at county fairs in an effort to drum up enthusiasm for the new technology. When his plane crashed at an exhibition in September 1911, he promised his new wife that he would end his career as a barnstorming pilot, although the pledge apparently did not apply to flying in other contexts, such as demonstrating new aircraft designs to potential customers. His wife had persuaded him to fly less often, but not to give up piloting aircraft completely.[5]

At the beginning of 1912, Allan went to San Francisco, where he picked up work as an auto mechanic, all the while hoping to build a hydro-airplane of his own design. By this time, Malcolm was an experienced supervisor at an auto factory, and Allan roped him into helping him build his dream plane. Malcolm helped raise $2,200 toward the $4,000 cost of building their first plane, which successfully landed in San Francisco Bay in June 1913 on its first test flight. It was called the Model G, because models A through F never made it off the drawing board. The plane had twin seats and an open cockpit. It was powered by an eighty-horsepower engine. It could reach a speed of sixty-three miles per hour and weighed up to a ton if fully loaded with supplies. It was an impressive achievement.[6]

In their first effort to make a profit in the business, Malcolm and Allan established a charter service that took customers on flights around San Francisco Bay for $10 a flight. The business never turned a profit, and after the plane crashed while Allan was showing it off to area sportsman and society figure Ferdinand Thierot, the main investor in the venture seized the aircraft and put it under lock and key in a San Francisco warehouse. Nevertheless, the failure of their initial venture didn't seem to discourage the Lougheads.[7]

With no money to build another plane, the brothers spent part of 1914 prospecting for gold, with little success. Allan took work as a mechanic, while Malcolm traveled the world as a salesman for Curtiss Aircraft in Hong Kong and then as an "adviser" to the air force of a wealthy, politically connected Mexican by the name of Elias Calles. "Air force" was a kind way of putting it—Calles owned just one functioning aircraft.[8]

In 1915 their prospects began to improve. Allan found an investor who helped them buy back their original Model G and bring it out of storage so they could bid on a passenger-flying concession at the Panama-Pacific Exposition being held that year in San Francisco. They lost the competition, but ended up running the concession anyway when their rival crashed and destroyed his only plane. Business was relatively brisk—600 passengers at $10 a head—and they earned enough to buy out their new investor with $4,000 left over to put toward their next venture: a "flying boat" that they hoped to sell to the U.S. Navy.[9]

The outbreak of World War I, the first war in which aviation played a part, served as a dynamic backdrop for the Loughead brothers' high-flying efforts. Britain fielded 1,232 planes in the conflict, losing most of them in combat. No American firms were able to design and build anything that was ready in time to do battle. For example, Douglas Aircraft Corporation had a contract with the Army Signal Corps for its MB-1 bomber, but early hopes of a large purchase were dashed when the Army bought only four of the planes. In the meantime, the Loughead brothers realized that they had neither the staff nor the capital to keep up with orders for the Model G aircraft. In part to rectify that gap, in the summer of 1915 they hired Jack Northrop, a self-taught engineer and aircraft designer who would later go on to found one of the most successful aerospace companies in the history of American aviation.

Northrop introduced a certain level of order and rigor to the Loughead company's design process, which he described as having been an ad hoc "by guess and by golly" approach before he joined the firm.[10] The "flying boat"—designated the F-1—had its first flight in March 1918, too late to win a major Navy contract, which went instead to Curtiss Aircraft for its HS-2L plane. With a push from Burton Rodman, the principal investor in the F-1 project, Allan pressed for and received a meeting with Rear Admiral David W. Taylor, a member of the Aircraft Production Board. Taylor wasn't exactly accommodating; he told Allan that he was "being pestered by every Tom, Dick and Harry who ever built a coffin, a toilet seat, or a chicken coop."[11] Despite this inauspicious beginning, Allan convinced Taylor that the F-1 was a legitimate aircraft worthy of consideration by the Navy. Taylor passed Allan on to Jerome Hunsaker, the head of aircraft design for the service.

Hunsaker was skeptical at first, but he did throw the Loughead brothers a contract of $90,000 to build two copies of their rival's HS-2L. He also gave them the chance to demonstrate the F-1 in a flight from Santa Barbara to San Diego, a trip of over two hundred miles. While the F-1 flight yielded no immediate business, the work on the two HS-2Ls allowed the company to expand its workforce nearly sixfold, from fifteen to eighty-five. Ultimately the Navy decided not to buy the F-1, leaving the brothers to seek other markets for it. An ill-fated attempt to demonstrate that a version of the plane dubbed the

F-1A could make a transcontinental flight from Santa Barbara to Washington—a stunt that they hoped would interest the U.S. Postmaster General in adopting the plane for long-range deliveries—failed miserably. The F-1A attracted no major customer and ended up being used for flight demonstrations for interested civilians at $5 each.[12]

The perceived failure of Loughead and its competitors during World War I drew harsh criticism in Washington. General Hap Arnold summarized the situation as follows: "No American-designed combat plane flew over France or Italy during the entire war. The foreign planes built in this country failed to arrive in Europe either on schedule or in the promised numbers, until what started out as a triumphant exhibition of American know-how turned into a humiliating series of Congressional and other investigations."[13] This situation was particularly galling given that over 7,700 planes had been built during 1918 by an industry that had never built more than a few hundred planes per year before. A congressional investigation blamed the failure to have combat planes ready for use in the war on "incompetence, inexperience, blundering, or personal interest," all of which combined to "jeopardize the winning of the war."[14]

Despite the criticisms, World War I established a business model that was to serve the aircraft industry well in the following decades. It all began with cost-plus contracts—an arrangement in which the company had all of its expenses reimbursed and then received an automatic profit on top of that. These generous deals were compounded by a lack of effective oversight and minimal accountability for any malfeasance or misfeasance carried out with the taxpayers' money. As evidence for this, the companies and investors that bore the brunt of the criticism for their conduct during the war eventually reemerged as leaders of the industry in the war's aftermath.

Loughead was not a major target of this criticism of the industry, in part owing to its minimal involvement in war-related production. But it suffered from the postwar slump nonetheless. According to the aircraft manufacturer's association, total aircraft produced dropped from 4,435 in the last three months of the war to just *26* for the same period a year later. The Loughead brothers continued to eke out a living doing tourist flights, the most notable of which was a $10 fee from

the State Department to fly the King and Queen of Belgium from
Santa Barbara to Santa Cruz Island for a picnic. And even the tourist
business was a shrinking proposition economically, as competition for
demonstration rides drove prices down to as little as $1 per ride. Mal-
colm Loughead had had enough. He left aviation to go back to the
auto industry, where he invented a four-wheel hydraulic braking system that became the industry standard.[15]

Without his brother and with little money to carry on, Allan
started a new company built around the design and production of what
the company materials described as a "Sport Biplane"—later named
the S-1—and designed from scratch by Jack Northrop. But this plane
too failed as a business proposition, since it was designed as a personal
aircraft. Taking it on the carnival circuit didn't produce any buyers, so
the plane went out of production, bringing down the Loughead Aircraft Manufacturing Company with it.

That should have been the end of it. Allan moved to Hollywood
and went into the real estate business while serving as a sales agent
for Malcolm's hydraulic brake company. Jack Northrop eventually took
a job with Loughead's rival, the Douglas Aircraft Corporation, but he
found the work unstimulating and spent time on the side designing his
own small aircraft.

In the meantime, Allan Loughead found some new investors,
most prominently Fred Keeler, a man who had invested in Malcolm's
hydraulic brakes company. In December 1926, the Lockheed Aircraft Corporation was incorporated in Nevada.[16] The change of the
company name to Lockheed was to match what Malcolm had done
with the name in starting his hydraulic brakes company; as noted
earlier, neither brother changed his own last name to Lockheed until
the 1930s.

Northrop was made chief engineer of the new company. The company's first product was the Vega, a sleek plane that didn't have the
traditional "struts" on the outside to hold up the wings. The Vega came
into being just six months after Charles Lindbergh's transatlantic
flight had created the conditions for a new aviation boom. The general
increase in aviation sales that followed on Lindbergh's feat helped
Lockheed sell more Vegas.[17] In 1929 and 1930, Lindbergh was to un-

dertake a series of demonstration flights (seeking to help airlines like Pan Am figure out which routes were practical), using a modified version of the Vega known as the Sirius.[18]

The Vega's record in high-profile flights was mixed, but it didn't seem to slow down sales. In August 1927, the Vega entered a race from Oakland to Honolulu funded by the eldest son of William Randolph Hearst. Of the seven aircraft entered in the competition, only two made it to Hawaii, and the Vega was not among them. It crashed into the ocean, never to be found, despite a search-and-rescue mission conducted by the U.S. Navy's Pacific fleet.[19]

The Vega's next venture was a rousing success, as Arctic explorer George Wilkins used it to complete the first flight over the Arctic Circle, from Barrow, Alaska, to Spitzbergen, Norway. Although this feat did not generate nearly the level of public enthusiasm as Lindbergh's transatlantic journey, it did help stoke the market for the Vega among everyone from individual pilots to up-and-coming airlines. Lockheed built twenty-nine Vegas in 1928 and over twice that number in 1929. The company's stock value increased more than tenfold. But even as the financial fortunes of the company soared, it lost its most talented designer, Jack Northrop, who had been anxious to develop a new plane, a "flying wing" design. Lockheed's principal investor, Fred Keeler, declined to invest in the concept, so Northrop left Lockheed to seek more interesting work elsewhere.

Because their markets had begun to grow dramatically and because they had not borrowed heavily to reach their current state, aircraft companies like Douglas Aircraft and Lockheed were attractive takeover targets. When a group of prominent Detroit investors—including Charles Mott and Charles Kettering of General Motors and William May of Ford Motors—decided to buy Lockheed, the company became a division of a larger holding company known as the Detroit Aircraft Company, which was being promoted as "the General Motors of the Air."[20]

While Fred Keeler (wisely, it turned out) decided to bail out while the company's value was at a historic high, Allan Loughead, angered by the sale of his company to a group of auto industry executives and investors, resigned instead, citing "mistakes in general policy and operation of the company" as his official reasons. In 1930 Allan started a new company called Loughead Brothers Aircraft, but the only plane the firm developed was destroyed in a crash, and the company went out of business just four years later. In 1937 he started another company, Alcor Aircraft Corporation, but it also folded after its only design crashed in a test flight over San Francisco Bay. He ran a division of another aircraft company during World War II, then went back to being a real estate salesman, in Palm Beach, California, before moving to Tucson, Arizona, in 1961 to enter a state of "semi-retirement," as his official biography from the National Aviation Hall of Fame put it. He maintained little connection to Lockheed, although he did some part-time consulting in 1969, the year he died at the age of eighty.[21]

At the end of July 1929, the Detroit Aircraft Corporation purchase of Lockheed was consummated. It was just a few months before the stock market crash that marked the beginning of the Great Depression, and the company faced an uphill battle just to survive.

By this point, the aviation industry's biggest client was the military, which accounted for two-thirds of the value of aircraft purchased in 1930, more than a decade prior to U.S. entry into World War II. Lockheed bucked the trend, however, selling the bulk of its planes to commercial users and celebrity pilots like Amelia Earhart. As aviation historian Wayne Biddle puts it, "For a while, Lockheed was the most illustrious example of a small company that had hit the jackpot with an innovative product without turning to the military."[22] But this was about to change. In early 1930, the company lost a big order when the client went bankrupt, and the company's income was soon coming not from selling new aircraft but from providing parts for aircraft that had already been sold. Meanwhile, its parent, the Detroit Aircraft Corporation, was hemorrhaging cash. The company's best hope of turning its fate around was the prototype XP-900 fighter plane, which proved to be faster than the Army's existing planes. But neither Lockheed nor its parent company had the connections in Washington to drive the deal home, and by early 1932 the Detroit Aircraft Corporation—along with its Lockheed division—went out of business.

Lockheed's remaining assets were auctioned off by the bankruptcy court to a company named Stearman-Varney, which wanted to produce Vegas as airliners for a new route from San Francisco to Los Angeles. A major investor in the new firm was Robert Gross, who went on to become one of the most influential figures in the history of the Lockheed Corporation. Gross was not a product of the aviation-crazed culture that suited Allan Loughead so well. He was a businessman with no experience with engineering and only a modest prior involvement in aerospace. He was an easterner who grew up in comfortable circumstances, went to Harvard, and earned his first million dollars before he was thirty years old. The contrast with Allan Loughead could not have been starker.

Gross was convinced that Lockheed could produce a good product, and he appeared to agree with Allan Loughead that most of the company's troubles had been the result of bad management. Gross also laid a bet that he would be getting a good deal by "buying low": "The world was flat on its face, at an all-time low. Aviation could only go one way: up. And the Lockheed company looked like it could go there with it."[23] In the end, Gross, Stearman-Varney, and a small group of individual investors bought Lockheed for the bargain basement price of $40,000. Their bid was matched by that of a salvage company, but the bankruptcy judge ruled in favor of Gross and his partners on the theory that they would do something constructive with the assets. Nevertheless, the judge was skeptical as well, saying to Gross, "I hope you know what you're doing, young man."[24]

Time would tell. In a May 1932 letter to his brother Courtlandt—who later became a major executive at Lockheed—Gross noted with respect to the Lockheed purchase that, "if I am not required to put up my own money, which I have not got, it undoubtedly has real possibilities."[25] In an earlier letter, he had indicated to Courtlandt that there was something for him in the pending deal: "We are still fussing around with Lockheed, and if we get our hands on it in any way I will certainly arrange to have you made eastern representative."[26] Gross did not seem to be overly concerned about the prospects of taking over an already troubled company in the midst of the worst depression in the history of the United States.

A June 28, 1932, article in the *Burbank Daily Record*, the hometown of the company's southern California production site, quoted

Lockheed Aircraft Corporation Vice President Carl B. Squier to the effect that the "company is now ready to take care of all orders for new planes as fast as they come in." Squier warned, however, that the plant would not resume operations on "an extensive scale" until new orders actually came in. Squier was concerned, according to the article, about "avoid[ing] an unwarranted rush of men to the factory seeking employment."

In its new incarnation, Lockheed looked in two directions for growth: to the airline industry, on the strength of its new Electra transport plane, a twin-engine aircraft that could carry ten passengers; and to the export market. This was an abrupt turn from the company's business base during Gross's first month at the helm, when the biggest clients were Amelia Earhart ($156) and Hal Roach Studios ($771.89), the latter being for aircraft used in motion pictures. The most famous use of a Lockheed aircraft in films came later, when an Electra was used as the getaway plane in the film *Casablanca*. But that was during World War II, when the company was already well established. From the vantage point of the early 1930s, Lockheed had a long way to go.[27]

Full funding for the Electra's development depended on up-front orders from Northwest Airlines (one plane for $35,000 and an option for two additional aircraft) and American Airways (six planes at $19,200 each). An additional order of one aircraft from the Navy, three from Pan Am, and the proceeds of a public stock offering were enough to underwrite the construction of a prototype plane, which had its first flight in early 1934.[28]

Lockheed was playing catch-up in the air transport market, in which both Boeing and Douglas Aircraft had strong entrants, including the Douglas DC-1. Lockheed turned a profit in 1933, but ran into difficulty during 1934 owing in part to the high development costs of the Electra. The problem was solved by going to the Roosevelt-created Reconstruction Finance Corporation (RFC) for a revolving loan of $150,000.[29] In justifying the loan, Gross debuted the arguments that were to figure so prominently in later debates over government aid to the company—creating jobs and preserving the industrial base. He suggested approaching the RFC "using the argument that the government wants to do something for aviation, that the Post Office realizes this airplane is a national asset, and that we could give employment to many men."[30]

The RFC was apparently the only aspect of the New Deal that Gross—a conservative Republican—could abide. His biggest concern was what impact the New Deal reforms would have on his ability to control his labor costs. In 1937, as sit-down strikes shut down Douglas's Santa Monica facility and other companies faced similar actions, Gross took systematic steps to "head off agitation," as he put it. His first move was to stop hiring new personnel, on the theory that "radicals and subversive aliens" would use "assumed names" and "forged references." So the hiring freeze was, in Gross's words, a means to "be absolutely sure that no undesirables get on here."[31]

As a second tactic, Gross moved to block the United Auto Workers (UAW) union—an affiliate of the Congress of Industrial Organizations (CIO), the more militant wing of the labor movement—from organizing Lockheed workers. Instead, he struck a deal with the International Association of Machinists (IAM), a member union of the reputedly more conservative American Federation of Labor (AFL). Gross maintained that no one at Lockheed really wanted any sort of union, but that the move to let in the IAM was designed to "combat this infectious spread of radicalism which is sweeping the country."[32]

Finally, Gross decided to grant a wage increase to Lockheed workers and to offer time and a half for overtime. On the one hand, this made Lockheed the highest-paying employer in the industry; on the other hand, from Gross's point of view, it was a bulwark against costly work stoppages, slowdowns, and other worker actions that might cut into short-term profits and productivity. His approach worked, at least to the extent that Lockheed was the only major aircraft maker in southern California that was not the target of a strike during the activist period of early 1937.

With the labor situation under control, Gross's company was well positioned to produce marketable aircraft in substantial numbers. In all, 148 variations on the M-10 Electra were sold to thirteen different airlines and the U.S. military, with sales split evenly between domestic and foreign customers. A scaled-down version, the M-12, sold an additional 136 copies. The plane helped the company survive in the heart of the Depression; with $2.1 million in sales and a profit of $217,000 in 1935, the losses suffered the year before were reversed.[33]

Far from confirming Gross's hope that he could run the company largely via sales to commercial buyers, the Electra experience led him to grudgingly acknowledge the need for sales to the military: "I have been loath to go into the military thing at all feeling that it was nicer not to have to depend on the light and shadow of politics, but the job of putting out the Electra has proved such an undertaking that some way or other we have got to scare up a lot of business to support it."[34]

As early as 1933, Gross had ticked off in his mind the company's most likely customers. The Post Office was ruled out: The Postmaster General felt that Lockheed's single-engine planes were too fast to fly safely in either a passenger or mail-carrying mode. As a result, Gross said, "it seems to me that we have only two places to drive at: one the organization ourselves of transport lines, and secondly, the possible getting of government contracts for war machines."[35]

So it seemed to be settled. Gross's concern about military business had never been grounded in any moral qualms. In fact, even as he was debating whether seeking large orders from the *U.S.* military made sense, Lockheed received an order for Electras from Japan. While the nominal buyer was commercial, Gross asserted that "we assume the plane is for the Japanese army."[36]

This was not to say that Gross did not proceed cautiously at first, at least with respect to sales to certain customers. In a back-and-forth exchange with his brother Courtlandt about whether to sell aircraft to Brazil, which was at that moment engaged in an air war against indigenous guerrilla forces, his concerns were entirely financial. Could the customer be counted on to pay up in full, or could a contract be "cancelled out on us just because somebody did not get paid enough down below?" Gross's solution was to seek large down payments and the best assurances available of payment in full. He expressed some concern about the practice of bribery to secure foreign contracts, but only out of fear of liability: "If . . . our agent was shown to have been bribing the officials of that country, might we not ourselves come in for certain international litigation with some chance of a recovery being had from us?"[37]

Gross was not opposed to military exports per se. In a letter to one of his European sales agents, Gross explained his attitude toward licensing Lockheed technology for use by companies in other countries: "I . . . am not interested in licensing a country which might become a serious competitor in the markets we are now developing. On the other hand, I have no particular objection to licensing . . . where I am positive it is never going to become a competitive factor and take bread from our mouths. Japan is a good example . . . I would quote them on the theory that they never will have anything for export in our game and I do not believe they ever will."[38] Gross's approach ignored the fact that Japan might become a *military* competitor of the United States, as began with its December 1941 attack on Pearl Harbor. While not a central factor by any means, Lockheed's sales of items that the company knew were destined for the Japanese military helped strengthen the fascist regime there in the run-up to the war. For example, a larger version of the Electra known as the "Super Electra" was licensed to a Japanese company in 1938, and 119 versions of the plane adapted for military use were delivered to the Japanese Army Air Forces between 1940 and 1942.[39]

Robert Gross's enthusiasm for selling to Japan came through in an August 1937 letter to a Japanese intermediary company in which he welcomed the arrival of a Japanese military delegation: "Having received permission from our government to receive General Okada and his party on August 4th, I will be very glad to show them through our factory and give them as much information as possible on our transport type."[40] Along with U.S. government contracts, exports to foreign governments were viewed as the possible salvation of Lockheed. In a letter to one of his sales representatives a few weeks after the note regarding the Japanese visit, Gross cited the sale of a "couple of planes" to Venezuela and the visit of a company pilot to the "Argentines" to train local pilots on an advanced model of the Electra as signs of potential progress. The important thing, however, was to push as aggressively as possible, wherever possible, wrote Gross: "Remember the Swiss, remember the Swedes and in fact remember anybody who has got the cash!"[41]

As was the case with its competitors Douglas Aircraft, Boeing, and the Glenn L. Martin Company, Lockheed's foreign sales activities attracted the scrutiny of the Senate Special Committee to Investigate the Manufacture and Sale of Arms and Other War Munitions. The committee was established in 1934 in the midst of a growing public outcry over the activities of the so-called merchants of death, including suggestions that they had maneuvered the United States into involvement in World War I. It was chaired by Senator Gerald Nye, a populist Republican from North Dakota who viewed arms exports as a dangerous form of entanglement that could embroil the United States in foreign wars.

The aviation industry drew Nye's attention relatively late in the game. His committee's investigations, which began in 1934, drew the greatest media attention for its revelations regarding the practices of gun makers and explosives companies, with a special focus on the DuPont Corporation. The focus on the aircraft industry didn't come until 1936.

Nye had an ambitious agenda. He described the committee's mandate as seeking to "take the profits out of war"; to ensure that "there will be no more profiteering in the unhappy eventuality that this Nation should again be engaged in war"; and to seek legislation to "strengthen our neutrality laws." As if this were not enough, the Nye Committee also declared that "the matter of national defense should be above and separated from lobbying and the use of political influence."[42] A noble goal, but extremely difficult to achieve, as we shall see.

Although the aircraft industry came under scrutiny last, the Nye Committee noted that it was actually more dependent on foreign sales than the large conglomerates like General Electric, General Motors, Westinghouse, and DuPont, in that aviation companies "supply the greatest portion of their output to the military services."[43] And this was in 1936, well before the huge World War II buildup.

The committee was particularly concerned with the apparently routine practice of bribery in the sale of munitions. It was so prevalent that the correspondence of weapons makers obtained by the committee referred to it by a whole range of names: "grease, palm oil, doing the necessary, doing the needful, bachshech, cumsha, and others."[44]

The Nye Committee's ultimate objection to bribery was not just that it was corrupt but that it could stimulate arms races, "culminating in economic strain and collapse or war" in the recipient countries. But contrary to later caricatures of the Nye Committee as a one-note, overly simplistic operation that blamed the arms companies for everything to do with conflict, the committee report noted that it was not suggesting that wars had been started solely as a result of actions of munitions makers. As noted earlier, Nye and his colleagues did want to keep the United States from arming one or both sides in active conflicts, as a way to limit the risk of U.S. involvement in another major war. These senators played a role in the passage of the Neutrality Act of 1935, which prohibited munitions exports by U.S. companies to countries engaged in conflict. In defining what constituted implements of war for purposes of the act, President Roosevelt included "aircraft, assembled or dismantled . . . adapted or intended for aerial combat."[45]

Luckily for Lockheed, Douglas, and the other major aircraft suppliers, the Neutrality Act was far from airtight. For example, an issue was raised about whether the Lockheed Electra—originally designed as a commercial air transport—was covered by the law. Never mind that it could be easily adapted to military use by the recipient country.

One indicator of the weakness of the Neutrality Act was the rapid growth of U.S. aircraft exports to Europe in the three years after it was passed. From 1935 to 1938, U.S. sales amounted to over $42 million, more than 40 percent of all U.S. exports to Europe during that time span. Although the largest recipients were Russia, the Netherlands, and the United Kingdom, Nazi Germany and the fascist regime in Italy each took in over $2 million in U.S. exports. In Asia the situation was even more dramatic, with Japan on the receiving end of $15.5 million in U.S. aircraft sales.[46]

Contrary to the spirit of the Neutrality Act, some manufacturers continued to seek opportunities to sell to areas of conflict. For example, in a letter bemoaning the settlement of a dispute between Peru and Chile in a conflict known as the Chaco War, a representative of the Electric Boat Company—which years later would become a division of General Dynamics—wrote the following: "It is too bad that the State Department have put the brake on armaments orders from Peru by forcing resumption of normal diplomatic relations with Chile."[47] A salesman for another exporter, Federal Laboratories, remarked on the perverse nature of his job: "We are certainly in one hell of a business where a fellow has to wish for trouble to make a living."[48]

Lockheed escaped the investigation relatively unscathed, except for one troubling episode. The company's agent in Europe, Anthony Fokker, had approached a subsidiary of the Skoda Works, a Czechoslovakian company that was believed to be a front for Hitler's armed forces, about producing a military version of the Lockheed Electra. Robert Gross's brother Courtlandt, speaking on behalf of the company, told the committee that the Czech deal was "in abeyance" and claimed that Lockheed had "never built a military airplane," but rather that it had exported "commercial airplanes with military modifications."[49] So, aside from an indication of questionable intent, it appeared that Lockheed was free and clear regarding the possible third-party deal with Germany. But as noted earlier, it was criticized by the committee for its deal with Japan. There were later rumors from Lockheed's Wall Street connections that Senator Nye might ask the company to halt all of its deals to Europe through Anthony Fokker unless it could guarantee that aircraft sold in Europe would not be used for military purposes. Lockheed's contact even suggested that Nye might seek to block the company's pending loan with the Reconstruction Finance Corporation if Fokker didn't adhere to these standards. In the end, the rumor was never put to the test because Fokker canceled his agreement to serve as Lockheed's agent for other reasons.

Although its sales to Japan and outreach to Nazi Germany brought controversy to Lockheed, its biggest export deal was to a U.S. ally—Great Britain. Embroiled in a fierce air war with Germany, the British armed forces were looking for new military aircraft wherever they could find them. In 1938 the Royal Air Force signed a contract for $25 million to buy 200 Hudson bombers (a military variation of the Super Electra), with an option for 50 more.[50] This represented the largest single order ever received by an American aircraft manufacturer up to that time. After the passage of a September 1939 law forbidding any U.S. citizen from delivering military goods to countries engaged in the war in Europe, Lockheed had to resort to some fancy footwork to carry out the order. The company bought an airfield that straddled the U.S.-Canadian border. Hudson bombers destined for Britain were flown to the American side of the line and then pulled over into Canada. They were then flown to Britain from there, in keeping with the law—on the theory that they were being delivered to Canada, not Britain. The Roosevelt administration winked at this clear violation of the spirit, if not the letter, of the Neutrality Act. Wayne Biddle describes the Hudson deal as having a transformative effect on Lockheed: "In one swift stroke, Lockheed left the ranks of small business forever and became a major power in the weapons industry."[51]

To meet the British demands and continue to produce the other aircraft on its order books, Lockheed had to purchase more land at its Burbank location and double its workforce. In 1939 the company earned $3 million in profits, the largest figure in its history. And it cemented its dependence on the military, delivering 356 planes, 329 of which were military. By 1941 Britain had purchased 1,700 Hudsons and Lockheed employed 50,000 workers—growth that catapulted it beyond its heretofore bigger rivals to make it the largest company in the industry.[52]

The move from 250 planes for Britain to 1,700 was not without its anxious moments for Lockheed. In a March 1939 letter to the company's English representative, George Swayne, Gross indicated that he had "heard a rumor" that "England is going to come into the American market again for a large quantity of airplanes." While making it clear to Swayne that "I don't want to give anyone in London the idea that we are unappreciative of the splendid order they have already given us," he did want Swayne to make it clear to the British leadership that Lockheed would be glad to deliver more planes on reasonably short order should they choose to buy more. In his reply, Swayne noted that Commander Sims of the Directorate of Equipment for the British Air Ministry had suggested that 250 planes "wouldn't really be of much use to the Royal Air Force if it ever came to a showdown with a foreign power."[53]

And the growing feeling in Britain was that the showdown would come soon, according to Swayne: "People are more jittery now than ever . . . they are even now visualizing Hitler as ruling England, which may seem far-fetched, but I . . . mention it to give you a sense of the feeling here at the moment. . . . The feeling is that they should go out and buy all the armament they can get their hands on for the final showdown, which no one seems to feel can be avoided now."[54]

When it came time to make a deal, Gross offered to provide the British Air Ministry with an additional 1,500 planes beyond the original 250 pledged for delivery between March 1939 and the end of 1940. The new arrangement would require an impressive turnaround time for that volume of planes. Gross planned to achieve it by producing 500 of the planes in Lockheed plants and farming out the other 1,000 to subcontractors. Gross waxed poetic about his company's commitment to Great Britain: "Our loyalty has resulted in our pledging you virtually all of our resources and facilities. . . . We align ourselves to your cause through commitments already given and it is our sincere desire to continue to render all possible assistance in furthering your program."[55]

This was not to suggest that this was all some sort of charitable venture. Gross noted that the new planes would have to be supplied "at a slight premium over our current price."[56]

As the scale of the British deal suggested, the "mom-and-pop" days of Gross's predecessors were long gone. He wrote to a colleague that "it is almost unbelievable to realize that our peaceful and happy community, which has been living in . . . comparative calm, has suddenly been transformed into an armed camp."[57]

But even as the company reached unprecedented levels of sales and profitability, Gross was focused on the deals that got away. In a March 1939 letter, he made it sound like the worst consequence of Hitler's march through Europe was its impact on a number of smaller export deals that had to be abandoned: "The unchallenged advance of the German march across Eastern Europe gives me furiously to think . . . I see our gallant little markets like Roumania, Jugoslavia, and Poland falling before Hitler's steamroller every week and it makes me realize how quickly the work of years' cultivating can be swept away overnight. Not a very pleasant thought."[58]

The highly profitable British deal was only the beginning. In mid-1937 the company had won an Army design competition for a new twin-engine fighter, beating out Douglas Aircraft and Boeing. The

$157,000 contract to build a prototype of the plane, which was designated the P-38, launched what may have been the most lucrative aircraft in Lockheed history. By the end of World War II, the U.S. military had purchased over 10,000 P-38s in various configurations. In tandem with the World War II boom, company employment nearly doubled yet again, reaching a peak of nearly 91,000 by 1943.[59]

Workers flooded into the Burbank area to meet the demand as everyone from refugees from Oklahoma and Arkansas to teenagers and out-of-work actors were hired to build Lockheed's military aircraft.

With money flowing from the U.S. government to weapons manufacturers as never before, the issue of war profiteering naturally arose. Smaller companies were the first to be caught engaging in price gouging: For instance, a Cleveland manufacturer charged the government nearly three times as much for aircraft engine starters as it had cost to build them. The immediate result was legislation aimed at curbing excess profits. Even prior to that, Congress had moved to bar the use of cost-plus contracts of the type that had proved so controversial during World War I and its aftermath. An attempt to impose an 8 percent ceiling on profits was overturned, and government procurement officers pushed normal rates up to 9 to 10 percent. This represented a huge windfall for companies like Lockheed and Douglas, given the volume of orders they were receiving and the fact that there was very little risk that their customer—the U.S. military—would fail to hold up its end of a contract.

As the war proceeded, the War Department gradually put a squeeze on profit levels, bringing them down to the 4 percent range. While companies complained about the shift—Douglas even refused to accept the voluntary limits—everyone fell into line once the War Department threatened to make the curbs mandatory.

As for Lockheed, Robert Gross had to acknowledge that even at these lower nominal rates the company was thriving. In a note to a concerned stockholder, he noted that although "we must recognize that we shall probably never again during this war be able to make the money that we made in the years 1942 and 1943 . . . you will be pleased to learn that we ended [1944] . . . with our company in the best financial position it has ever enjoyed."[60]

The presentation of the company's position was quite different when it was intended for broad public consumption. In mid-1943 a representative of western aircraft manufacturers like Lockheed and Douglas told a congressional hearing that "our stockholders are risking every penny of their capital . . . in the war effort. The general belief is that we have benefited from the immense volume of business that has been entrusted to us. This is far from being the case."[61]

The aviation industry's complaints over the allegedly onerous wartime restrictions imposed on it were soon to be outstripped, however, by a real threat to its profitability: the end of the war and the adjustment to the relatively short-lived peace that followed.

Chapter 3

FROM WAR TO COLD WAR

The military buildup for World War II resulted in an aircraft industry that was on a whole different scale from the struggling, on-again-off-again business that companies like Lockheed struggled with in the early to mid-1930s. Demand for supplies for the war predated U.S. entry into the conflict, most notably in the case of Lockheed's provision of Hudson bombers to Britain. But it was the war itself that transformed the industry. Output increased by an astounding 13,500 percent during the war: The U.S. aviation industry produced more than 300,000 aircraft for the military services.[1] It was hard to imagine how a peacetime economy could sustain anything approaching those production levels, and initially it didn't.

As Lockheed President Robert Gross put it in his reflection on the immediate postwar situation, "As long as I live, I will never forget those short, appalling weeks."[2] Whatever his personal feelings may have been about the conflict, from his perspective as a businessman it was not the war itself but the drop-off in business that followed that appalled him. As he put it in a 1946 letter, "After the end of the Japanese war we had what looked like a very healthy production program," but difficulties with key programs, like the Constellation airliner, required that operations be "cut to the very bone."[3] By the following March, Gross was pining for the good old days of World War II: "We had

one underlying element of comfort and reassurance during the war—
we knew we would get paid for whatever we built. Today we are almost
entirely on our own, the business is extremely speculative, and with a
narrowed market, the competition is very keen."[4]

As the end of the war neared, Gross had hopes that his firm would
have a leg up by virtue of the fact that it had built a substantial number of military transports that could be readily adapted to serve as
long-range airliners, but he feared that the timing was wrong: "If the
war had ended six months ago, our development position would have
been so favorable compared to anybody else's except Douglas that we
would undoubtedly have been guaranteed a leading position in the
market. . . . Now, however, the war has dragged on and every month
that it lasts gives other companies an opportunity to get development
work going."[5]

The shifts in the business took a personal toll on Gross, who wrote
to his associate Henry F. Atkinson that "life is really hectic these days,
what with the airplane business nearly flat on its face and me having
my 50th birthday and feeling old age as a real flat tire. Seriously, we
have lived a lifetime these past few years, but I am fundamentally a
man of hope and faith and I believe in the end things will come out."[6]

Part of Gross's "hope and faith" stemmed from his sense that he
and his colleagues could successfully lobby for a policy of peacetime
government subsidies for the aerospace industry, even if it did not
compare to the levels of government business achieved during World
War II. In August 1945, just a few months after the end of the war,
Gross testified on the topic of "aircraft reconversion and America's airpower policy" at hearings held by the Aviation Subcommittee of the
Senate Committee Investigating National Defense Programs. The
theme of Gross's testimony was that just as the aircraft industry had
answered the nation's call during wartime—providing America with
the "greatest air force in the world, and a production capacity of 50,000
planes per year"—the U.S. government had an obligation to sustain
the industry in peacetime. And while Gross acknowledged that "peacetime aviation will not be able to *immediately* [emphasis added] support this war-expanded industry," he had a number of suggestions on
how to start that process.[7] First, he wanted government to give the

production equipment it had paid for during the war to industry on a free or low-cost basis. Gross argued that it would otherwise be sold for scrap with little benefit to the government. He also wanted to avoid having the government dump military transport planes onto the commercial market, a move that would deprive Lockheed and its cohorts of potential business. And he wanted the development of a peacetime aviation policy that would provide subsidies in areas such as support for civilian transport planes that could be converted to military use in time of war.

Gross was far from shy in making his case. Without "steady encouragement and financial backing" from the taxpayers, the technical marvel that was the modern aircraft industry would atrophy, he suggested. "One road leads to retrogression and mediocrity," Gross said. "The other leads to progress and continued world leadership in the science of flight. The choice is one which the public must make, and the hour of decision is here."[8]

Gross's ultimate argument, however, had little to do with science and technology for their own sake, or even the economic benefits of a thriving aircraft industry. It had to do with national security: "I find it very difficult to talk about the airplane as a weapon of war . . . the prospect of an airplane maker pleading the case for air security is somewhat tragic. It is a cause I would not be selfish enough to plead as a businessman, but it is my duty to plead for it as a citizen."[9]

To Gross's mind, the case was clear: "Having made these new discoveries, we have to decide whether we will advance them as a means of security for our country or abandon them only to have other countries use them against us."[10] Gross's case appeared to offer no middle ground, no policy that would provide modest support to the industry without being viewed as "abandoning" it and its technological capabilities. His reflections sounded suspiciously like a recipe for a new arms race.

In spite of his fears—and his special pleading on behalf of his industry—once the initial shock wore off, Gross managed to regain his emotional footing and come out on the other side more bullish on his company's prospects than ever. In an extraordinary address to the Southern California Council of State Chambers of Commerce, Gross plugged both the military and the civilian sides of the business. First, he suggested that the technological gains in military uses of aircraft had to be sustained through ample ongoing investments during peace-time. Then he forecast "extraordinary advances in transport of passengers and mail all over the world," to the point where flying would become a regular part of everyday life, not a luxury for a relatively few well-heeled customers. He even predicted that private flying would increase to such a degree that it might eventually be possible to have "an air buggy [helicopter] for everyone."[11]

Gross's rivals were not so upbeat. Jack Northrop suggested that there would not be adequate orders to hold together the talent and facilities that had been built up in the industry during the war. And Donald Douglas seemed more angry than hopeful. He sent a letter to Congress arguing that "after telling industry to drop everything and concentrate on war production . . . Government should not, now that the war is over, say to industry . . . you're on your own."[12]

In the early months after the war, Wall Street seemed to agree with Gross's rosy outlook, and the company enjoyed a surge of investment in 1946. But by 1947 Lockheed's share price had dropped by two-thirds. Hopes had been boosted in early 1946 when the company delivered the first postwar copy of its Constellation airliner—a four-engine transport that had been in the works before U.S. entry into World War II—but it was not enough to stop the slide in its share price. Matters got worse when the Constellation suffered numerous mechanical failures, including a crash over Bozeman, Montana, that forced the Civil Aeronautics Board (CAB) to ground the plane in the summer of 1946.[13] Despite this setback, the various versions of the "Connie"—the nickname for the Constellation—proved to be good business for the company. As early as 1941, the year America entered World War II, Lockheed had already taken orders for 80 Constellations, 40 each from TWA and Pan American.[14] In the 1950s, the next-generation Super Constellation sold over 160 copies at roughly $1.7 million per plane.[15]

In the end, the company held on, not by finding commercial business but by selling fighter planes and patrol aircraft to the Air Force and the Navy. The postwar increase in commercial airliner sales had been expected to amount to only $400 million in business over two to three years, versus projections of $1.2 billion *per year* in military aircraft sales. On an annual basis, military sales to the government would average about ten times the amount of sales of commercial planes to the airlines. As the *Wall Street Journal* put it in August 1945, "Continuing military contracts are expected to keep the plane makers eating regularly, but airline business may well prove to be the butter on the bread."[16]

In his speech to the southern California business group, Gross reiterated the ambivalence he had felt about doing military business prior to the World War II boom. "We have always had the ambition to make the business pay, just on the basis of commercial and private type airplanes, without having to be dependent on military orders. . . . [But] in spite of my personal feelings on the subject, the aircraft industry needs substantial Government support."[17]

Gross and his allies in the industry went about rallying that support, not by developing new products but by injecting themselves into the political process in the hopes of creating the conditions for permanent high spending on military aircraft. The mechanism of choice was to be a blue-ribbon panel—modeled on one appointed in the mid-1920s known as the Morrow Board—that could make the case for what in essence would be a large, permanent arms establishment.[18] Gross and his associates turned their attentions to the Congress, where they prevailed upon key members of the majority Republican caucus to seek the creation of a pro-industry advisory board made up of representatives, senators, and former cabinet officials. Gross was thrilled, crowing that "I cannot overestimate the good effect the creation of such a board might have on our whole industry. . . . That is the 1947 version of the 1926 Morrow Board, which laid the foundation for America's air power."[19]

In the meantime, President Truman decided to create his own commission, which he appointed on July 18, 1947. Initially Gross was concerned about whether to continue to push for the congressionally mandated Air Policy Board, but he ultimately decided that two boards were better than one.[20]

In the end, Truman's body, officially known as the Air Policy Commission, had the greatest impact. Chaired by Thomas Finletter, a lawyer and former State Department adviser with no background in the aircraft industry, the commission interviewed 150 witnesses, including all of the captains of the aviation industry, from Robert Gross to Donald Douglas to Jack Northrop to Glenn Martin. As Wayne Biddle notes, the deck was stacked to the degree that, of all the witnesses, "none came from outside the circle of business, military, and government officials who had a direct stake in the expansion of air power."[21]

To say that the Finletter Commission came out with hard-line recommendations would be putting it mildly. In its preamble, it asserted that "this country . . . must be ready for modern war. . . . It must be ready not for World War II but for a possible World War III."[22] Noting that the bulk of U.S. government expenditures over the prior three decades had been for military purposes, the commission suggested that in the new environment "even this amount is not enough." This hawkish rhetoric was followed up with specific recommendations for military aviation, suggesting a sharp increase in Air Force and Navy combat planes. The commission also called for an overall 80 percent increase in military spending.[23]

In the meantime, Robert Gross and his industry colleagues used congressional hearings on the wisdom of creating an Air Policy Board to make the economic case for a more strategic approach to supporting the aviation industry in peacetime as well as in time of war. The first witness at a crucial May 1947 hearing on the subject before the Senate Subcommittee on Interstate and Foreign Commerce was Oliver P. Echols, the president of the Aircraft Industries Association of America. Echols knew a great deal about industry-government interactions, having been in charge of overseeing and directing the U.S. government's aircraft procurement effort during World War II. Echols's move from an influential government post to a position representing the industry he used to oversee was an early example of the so-called revolving door. The practice, and the conflicts of interest it entails, was to draw periodic criticism in the ensuing decades. Echols came out fighting, arguing that "our country has spent too many lives and too many billions to achieve leadership in air power to let it slip away from us by default. That would be a national tragedy."[24]

Having set the tone, Echols got down to brass tacks. He suggested that in the nuclear age, "never again will the Nation have three or four years to build up its aircraft industry to a winning level," and that therefore there needed to be a sharp upturn in annual military purchases, to as much as three times the levels that obtained in 1947. To do so, he recommended "a firm five-year program established by law."[25]

Speaking later in the same hearing, Lockheed's Robert Gross made one of the most detailed cases up to that point on the need for a steady approach to military aircraft procurement. As Echols had done, he prefaced his remarks in lofty terms: "I am not talking for the Lockheed Aircraft corporation. . . . I am here speaking for every aviation element, and in many senses, for everybody in America."[26]

That being said, Gross turned to the question of why the aviation industry was special and why it needed special treatment: "We do not have volume markets. We do not have consumer goods to go on." This was particularly difficult in the postwar period, Gross suggested, because "from a small business, we were catapulted to a high one, and have had nothing sure to go back to."[27]

In setting up his plea for dramatically increased government investment in his company and his industry, Gross suggested that his organization had already made every effort to achieve as much independence as possible by seeking commercial markets, rather than "throwing ourselves in the lap of a paternal Government and saying, in effect, 'If you do not fully support us, we are through.'"[28]

From here Gross's argument turned toward justifying greater government purchasing to sustain the "defense industrial base," a term that the Lockheed chairman did not use directly but that evolved later to describe precisely the points he was making.

First, he asserted that more reliable purchases, stretching beyond one year at a time, could establish a "clean steady flow" that would avoid "wasteful expenditure . . . caused by peaks and valleys in our industry."[29] In short, if the military bought more, the unit price of each aircraft would go down.

Otherwise, Gross suggested, a situation would continue in which "the whole paraphernalia of production is thrown into a stop and start, turkey and feathers, feast and famine psychology and we do not know from one year to the next what we can plan."[30] Among the downsides Gross underscored was a projected $8 million gap in the funding of its highly successful P-80 fighter plane—a gap that, he implied, might have to be filled in some form by Lockheed to keep the production line ready for the next round of orders. "Would not the United States be better off," suggested Gross, "if we had enough long-range planning to give it that $8,000,000 in airplanes, instead of throwing it out the window and getting nothing?" Put another way, he argued that, "if we have to dismember the P-80 program and stop it," costs for any planes built later could go up to $100,000 or more each, a 25 percent increase.[31]

Gross was aided in making his case by a series of friendly questions from industry advocate Senator Warren Magnuson of Washington State, the home of the headquarters and main operations of the Boeing Corporation.

When Magnuson argued that maintaining the relatively low postwar levels of aircraft spending could mean a "dry spell for aeronautical growth," Gross jumped on his point. "It means the loss of it . . . these things are not the product of one or two men."[32] Unsteadiness of demand not only risked losing skilled personnel but "works material hardships on our vendors" that might make them unavailable when needed for future projects. These were precisely the kinds of arguments that were to be made over sixty years later when Lockheed Martin was trying to save the F-22 combat aircraft program.

While Magnuson and the subcommittee chairman, Owen Brewster of Maine, were highly sympathetic to Gross's case, Senator Edwin Johnson of Colorado was not. He expressed his fear that the kind of planning that Gross was propounding would lead to "a totalitarian system" in which "we had one customer, and that customer was Uncle Sam, with bags and bags of money."[33] Instead, he suggested a return to the free enterprise model that had existed before World War II. Gross took an opposite tack, suggesting that lack of planning was what could bring "a totalitarian system in this country or something worse," presumably referring to the possible conquest of the United States if it let its guard down by failing to sustain its edge in air power.[34]

Gross built up to his final pitch: a call for a board of "disinterested, far-sighted, public-spirited Americans that will get for their country an air power that is adequate, continuous, and permanent, and this in so doing it will secure for a world that certainly needs it, peace, but peace with justice."[35] This practice of equating the aircraft industry's interests with the national interest was to serve Lockheed and its rivals well in the decades to come.

Although it was far from disinterested, as noted earlier, Finletter's Air Policy Commission met Gross's requirements for a board that would make the case for permanently high expenditures on military aviation.

The prospects for enacting the commission's agenda seemed promising, particularly after Finletter, its chair, was appointed Secretary of the Air Force in 1950. At first President Truman held the purse strings tight. Ideological developments—such as State Department official George Kennan's "long telegram" describing an aggressive and implacable Soviet foe that had to be contained at every turn—did not spur a dramatic upsurge in defense budgets. Likewise, Truman's 1947 speech calling for increased aid to anti-Communist forces in Europe and outlining the approach that came to be known as the Truman Doctrine offered little aid to the aviation sector.

Ultimately, it was not words or arguments or an abstract fear of communism that opened the military spigot, but war—the Korean War. The war broke out in June 1950, with U.S. intervention following shortly thereafter. The new conflict offered Lockheed President Gross a chance to wax even more patriotic than he had in making the case for post–World War II subsidies. In a draft of a September 1950 address on "The Air Transport Plane in War and Peace," Gross argued that, "for the first time in recorded history, one nation has assumed global responsibility. By its action in Korea, the United States set the plan for the restoration of order and progress in Asia, and to peace and freedom around the world." The greatest problem, therefore, was to "get enough of all the things and equipment needed to make this commitment good"—equipment that Lockheed was glad to supply, as in World War II, at a substantial profit. But it wasn't just about Korea, Gross pointed out. The question was "Are we committed to deal with all future armed aggressions against the peace of the world?" If so, we needed the means to provide transport of "huge quantities of men, food, ammunition, guns, tanks, gasoline, oil and thousands of other articles of war to a number of widely separated places on the face of the earth." And of course, it should be "fast transport . . . transport from the air."[36] In short, if we wanted to play the role of global policeman, we needed to buy more transport planes from Lockheed.

But Gross was getting ahead of the game. The first order of business was Korea, and that war was lucrative enough without looking ahead to the economic benefits to Lockheed of a policy of permanent "global reach." By 1952 aircraft purchases by the U.S. military had more than tripled from their post–World War II low, reaching over 9,300. Industry employment reached 600,000, up from 192,000 in 1947.[37] While there would be ups and downs, it was not until the post-Vietnam period in the 1970s that Lockheed would face anything approaching the tough times of the late 1940s.

Military aircraft and commercial airliners weren't the only products sustaining Lockheed through the 1950s. As the aviation industry morphed into the aerospace industry—adding missiles, space vehicles, and other non-aircraft products to the mix—Lockheed was at the forefront of industry diversification. A Navy contract for the Polaris submarine-launched ballistic missile put the company at the center of the nuclear buildup of the 1950s, driven by President Dwight D. Eisenhower's doctrine of threatening "massive retaliation" with nuclear weapons for any attack on the U.S. homeland. The company also acquired a new customer—the Central Intelligence Agency (CIA), which hired Lockheed to produce sophisticated spy planes that were used to keep track of the military capabilities of the Soviet Union.

The most urgent project taken on by Lockheed in the mid-1950s was an aircraft that could fly beyond the range of Soviet radar and anti-aircraft missiles and conduct detailed reconnaissance of that country's nuclear weapons testing and production facilities, as well as virtually every other aspect of its military and industrial capabilities. Up to that point, the Pentagon had been largely flying blind in its efforts to determine what Moscow was capable of, relying on often unreliable defectors and aircraft incursions that frequently ended up with the planes being shot down and the pilots being killed or captured. There had been at least forty such incidents in the 1950s alone.

The aircraft that was developed to solve this problem came to be known as the U-2, with the "U" standing for "utility aircraft." The cover story for the plane was that it was not a military aircraft at all, but a weather surveillance aircraft run by the National Aviation Co-ordination Agency (NACA), the predecessor to NASA.[38]

Understanding how the U-2 was developed requires a look at the development of the "Skunk Works," an elite aircraft development division of Lockheed that was created in 1943 to build a prototype for an upgraded version of the company's P-80 fighter plane. The new version was supposed to travel 200 miles per hour faster than any aircraft then in service and could be assembled in just 180 days. A top-secret location was created to house the new division, and it was run by Clarence "Kelly" Johnson, a thirty-three-year-old designer who had already distinguished himself through his central roles in developing the first P-80s and in transforming the civilian Electra airplane into the Hudson bomber, the workhorse of World War II that helped keep Lockheed afloat during the late 1930s via sales to Britain.[39]

Johnson was a unique character, believed by many to be the most gifted aircraft designer in the history of the industry. He was as aggressive as he was self-confident, as evidenced by the fact that he criticized Lockheed's latest design as a twenty-three-year-old recruit, even before he had been officially hired by the company. He is described by company biographer Walter Boyne as "physically prepossessing," appearing to be "much taller than his five-foot eleven-inch height and much more than his 200 pound weight. . . . His posture, walking or sitting behind a desk, was aggressive, leaning forward as if battling a wind . . . and winning."[40] In later years his colleague and protégé Ben Rich would offer a less flattering portrait: Johnson, according to Rich, waddled around with his shirt untucked and had "a thick, round nose that reminded me a lot of W. C. Fields, but without the humor. Definitely without the humor."[41]

Johnson inspired fear as well as respect in the small number of engineers, designers, and machinists he handpicked to work with him at the Skunk Works. The name was inspired by a running character in Al Capp's *L'il Abner* comic strip who built an outdoor still that he filled with all manner of garbage, from old shoes to dead skunks, all to make a concoction known as "Kickapoo joy juice." Capp referred to the still as the "Skonk Works." Workers in Johnson's top-secret operation started referring to it as such because it was run out of a circus tent—no buildings were available at the time of its inception—close upon a noxious plastics plant whose odor pervaded their work areas. The name was eventually changed to the more traditional spelling, "Skunk Works," after Al Capp's publisher objected on copyright grounds to the use of the word "skonk." The employees referred to each other as "Skunks."[42]

Whatever one chose to call the factory, Johnson ran a tight ship with very specific ideas about how things should be done. He wanted a lean, mean staff and tight coordination among engineers, production workers, and the "customer"—which in the case of the U-2 was the CIA. In his efforts to limit paperwork and bureaucracy, he suggested, for example, that financial rewards should accrue to men not based on how many people they supervised but on how effective their work was. He wanted succinct technical updates and cost projections at every stage of the process. His motto was "Be quick, be quiet, and be on time."

Unlike other units of Lockheed, which would have a hard time meeting Johnson's standards, by all accounts the Skunk Works was able to live up to its founder's vision. To the extent that it can be known—given that it was funded via a "black," or secret, budget that was scrutinized by only a handful of members of the executive branch and Congress—the U-2 came in on time and about 10 percent under cost, prompting Ben Rich to label it "probably the only instance of a cost *underrun* in the history of the military-industrial complex."[43]

But it was performance that counted. President Eisenhower was seeking a plane that could fly safely at 70,000 feet while staying still enough for its surveillance cameras to get usable photographs of Russian military installations many miles below. As Johnson's colleague Ben Rich points out in his memoir of his time at the Skunk Works, virtually every aspect of designing the U-2 involved solving an unprecedented engineering problem, from designing the engines to choosing the materials for the fuselage to pressurizing the cockpits in order to protect the pilots from the dangers of life at 70,000 feet. And it worked.

Even though the U-2 was a technical success, the ultimate test of its value came in how it was utilized. On that score, the aircraft worked quite well: It ran about thirty missions over Soviet territory during the three and a half years from August 1956 to January 1960. Early on, the Eisenhower administration was disappointed to learn that although the U-2 appeared to be well beyond the range of Soviet anti-aircraft systems, it could be picked up by Soviet radar. This led to an odd situation in which, on the one hand, Soviet authorities responded angrily to the flights, but on the other, they were embarrassed to mention them publicly for fear of revealing the weaknesses in their air defense system. So, both the United States and the Soviet Union kept the U-2 flights out of public view. As Richard Bissell, the CIA contact who helped run the U-2 program, put it, the Soviet leadership kept quiet because "if they [the flights] were ever revealed, the Russians [sic] would have to present us with an ultimatum and admit they were impotent in stopping these flights over their territory."[44]

At least from the perspective of the corporate and government officials involved with the U-2 program, it was a rousing success. Bissell described it as "absolutely the smartest decision ever made by the CIA," asserting that "the U-2 overflights of the Soviet Union made up the most important intelligence gathering operation ever launched by the West."[45] Hyperbole aside, the U-2 was a valuable asset. Among its most interesting findings was the fact that the Soviets were *weaker* militarily than the CIA had been assuming. For example, while the Eisenhower administration believed that Moscow had roughly one hundred long-range "Bison" bombers capable of reaching the U.S. mainland, U-2 flights put the number at twenty to thirty—one-third to one-fifth of the original estimate. Bissell reported that, as a result of these findings, he was able to "assure him [the President] that the so-called bomber gap seemed to be non-existent."[46]

The lessons of the U-2 flights seemed to be that intelligence is only as good as the way it is used by decision-makers. The revelations that the United States had been overestimating Soviet military capabilities did little to slow the pace of U.S. military spending. In fact, the pace of spending increased during the early years of the Kennedy administration, until the Vietnam War escalated and brought the Pentagon budget to its highest levels since World War II.

Useful as it was, Eisenhower decided to stop the U-2 flights over Russia for a combination of performance and political reasons. The most dramatic turn of events came on May 1, 1960, when an experienced U-2 pilot named Gary Francis Powers was shot down over Soviet territory and captured. The CIA had chosen May Day on the theory that Soviet anti-aircraft personnel would have their guards down on one of the Soviet Union's most important holidays. Unfortunately, they were wrong. A few hours into his flight, which had taken off from Peshawar, Pakistan, with the goal of photographing Soviet ICBM (intercontinental ballistic missile) sites in the cities of Pisetsk and Sverdlovsk, Powers was shot down by up to fourteen Soviet SA-2 surface-to-air missiles described by one analyst as being the size and shape of telephone poles. Powers was able to bail out and open his parachute in time to land unhurt, after which he was captured by Soviet military personnel.

Eisenhower, who had been reluctant to authorize the Powers mission in the first place, was both angered and humiliated by the incident. The CIA's Richard Bissell claimed that "I was constantly pressing Eisenhower for more flights and he was constantly resisting me. I had to go to the mat on nearly every authorization because he was following the advice of the other Dulles brother, John Foster [Secretary of State and the brother of Bissell's boss, CIA Director Allen Dulles] . . . who was wringing his hands over the spy flights from the beginning."[47]

When the downing of the U-2 was first announced, the Eisenhower administration tried to tough it out, asserting that the plane was a weather surveillance aircraft that had strayed off course. What they hadn't counted on was that not only had Powers survived, but he had confessed the purpose of his mission to the Soviets. Soviet Premier Nikita Khrushchev had a field day at Eisenhower's expense, chiding him repeatedly at a U.S.-Soviet summit two weeks later. Eisenhower tried to save face by promising the Soviets that the flights would be halted, but when Khrushchev demanded an apology, the President refused, and the summit ended on that sour note.

In the meantime, the missile buildup in the United States continued, despite indications from the U-2 flights that the Soviet missile program was much less advanced than the official U.S. government position suggested. President Eisenhower's administration had been attempting to hold the line on defense expenditures even in the face of pressures from the military leadership and the Democratic Party, but the Soviet Union's successful fall 1957 launch of the Sputnik satellite made it increasingly difficult to do so. Pressures mounted in the run-up to the 1960 elections, when Democratic presidential candidate John F. Kennedy repeatedly slammed Eisenhower for allegedly leaving the United States vulnerable to a Soviet first strike. The tragedy of all of this was that Eisenhower knew from the U-2 flights that Soviet capabilities were substantially less than the missile gap crowd was asserting, but felt restrained for security reasons from providing proof of that fact.

It wasn't as if Eisenhower's administration had been sitting on its hands before the Sputnik flight. As of mid-1955, there were four separate ballistic missile programs under way in the Army and the Air Force. But when the Navy tried to get into the act, the administration cited budget restrictions as a bar to starting a fifth separate program and told the Navy to team up with the Army to see whether a variation of that service's Jupiter missile could be adapted for use on surface ships and submarines.

The Jupiter experiment was a failure, as became evident during the one-year joint Army/Navy project. As Rear Admiral W. F. Raborn explained to a congressional hearing, at 185,000 pounds the Jupiter was a "grotesque missile," far too large to be deployed on a ship of any reasonable size. An added problem was that Jupiter was a liquid-fueled missile that would be difficult and dangerous to handle in the close quarters of a submarine.[48]

Given these problems, as well as the growing concern that the Soviets might develop a capability to take out stationary land-based ballistic missiles in a first strike, the Navy was given its wish for its own program, and the Polaris project was born. The advantage of a submarine-launched ballistic missile (SLBM) was its mobility, which made it difficult to find and target. Thus, it was argued, the SLBM offered the best chance of making the U.S. nuclear force invulnerable to an enemy attack. It was this argument more than any other that sustained funding for the Polaris program even as financing for other major programs ebbed and flowed. And the biggest beneficiary of the program was Lockheed, which was selected by the Navy as the principal contractor, in part as a result of relationships built while the company was helping the Navy develop solid fuel for use in the submarine-launched missile. The program was to become a steady revenue source for the company for over a decade, during which time the company received $3.5 billion in prime contract awards for building 656 Polaris missiles, plus spare parts.[49]

This is not to suggest that the ramping up of the Polaris program was a slam dunk. It faced initial resistance from within the Navy, where top officials were concerned that the program would eat up large parts of the budget, undercutting funding for surface ships and fleet maintenance as well as cornering the market on the bulk of modernization funds. Even the submarine operators had their doubts: They feared that the advent of submarine-launched missiles would take the skill out of their jobs. As Harvey Sapolsky puts it in his landmark study of the Polaris program, "In their view, the submarines were made to sink ships with torpedoes, not to blast land targets with missiles; submarine warfare was a battle of wits against an opponent, not a demonstration of technological sophistication."[50] Ultimately these internal criticisms would be overcome, and Polaris development would be removed from traditional Navy agencies and placed in the hands of the Special Projects Office (SPO), run by Rear Admiral W. F. Raborn, who was as skillful an advocate as the Navy had seen.

Raborn quarterbacked an all-hands-on-deck lobbying effort on behalf of Polaris, touring plants and shipyards around the country to stimulate enthusiasm for the project. His efforts were reinforced by the work of a team of "technical information officers" who made presentations to business groups, military reservists, and professional associations, spreading the word about the need for Polaris as a response to what they asserted was a growing Soviet missile threat. Newly elected members of Congress were offered special classified briefings on the program, and contractors like Lockheed, General Electric, Westinghouse, and Aerojet General engaged in special outreach and advertising campaigns, both in areas where they had factories and for national audiences.[51]

Polaris was not free of technical glitches, but it was generally seen as one of the most successful military procurement efforts of its era, coming in on budget and ahead of schedule (although the missile had a slightly shorter range than originally claimed). Polaris took less than four years from the authorization of early development in late 1956 to its first successful launch from a submarine in July 1960, a creditable record for such a complex system. Although much of the credit for this success went to the Navy's Special Projects Office for its management of the program, contractors like Lockheed clearly played a central role, as it was their job to develop the technology and deliver the final product. Even given this relative success, there were criticisms of the program along the way. The House Committee on Science and Astronautics held hearings in July 1959 that focused in part on high-profile test failures of the project, drawing headlines such as "Undersea Firings of Polaris Missile Beset by Troubles" and "Polaris Missile Blown Up in Test."[52] But Admiral Raborn was able to reassure the committee that the program was on track, and from that point onward, criticisms from Congress were nearly nonexistent.

The critical press coverage was far outweighed by positive media accounts, including a gushing report by *New York Times* reporter Hanson Baldwin filed from aboard a naval observation ship during the first launch of a Polaris from a submerged submarine. Baldwin asserted that "the Navy opened a new chapter in warfare today as a submarine—for the first time—successfully fired a ballistic missile from underwater."[53] Edward R. Murrow and Fred Friendly did a positive account of the Polaris program's development in a documentary for the now-famous *CBS Reports* program, tempered only by Murrow's observation that, "if the Polaris missile is ever fired in earnest, it has been a failure."[54]

From a business perspective, the U-2 and Polaris programs helped Lockheed make the critical transition from an aviation company involved primarily in the production of combat aircraft and transport planes to a genuine aerospace giant involved in projects that were central to the evolving Cold War military force of the United States.

But even these successful projects were not enough to keep the company's finances on an upward path. Problems with the Electra aircraft—including expensive retrofits of existing planes after two crashes tied to design flaws—cost the company over $24 million. And cuts in the non-nuclear parts of the military budget left Lockheed high and dry on its JetStar transport plane, a project that had cost the company $31 million to develop. As a result of these and other losing propositions, the company's stock value fell by nearly one-half during 1960, reaching its low point in August, just one month after the high-profile success of the first underwater test of the Polaris.[55]

Bob Gross, still running Lockheed after all these years, decided that the company should take the hit from its series of misfortunes all at once, leading to a record $55 million loss in the first quarter of 1960. The Polaris—poised for possible sales to Great Britain, America's closest NATO ally—was the brightest spot in an otherwise grim picture, accounting for most of the company's $1.1 billion backlog.[56]

It would take nearly two years for the company to bounce back. By March 1962, Lockheed had ridden the wave of the Kennedy administration's defense buildup to post its largest profits ever, aided by its decision to leave commercial markets behind and focus on garnering military and aerospace orders, including substantial earnings from its Agena rocket, which by that point had accounted for three-quarters of the payload launched into space by the United States. But as a *Time* magazine profile of the company noted, the Polaris missile was still the "Sunday punch of the nation's fastest growing defense system," bringing in $372 million in 1961 alone. Missile gap or no missile gap, the Kennedy administration nearly tripled spending on the Polaris program (submarines and missiles) and moved from a modest goal of building six ships to a target of forty-one total by the late 1960s. Kennedy's projections proved out: The forty-first boat was christened on July 21, 1966.[57]

But the company's successes of the early 1960s were not long-lived. After a series of cost overruns and canceled programs, the company was soon in its worst financial condition since the bankruptcy suffered in the early 1930s. At the center of Lockheed's troubles was the largest aircraft ever conceived—the C-5A Galaxy.

Chapter 4

THE C-5A SCANDAL

The Vietnam War put tremendous pressure on the U.S. military's transportation systems—the planes and ships that were needed to deliver millions of tons of military equipment to battlefields ten thousand miles away. One of the workhorses of this effort was the Lockheed C-130, a transport aircraft developed in the mid-1950s. But well before the peak of the U.S. intervention in Vietnam, the Air Force decided that it needed a larger aircraft—something much larger. The rationale was to get troops quickly to any part of the world, within days rather than weeks or months. Even as one war was ramping up, the Air Force appeared to be easing the path toward future conflicts.

This impulse was the genesis of the C-5A Galaxy, the largest military aircraft ever built. As author Berkeley Rice notes in his 1971 book on the C-5A, its dimensions alone are awe-inspiring. At over 260 feet long, with a 223-foot wing span, one C-5A just barely fits into an average-sized football stadium. And with a tail wing that reaches six stories in height, it makes for an intimidating presence.[1]

Even the name was huge. Its predecessors in the military transport field had pithy names like Hercules and Starlifter. But as Senator William Proxmire (D-WI) observed: "It was so gigantic . . . that instead of being named for only one star or planet in the firmament, it was called the Galaxy."[2]

The proposed performance characteristics of the aircraft were equally impressive. The plane's engines were meant to produce electricity equivalent to that needed to power a city of fifty thousand people. And despite its size, the original specs called for the aircraft to be able to land on a dirt runway of just four thousand feet—less than half the length of the landing field needed for a normal (much smaller) airliner.[3]

One of the more controversial aspects of the proposed plane was its projected ability to get war matériel to any spot in the world on extremely short notice—"like having a military base in nearly every strategic spot on the globe," as a Lockheed marketing brochure put it.[4] But this military strong point was viewed as a political liability by Senator William Fulbright (D-AR), then the Senate Foreign Relations Committee chairman. He argued in 1969, when the first C-5As were nearing production, that "if we have big planes which will, on a moment's notice, take two or three divisions to every outbreak that may occur, we will be tempted to do it. . . . But I don't think we should be projecting our military power all over the world, and undertaking to settle every quarrel that breaks out anywhere."[5] Fulbright was not alone in his anti-interventionist sentiments—the fiasco in Vietnam had generated similar feelings among many members of Congress and much of the public.

Its strategic merits aside, Lockheed's C-5A Galaxy might never have been built in the first place if the Air Force's own procurement advisers had had their way. The original bidders for the enormous new transport plane were Boeing, Lockheed-Georgia, and the old Douglas Aircraft Corporation. Douglas later merged with McDonnell Aircraft to form McDonnell Douglas, which in turn was swallowed up by Boeing in the 1990s defense merger binge.

After wending its way through two layers of Air Force bureaucracy— a four-hundred-person C-5A evaluation group and the C-5A Source Selection Board, composed of four generals—the Boeing design was deemed superior, even though its bid price of $2.3 billion was $400 million more than Lockheed's offer.[6]

Lockheed had been given every opportunity to win the bid from Boeing. After its original design failed to meet the Air Force's requirements for short takeoff and landing capabilities, the evaluators gave Lockheed a chance to fix its design, which it did by proposing larger wings and wing flaps for the aircraft. Curiously, despite these additions, Lockheed's proposed price held firm at $1.9 billion.

But the fight wasn't over, and the selection board's recommendation was not the last word. The Lockheed lobby burst into action, beginning with the mayor of Marietta, Georgia, Howard Atherton, whose city depended heavily on the Lockheed plant that had produced both the C-130 and C-141 transport aircraft. Without the C-5A contract, Marietta stood to lose up to twenty thousand jobs, not to mention the economic activity generated by the wages spent in the area by Lockheed employees. So it was natural for Atherton to turn for help to his state's most powerful politician, the late Senator Richard Russell, who chaired not only the Senate Armed Services Committee but the Senate Appropriations Committee's defense subcommittee and who was also a close friend and mentor of President Lyndon Johnson. Atherton later noted that despite the fact that "Russell didn't think the C-5A was really needed," Marietta "wouldn't have gotten the contract" without his efforts.[7] Lyndon Johnson confirmed Atherton's assessment a few years later when he attended the rollout of the first C-5A: "I would have you folks know that there are a lot of Marietta, Georgias scattered throughout our fifty states. All of them would like to have the pride that comes from this production, but all of them don't have the Georgia delegation."[8]

Lockheed did its part in winning the battle for the C-5A, most notably by suggesting that it might place a sub-assembly factory for the plane in Charleston, South Carolina, in the heart of the district of House Armed Services Committee Chairman L. Mendel Rivers.[9] Two other C-5A contractors, AVCO and General Electric, had already done so. Lockheed was so intent on getting on Rivers's good side that it even pitched in to help pay for a bust of the congressman that was placed on the main drag in Charleston. Rivers became one of the fiercest congressional defenders of the Galaxy.[10]

Rivers was a good friend to have. An unapologetic practitioner of pork barrel politics, he openly bragged about the number of military bases and arms factories he had helped attract to his part of South Carolina. His campaign slogan—"Rivers Delivers"—was largely based on his ability to steer Pentagon funds into his district. The word in South Carolina was that if Rivers got one more base for the Charleston area it would sink into the Atlantic Ocean. Rivers was the primary reason that the House Armed Services Committee never made a serious inquiry into the problems of the C-5A program, even when it became clear from the work of other committees that it had enormous cost and performance problems. At one hearing Rivers took the opportunity to tell Lockheed CEO Dan Haughton what a great plane his company was building and railed against those who had "lambasted" the C-5A: "It is ridiculous, the fine showing this plane has made. I understand—you can tell me—it has exceeded every expectation anybody in the know had of this plane. Is that a fact?"[11]

Haughton heartily agreed, even putting a number on the plane's superiority by asserting that it had exceeded expectations by "about 7 per cent." As for the cost problem, Rivers had no qualms: "Regardless of what the plane costs, we need it, and we must have it." Case closed, as far as Rivers was concerned.[12]

Although having Russell and Rivers in their corner couldn't hurt, the most powerful tool in Lockheed's lobbying arsenal may have been the Pentagon's desire to keep Lockheed-Georgia in business as a part of the "defense industrial base"—the reserve of factories, equipment, laboratories, and skilled personnel that the Department of Defense would draw on in the event of the need to mobilize for war or increase weapons production in response to new global threats. While Boeing was flush with orders for airliners and other military aircraft, Lockheed-Georgia had specialized in military transports, and it was running out of work on that front.

The practice of doling out contracts according to the financial needs of the arms makers rather than the merits of a particular weapons design is a long-standing practice in the military-industrial complex, where the investments needed to keep factories at the ready to build modern armaments can run into the billions of dollars. As a result, a symbiotic relationship has developed between the Pentagon and its top contractors in which each needs the other to survive and prosper. But the decision to bolster Lockheed by awarding it the C-5A contract directly contradicted the rhetoric of Defense Secretary

Robert McNamara, who argued in his 1966 budget submission that the Defense Department should not "depart from the strictest standards of military need and operating efficiency in order to aid an economically distressed company or community."[13] Fine words, but completely out of step with what his department ended up doing in the C-5A case.

Without giving any rationale beyond vague platitudes about the Lockheed design serving the "national interest," the Air Force overruled its own selection board and opted to buy the company's C-5A Galaxy rather than Boeing's proposed design. One specific factor it cited was the C-5A's lower price—a claim that proved to be a cruel joke on the American taxpayer once the system's record cost overruns began rolling in like waves at high tide. There is no question that having friends like Richard Russell and Lyndon Johnson was a huge help in switching the contract over to Lockheed, but the budgetary and security costs of this successful lobbying effort were to have devastating repercussions for the company and the country.

The Pentagon and the Air Force, predicting unprecedented performance delivered on budget and on time, had high hopes for the C-5A. To ensure this result, a protégé of Robert McNamara designed a new kind of contract that was supposed to institute new safeguards against excess costs. It may be hard to remember in light of his disastrous performance as Johnson's Defense Secretary during the Vietnam War, but Robert McNamara came into office touting his skills as an efficiency expert. He promised to put his private-sector experience as President of Ford Motor Company to work toward that end. His partners in this effort were a group of bright young civilians, including numerous MBAs from Harvard, who came to be known within the Pentagon as "the Whiz Kids." They engaged in complex computer analyses designed to determine the cost-effectiveness of a given weapon system relative to viable alternatives.

In keeping with the spirit of McNamara's enterprise, Robert Charles, the Assistant Secretary of the Air Force for Installations and Logistics—and a former vice president of McDonnell Aircraft—developed an innovative contract known as total package procurement (TPP), which received its initial tryout on the C-5A.[14] TPP was a departure from the existing method, which allowed companies to bid on the research and development (R&D) phase of a contract without having to project production costs. As a result, the firm that won the R&D contract usually won the production award as well, since that firm and that firm alone had developed the technology for the weapon system in question. The Pentagon would then generally be forced to accept the company's production bid, no matter how high. The alternative would be to start over with a new R&D contractor, an option that neither time nor money would normally allow. By contrast, the new TPP method required companies to estimate research, development, and production costs up front, including commitments to meeting timelines for delivery and achieving key performance characteristics. In the case of the C-5A, slipping on schedule would bring penalties of $12,000 per day—with a maximum fine of up to $11 million. Lockheed would also be responsible for absorbing the cost of structural deficiencies. Charles bragged that the arrangement was "probably the toughest contract for a major defense system ever entered into by the Pentagon."[15] McNamara concurred, telling Congress that it was a "damned good contract" that "represents a major breakthrough in contracting techniques."[16]

The problem with TPP contracting, as would emerge during the history of the C-5A project, was that companies were being asked to project prices out over a long time period—up to ten years in some cases. This left ample room for the time-honored concept of "buying in": An arms manufacturer would bid low in order to get a contract and then receive hundreds of millions, or even billions, of dollars more once it charged the Pentagon for the final—and much higher—cost of actually building the system. Under the TPP contract, the maximum fine of $11 million for falling behind on the schedule was next to nothing compared to the multibillion-dollar price tag of a system like the C-5A. And the C-5A was to be the test case for the TPP contracting method. Beyond that, the Pentagon had often been lax in enforcing even those modest penalties that were included in major contracts. So even from the outset, Lockheed executives wouldn't exactly be staying up nights worrying about the allegedly "tough" TPP contracting method.

In addition to the relatively modest scale of the financial penalties for cost overruns and schedule delays, Robert Charles's new state-of-the-art contracting method was riddled with loopholes. For example, the government was on the hook for 70 percent of the costs of project overruns, up to the first 30 percent of excess costs. And most importantly of all to Lockheed's bottom line, there was a "repricing" formula that would essentially allow the overruns experienced on the first batch of C-5As to be folded into the cost of the second batch. In other words, the hidden rewards for ramping up costs ended up far outweighing the explicit penalties that Charles had built into the contract. The provision that allowed Lockheed to overcharge on batch two to make up for cost problems with batch one was dubbed the "golden handshake" by its critics.[17]

The C-5A pricing scandal might have been just another quiet scandal hidden in the fine print of Pentagon paperwork if it hadn't been for A. Ernest Fitzgerald, a courageous cost estimator in the Air Force who repeatedly blew the whistle on the problems with the C-5A program until Congress and the press could not ignore them. Fitzgerald had a reputation within the Air Force for being stubborn and inquisitive. These qualities helped him unearth the C-5A scandal, but they also got him in and out of hot water with the bureaucracy on a regular basis. He was not the sort of person who would "go along to get along."

Ernie Fitzgerald joined the Pentagon in September 1965 after a successful career running an industrial engineering consulting firm that had done work for the likes of General Electric and North American Aviation. Born in Birmingham, Alabama, and schooled in industrial engineering at the University of Alabama, Fitzgerald described himself in his memoir as "a country boy in the aerospace industry."[18] He was far more sophisticated than he let on, however, and it was clear that Fitzgerald felt that he could have a greater impact working in the Pentagon than he could running a small private firm. He took the job at the Department of Defense over the objections of his wife, who was less than thrilled with the fact that he would have to take a pay cut to enter government service. But Fitzgerald was attracted by McNamara's public commitments to efficiency and cost control, and he wanted to help turn the Defense Secretary's rhetoric into reality.

Fitzgerald's initial misgivings about the costs and performance of the C-5A were bottled up inside the Pentagon and the Air Force, hidden from scrutiny by the Congress, the media, and the taxpayers. His first hint that something was wrong came in a VuGraph briefing (the predecessor to today's PowerPoint presentations) by Air Force officials in which Fitzgerald was introduced to the concept of incorporating cost overruns from the first batch of C-5As into a second batch. The tip-off was the Air Force briefers' reference to "an upward revision of planned costs" in round two of the procurement. Fitzgerald dug further and found that since the initial estimates were made in early 1964, projected costs for the program had increased by nearly $2 billion, with no relief in sight. Even before the cost overruns, the C-5A had been the most expensive aircraft project ever undertaken by the U.S. Air Force; now it was about to set records for excess costs as well.[19]

Although internal documents in Fitzgerald's possession made it clear that the Air Force knew of the cost problems from early on, its representatives continued to tell Congress that all was well with the program. Given their parochial interests in the C-5A, neither House Armed Services Committee Chairman Mendel Rivers nor Senate Armed Services Committee ranking Democrat Richard Russell were inclined to ask tough questions of the Air Force briefers. And Senator John Stennis (D-MS), who replaced Russell as Armed Services chair in 1969 when Russell moved up to run the even more powerful Appropriations Committee, was a good friend of the military who had done prodigious work in steering military bases and weapons projects to his home state of Mississippi. He wasn't about to bite the hand that fed him billions in pork barrel projects for his constituents.

Given these realities, the main criticism of the C-5A emanated from two other committees: the Joint Economic Committee's Subcommittee on Economy in Government, chaired by the legendary opponent of government waste, Senator William Proxmire of Wisconsin; and the House Government Operations Committee's Subcommittee on Military Operations. The House committee had one particularly skeptical member, Representative William Moorhead of Pennsylvania, who put his staff member Peter Stockton onto the task of trying to separate truth from myth in the C-5A affair.

It was Proxmire's committee that drew first blood, in November 1968, when his staff contacted Fitzgerald and asked him to testify about problems in military procurement. Proxmire was able to prevail over the objections of Fitzgerald's bosses in the Pentagon—who had tried to prevent him from testifying—and scheduled an appearance for November 13.[20] It was here that the public first learned of Fitzgerald's estimate of a $2 billion cost overrun on the C-5A.

Fitzgerald had never before attended a congressional hearing, much less testified at one, and he described himself as being "somewhat surprised to see so many spectators, reporters, and television camera crews present."[21] His opening statement was a relatively innocuous review of the importance of "sound management systems" in curbing weapons costs. Fitzgerald had been urged by Robert Charles to lay off the C-5A in his testimony, but he couldn't control Proxmire's questions. When Proxmire asked point-blank if it was true that the C-5A program would cost "approximately $2 billion more than was originally estimated and agreed on," Fitzgerald was forced to address the issue. He acknowledged the *possibility* of such an overrun, but he tried to leave himself some wiggle room so as to avoid angering his supervisors at the Department of Defense. His answer was as follows:

> If the total amount of estimated cost variance were to come to pass—and I have no way of knowing if it will come to pass—on both the Lockheed and General Electric contract—General Electric provides the engine for the C-5A airplane—if we were to buy the follow-on production runs using the repricing formula, and if our Air Force support items, things we have not yet contracted for, increase proportionately, your figure could be approximately right.[22]

Fitzgerald characterized his roundabout answer as a "maybe," but that's not how the press treated it. The stories the next day were all about the $2 billion overrun on the C-5A, not the "possible" overrun that "might" occur if a series of circumstances coincided. Once he realized that this was going to be how his remarks were interpreted, "I knew then that I was in the soup," Fitzgerald wrote.[23]

When he returned from his testimony, his secretary asked anxiously, "Have you been fired yet?" to which Fitzgerald replied in the negative.[24] He was, however, iced out of any work related to weapons cost assessment. By March 1969, less than four months after his initial testimony, Fitzgerald had been formally removed from any work involving the acquisition of major weapon systems. Rather than serving on teams to evaluate projects like the new F-15 fighter plane, the F-111 combat aircraft, the Minuteman missile, and the C-5A, Fitzgerald was relegated to work on "the cost of food service" and "minor construction in Thailand." The main project he was tasked to monitor in Thailand was a bowling alley for Air Force personnel. In true Fitzgerald fashion, he questioned the need for the bowling alley in the first place and noted that the project had experienced a 300 percent cost overrun.[25]

Despite the Air Force's efforts to keep him out of the loop on information that he might use in continuing to criticize the C-5A, Fitzgerald carried on with the help of sympathizers within the department who sent him key documents anonymously—or, as Fitzgerald put it, through "unofficial personal channels." He also kept excellent files of memos and cost studies that had been done before his de facto demotion, so he had plenty of ammunition for fighting the Air Force's propaganda machine.

But Fitzgerald's decision to speak out came at a high personal cost. In May 1969 the Air Force's Office of Special Investigations (OSI) started an inquiry regarding Fitzgerald, a probe that was described by one Pentagon insider as a fishing expedition looking for personal information such as incidents of extramarital relationships, drug or alcohol abuse, or "homosexual contacts."[26] When none of these avenues of inquiry bore fruit, OSI hung its hat on false accusations that Fitzgerald had engaged in the unauthorized circulation of classified documents. In fact, the most sensitive pieces of paper distributed by Fitzgerald had been marked "confidential," and he had received assurances from his supervisor that copying and sharing the documents was neither illegal nor improper.[27]

Despite these efforts at harassment and intimidation, Fitzgerald felt relatively safe. In September 1968 he had received a letter granting him "career tenure" under civil service rules. He could still be fired, but it would be much harder to do so. In a Kafkaesque maneuver that was unprecedented even in the annals of the Pentagon, the Air Force moved to revoke Fitzgerald's career tenure on the grounds that the original letter bestowing it had been a "computer error."[28] The bureaucrats in the Air Force could cite no other example in which this had ever happened—besides which, as Fitzgerald noted, the letter in question was not computer-generated: It had an original signature from the chief of civilian personnel at Air Force headquarters.

On November 4, 1969, just short of a year after his original testimony on the C-5A cost overruns, Fitzgerald was given a "notice of separation"—in a word, fired—and told that the unit he worked in, the Office of the Deputy for Management Systems, was being eliminated in an attempt to "economize." The irony of asserting that a sharp-eyed cost-cutter was being canned in order to save money was lost on the Air Force bureaucrats, who were primarily concerned about getting Fitzgerald out of the way so they could continue to offer sweetheart deals to Lockheed and other weapons contractors without being pelted with impertinent questions about the costs of these arrangements to the taxpayer.

The Air Force's move to fire Fitzgerald drew strong opposition from his supporters in Congress. Sixty members of the House of Representatives signed a letter to President Nixon noting the crucial role of "honesty and candor" in government and urging the administration to "repudiate the type of action that was taken against Mr. Fitzgerald, and restore him to his former duties."[29] Senator William Proxmire went further: In a 1969 press conference, he asserted that a crime had been committed in the firing of Fitzgerald. He raised the issue of "whether there is law and order in the Pentagon" and called for the law to be enforced.[30] A Justice Department official assured Proxmire that the Fitzgerald case would receive "priority treatment," but its investigation was dropped a year later before Fitzgerald had even been interviewed. The department suggested that no further action be taken. The choice for Fitzgerald's replacement caused another ripple of outrage. Spencer Schedler, the Assistant Secretary of the Air Force for Financial Management, who "earned" his job through his work for Spiro Agnew during the

1968 presidential campaign, chose a consultant, John Dyment, to review the costs of major Air Force systems. Dyment was a partner in Arthur Young and Company, Lockheed's chief accounting firm and a partner in covering up the company's cost overruns on the C-5A. Dyment's hiring created a firestorm of criticism in Congress and the press. Representative William Moorhead (D-PA) said it was like "sending a bulldog to guard the hamburger." After futile attempts to explain that there was no conflict of interest, the Air Force gave in and fired Dyment after one day on the job.[31]

In the meantime, the actions of Fitzgerald's congressional supporters did him little good, at least in the short term. About four years later, Fitzgerald was finally allowed to return to the Pentagon, but his responsibilities were carefully circumscribed to make sure he couldn't cause any "trouble" by exposing waste, fraud, or abuse in contract pricing and performance. Once he got his job back at the Pentagon, it took another eight years before Fitzgerald was once again allowed to work on assessing the problems and progress involved in developing complex weapon systems. It took a lawsuit to get the job done. A June 15, 1982, consent decree stated that "the Air Force shall in good faith assign Fitzgerald tasks and work assignments commensurate with the position of Management Systems Deputy to the Assistant Secretary of Defense (Financial Management) and provide him with the resources to carry them out."[32] But Fitzgerald wasn't exactly welcomed with open arms. In a press interview, Secretary of the Air Force Verne Orr called Fitzgerald "the most hated man in the Air Force."[33]

One of the most frightening revelations that came out of Fitzgerald's lawsuit was that the decision to fire him went all the way up the chain, straight to the Oval Office.

On January 31, 1973, fresh from his landslide victory over George McGovern in the 1972 elections, Nixon was relaxing with aides John Ehrlichman and Charles Colson, reviewing his performance in a press conference he had just finished. Nixon was proud of himself: "Like out there today I was very informal today. I just, you know, talked quite a while when I wanted to. Even kidded around with Mollenhoff. He sure presses, though." The Mollenhoff referred to was Clark Mollenhoff, a journalist and former Nixon aide who asked a question about developments in the civil service hearing that dealt with the propriety of firing Fitzgerald. At six-foot-four, 250 pounds, Mollenhoff—nicknamed "Boomer" for his loud voice—was hard to miss, and hard for Nixon to ignore. In response to Mollenhoff's question, which related to whether the Secretary of the Air Force could claim executive privilege in refusing to answer questions in the Fitzgerald hearings, Nixon acknowledged that he had known about the Fitzgerald firing. Later, in his office, Nixon went further. "This guy that was fired . . . I'd marked it in the news summary. That's how it happened. I said, get rid of that son of a bitch." Nixon went on to say that Fitzgerald's sin was that he was "frankly, not taking orders" by exposing the overruns on the C-5A. Nixon seemed to think that Fitzgerald should have stuck to working inside the Air Force. This was a futile strategy, as Fitzgerald's account of his troubles makes clear.[34]

Despite the Air Force's campaign to silence him—backed up, as we now know, by the President himself—Fitzgerald was able to make a great deal of useful information public between his original testimony in November 1968 and his firing in 1969. One particularly impressive performance came in his May 1969 appearance before the House Armed Services Committee and its pro-C-5A chairman, Mendel Rivers. In hearings that occurred a week before Fitzgerald testified, Rivers had repeatedly served up softball questions to Defense Secretary Melvin Laird. "Those fellows in the other body [the Senate] are going to beat this thing to death," Rivers warned Laird. "From where I sit, at least, you are getting a plane that is going to work, that is fulfilling a very urgent need." Rivers then proceeded to let Laird enter into the record cost overrun figures of $382 million to $500 million—one-quarter or less of the figure that had been documented by Fitzgerald. When Rivers noted that "people over in the other body are talking about $2 billion," Air Force Chief of Staff John McConnell chimed in and said, "They have not got the right information, Mr. Chairman."[35]

It was into this less than sympathetic environment that Ernie Fitzgerald was called to testify just a week later at the behest of Representative Otis Pike (D-NY), one of a handful of C-5A critics in the House informally known as the "Fearless Five." Fitzgerald used a series of internal Air Force memos and documents to show that not only was the real cost overrun figure at least $2 billion, but that the top officials in the Air Force had known this since 1966. In other words, they had misled Congress about the problem for three years and would have continued to do so for as long as they could get away with it if Fitzgerald had not gotten involved. Ignoring the fact that Fitzgerald had been working on the C-5A cost issue for over three years, Rivers tried to undercut Fitzgerald's revelations by suggesting that he was somehow too inexperienced to know what he was talking about.

It was a bad day all around for Rivers. Not only did he fail to refute Fitzgerald's damning testimony, but he lost a critical argument with Otis Pike regarding the cost of spare parts for the C-5A. After getting an investigator from the General Accounting Office to acknowledge that he didn't "think even the Air Force knows exactly how much they will ultimately spend for spare parts on this aircraft," Pike noted that Lockheed was in the enviable position of having a provision in the contract calling upon them to provide spare parts, but there was no mention of the price. "I don't want to interrupt you," Rivers said disingenuously, "but there is no contract for spares." "There is a contract that says they can't get them anywhere else," replied Pike.

"I don't care what the contract says," Rivers acknowledged in frustration.[36]

In an argument that foreshadowed the fights in the Reagan era over $600 toilet seats and $7,662 coffeemakers procured for key weapon systems, Pike noted that "time after time in procurements, they get in trouble and so they make up their hole by laying it on the spare parts. There's not a darned thing the Air Force can do about it. . . . Once they start buying equipment, they have got to have the spare parts."[37]

In his assertions of an Air Force cover-up on the question of the C-5A, Fitzgerald was merely reinforcing what an Air Force official had acknowledged the month before in hearings before Representative Chet Hollifield's (D-CA) House Government Operations Committee. Hollifield, a Lockheed ally whose California district was chockfull of military contractors, had hoped to use the proceedings to announce a blue-ribbon panel on weapons procurement, under the well-worn theory that it is better to study an issue than to take action. Representative William Moorhead disagreed, and he came to the hearing armed with an internal Air Force memo acknowledging that the Air Force had purposely doctored the figures and kept information on the full overrun from the Congress. According to Moorhead's staffer Peter Stockton, when Hollifield realized what was happening, he leaned over his chair and grabbed Moorhead, saying, "You're a son of a bitch for bringing that thing in here." Things only got worse for Hollifield and his allies at Lockheed and in the Air Force when Colonel Kenneth Beckman, the Air Force official in charge of the C-5A program, acknowledged the cover-up. He said, "The nature of the estimates was such that if publicly disclosed, they might put Lockheed's position in the common market in jeopardy."[38] It soon became apparent that by the "common market" Beckman meant the stock market. Had the Air Force withheld vital cost information from Congress to boost Lockheed's stock?

The charge was plausible enough that it sparked an investigation by the Securities and Exchange Commission (SEC), which confirmed that the Air Force and Lockheed had both concealed the cost overruns on the C-5A—the Air Force in its dealings with Congress, and Lockheed in its official financial statements. The SEC found that Lockheed executives had sold off their stock in large amounts at around the time that the Air Force had expressed serious concerns about the C-5A. Company executives had withheld this information from other shareholders. One such shareholder, Colonial Realty, sued the company after it lost 50 percent on its Lockheed bonds at the same time that the company's leaders were selling off large chunks of their investments in their own firm.[39] The SEC ultimately decided that no law had been broken and no insider trading had occurred, but an SEC staffer told Congress that it had been a close call as to whether to pursue a criminal prosecution against one company executive. The SEC did express concerns about whether the company had adequately disclosed known problems with the C-5A in its filings with the agency, but it decided that these failures did not rise to the level of criminal conduct.[40]

The cover-up of Lockheed's sweetheart deal on the C-5A was only part of the story. After all, as the plane's proponents had argued, what's a billion dollars or two extra when you're building something that is absolutely essential for national security? The "need" for the plane hinged in large part on whether one thought the United States needed to have the power to intervene anywhere in the world on short notice. Lockheed and the Air Force viewed this capability as a plus, while critics like Senator Fulbright saw it as a dangerous tool that could embroil the United States in unnecessary conflicts. If we can intervene quickly and easily, we are more likely to do so, the plane's critics suggested. Supporters of the plane argued the opposite, that the capability to intervene might deter countries from taking actions contrary to U.S. interests, thereby reducing the need to intervene.

Even if one wanted a cargo plane suited to rapid intervention in foreign wars, in the end the C-5A had little to offer. In June 1969, Bernard Rossiter of the *Washington Post* reported on an internal Pentagon study that suggested that buying the second "batch" of C-5As—the batch that would help Lockheed recoup the money it had lost to cost overruns on batch one—was unnecessary. The study, by the Defense Department's Office of Systems Analysis, asserted that C-5As provided an advantage only in the first ten days of a conflict, after which existing ships and transport planes could get the job done just as quickly and at a far lower cost.[41]

What was not being discussed in all of this was whether the plane could perform as advertised. Could it carry as much cargo as promised, could it travel at the projected speed, would it be durable and sustainable, and would it in fact be able to land on small, unimproved airfields? Without answering these questions, the strategic debate about how, when, and in what circumstances the planes should be used would be rendered irrelevant.

The first official recognition of the seriousness of the technical problems plaguing the C-5A didn't surface until March 1971, years after Fitzgerald had first raised them and after a number of the planes were already in service. The GAO did a report that made the following revelations: "The Air Force is accepting the C-5A aircraft with major deficiencies, in the landing gear, wings, and avionics. The deficiencies have restricted the C-5A to perform its basic cargo mission only. The C-5A cannot perform its tactical mission until certain deficiencies are corrected."[42]

The GAO further noted that the plane could land only on paved runways, and that attempts to land on dirt runways were so damaging to the plane's engines and other key components that the Air Force had stopped testing to see whether the C-5A would ever achieve such a capability. The C-5A could not perform its most critical mission.

Congress had first heard about technical problems with the C-5A in November 1968, but they had begun to be noticed much earlier. As Berkeley Rice notes, "Early in 1966 the men down at Marietta [the site of Lockheed-Georgia's assembly plant] began to encounter a series of unforeseen technical problems referred to in the trade as 'unk-unks'—or unknown unknowns."[43] The fixes sometimes caused more harm than the problems they were meant to solve. For example, to deal with the fact that the plane was well over its projected weight, Lockheed decided to use lighter metals to connect the pieces of the aircraft's body, such as titanium fasteners. This decision was to be the seed of later problems.

In July 1969, a C-5A undergoing ground testing suffered a cracked wing. The Air Force claimed that the crack occurred because the plane was carrying 128 percent of its normal load. This assertion ignored the fact that by the terms of the contract the C-5A was supposed to be able to carry 150 percent of its normal load. Matters took a turn for the worse a few months later when a C-5A whose wings had been reinforced suffered a wing crack again, even though it was carrying only 83 percent of the plane's projected normal load. Despite this problem, the Air Force accepted the first C-5A in December 1970, in the face of charges by Representative William Moorhead that the plane was "inferior" and "defective":

> We were told it could do all sorts of marvelous things. How many of these marvelous things can the C-5A do? Not one. . . . As of now, the C-5A has been so severely restricted that it cannot land or take off from a rough field at all. So the "remote presence" that was so highly touted to Congress a few months ago is more remote than we were led to believe.[44]

Moorhead had good reason to make these charges. Just a few days before the Air Force accepted delivery of the first C-5A, the GAO delivered a report he had requested on the aircraft's technical problems. The report found twenty-five defects, including limits on the load the plane could carry of less than half of its projected capacity, restrictions on maximum speed, landing gear problems, and problems with the radar system. Far from the claims of the plane's supporters that the need for its capabilities was worth it even for a few billion dollars more, it turned out that the C-5A had not only run a record $2 billion cost overrun but could not perform its original mission. Regardless of one's position on the strategic necessity for the aircraft, its performance problems were so wide-ranging that it couldn't provide its proposed capabilities in any case. It was a colossal waste of money, and a potential danger to the U.S. pilots and air crews who were supposed to use the plane.

Observers seeking evidence of the problems with the plane didn't have to wade through the dry jargon of a GAO report. There were several spectacular operational failures that could not be swept under the rug. On September 29, 1971, in a takeoff from Altus Air Force Base in Oklahoma, one of a C-5A plane's two engines broke off and went whizzing down the runway without the aircraft, ending up in a ball of flames.[45] On another occasion, one of the plane's tires fell off and another blew out while the plane was landing in front of a delegation of dignitaries at Charleston Air Force Base in South Carolina. Included in the crowd was House Armed Services Committee Chairman Mendel Rivers, one of the plane's biggest boosters. Trying to make light of the incident, an Air Force public information officer told a reporter, "Don't worry, it's got 26 tires left."[46] And on October 17, 1970, the first C-5A delivered to the Air Force had caught fire and blown up on the runway after it had been returned to Lockheed for additional testing. One mechanic was killed and another injured. The plane burned for over two hours before Lockheed personnel could put out the fire.[47]

Ernie Fitzgerald had led the charge on exposing the problems of the C-5A, but it was up to another whistle-blower, Henry Durham, to give an insider's account of the process that led to the poor performance and staggering costs of the C-5A. While Fitzgerald uncovered

the malfeasance on the part of the Air Force in protecting one of its favorite contractors, Durham offered a bird's-eye view of what was happening in Lockheed's factories. In the summer of 1969, Durham was
working as a production supervisor of the C-5A as it moved from assembly to readiness for flight testing. Durham described "mismanagement and waste in all areas" of the factory. More disturbingly, he also
saw "what appears to be collusion with the Air Force to receive credit
and payment for work on aircraft which had not been accomplished."
Given these developments, Durham initiated his own investigation of
practices in the Marietta factory.[48]

His efforts were not well received by company executives. Durham
reported that the director of manufacturing at the plant, Mr. W. P. Frech,
tried to shut him up by asking him if he knew what had happened to
Ernie Fitzgerald when he raised questions about Lockheed in Washington. Durham said that no, he hadn't. According to Durham, Frech
then "said that Mr. Fitzgerald was now chief shithouse inspector for
the civil service and would never be able to get a good job." "I considered this intimidation and the inference of course was that anyone who
bucks Lockheed or the Air Force is in for trouble for the rest of his
life," Durham said.[49]

While Lockheed officials threatened his job, some of his fellow
workers and other members of the Marietta community threatened
his life. After *Washington Post* reporter Morton Mintz published an
article recounting Durham's charges against the company, he was subjected to a series of death threats, as well as threats that his daughter
would be disfigured as punishment for what he had dared to do. Signs
were put up in the Marietta factory saying, KILL PROXMIRE and KILL
DURHAM. The situation was dangerous enough that Proxmire requested and received the protection of federal marshals for Durham
and his family.[50]

To be clear, the threats against Durham appeared to arise sponta-
neously from a minority of members of the Marietta community who
feared that his revelations would hurt Lockheed and threaten their
jobs. This activity was by no means instigated by Lockheed management. Company CEO Daniel Haughton issued the following letter
to all company employees:

SPECIAL BULLETIN–All Divisions, All Plants, All Offices–July 22, 1971
To the Men and Women of Lockheed:

There have been reports that Lockheed employees are threatening Lockheed critics in various ways during the Congressional debate on the
loan guarantee issue.

It is understandable that we would become emotional about others'
threats to our jobs and our futures but it is not acceptable for anyone to
make threats of any type to our critics.

During the next week or two our elected representatives in Congress
will determine our fate. Their deliberations and their voting judgments
must be allowed in an atmosphere of calm deliberation and free opportunity for expressions from all sides. . . .

In spite of our strong feelings, I hope you will join me in expressing
those feelings in a calm and considered manner worthy of the tradition
of the men and women of Lockheed.

Dan Haughton
Chairman of the Board
Lockheed Aircraft Corp.[51]

Haughton's letter would obviously have been stronger if he hadn't
chosen to describe the efforts of men like Henry Durham to expose
waste and abuse at the company as "threats to our jobs and our futures," but it was clear that he did not condone the threats of violence.
The reference in the letter to a vote was to an upcoming congressional
decision on whether to bail the company out of its financial troubles
with a $250 million federal loan guarantee (see next chapter). Durham's
testimony on the company's malfeasance on the C-5A program was
bound to figure in that debate.

Threats notwithstanding, Durham testified before Proxmire's Subcommittee on Economy in Government on September 29, 1971, and
set out Lockheed's pricing practices in exquisite detail: $65 for a sim-
ple bolt; a 67-cent piece of sheet metal sold to the government for
over $19; forty-two tons of steel left to rust behind one of the com-
pany's factories; and dozens of other examples representing millions

upon millions of dollars wasted by Lockheed, all billed to the taxpayer. Many of the parts in question were available at the company's Chattanooga, Tennessee, facility, but lack of inventory control resulted in similar components being bought new at premium prices by officials at the plant in Marietta, Georgia. It was Durham's assertion that these practices permeated Lockheed's production processes and were a prime contributor to the cost overruns on the C-5A.[52]

There were safety problems as well. Planes were rushed through the production line with crucial parts missing so that the company could receive progress payments from the Air Force. Progress payments were installments against the full value of the contract that were transferred to the company as key pieces of work were completed.

Durham witnessed planes with thousands of parts missing that were on their way to be flight-tested, only to have most (but often not all) of them installed at the last minute. In the same hearings where Durham documented these abuses, Lockheed-Georgia executive H. Lee Poore admitted that many C-5As were delivered to the Air Force with parts missing, but he claimed that the parts were not critical to the operation of the planes. Proxmire took issue, questioning how the company knew which parts were "necessary" and which could be done without.[53] The company appeared to be gambling that the missing components would not impair the performance or safety of the C-5A. But given the lax inventory systems described by Durham, the odds of a problem occurring seemed far higher than Poore's bland assurances would have suggested.

Even as the C-5A scandal was unfolding, Lockheed's finances were rapidly eroding. The Air Force met the company more than halfway in paying for the cost overruns, but the company still lost close to $500 million on the contract. And equally or more important, the company's L-1011 Tristar airliner was being squeezed out of the market by the better-performing and far more popular Boeing 747. With its two biggest programs under siege, the prospect of bankruptcy was real.

The company's financial troubles would eventually lead it to receive a major loan guarantee package from the federal government, but long before that occurred the Pentagon and the Air Force did their best to bail the company out by offering to buy more C-5As on even more relaxed terms than had applied to the first batch of eighty-one planes.

The Air Force's efforts to cover up the problems with the plane—up to and including the firing of Ernie Fitzgerald—were closely tied to its interest in getting Congress to approve a second batch of C-5As. Under the "repricing" formula contained in the original contract, any increases in price on the first round of planes could be used as a rationale for increasing the *base price* of the second round. Robert Charles argued that this provision was included to prevent "catastrophic losses" on the part of the contractor, Lockheed. "Run A" of the C-5A was pegged at fifty-three planes, while "Run B" would entail buying fifty-seven, thereby leaving considerable scope to make up losses on Run A with increased charges for Run B.

As it turned out, the first fifty-three planes cost 100 percent more than projected. Thus, under the repricing formula, the second run of fifty-seven planes would cost 240 percent of the original projected cost. In a sense, Lockheed was being rewarded for its own cost overruns—but only if "Run B" was approved by Congress. Without Run B, it was estimated that Lockheed would end up owing $670 million on the first fifty-three planes, enough to potentially bankrupt the company.[54]

Faced with such large potential losses for one of its major contractors, the Air Force decided to ram through the order for the second batch of C-5As in January 1969, without notifying Congress or the incoming Nixon administration. The order was placed just hours before Proxmire was to hold hearings on the deal, and just four days before Nixon was sworn in as president. Even the pro-military *Armed Forces Journal* criticized the Air Force's decision: "With what amounted to embarrassing haste, DoD last week exercised one of its options for more C-5As—after giving Congress and the GAO only the barest details on its long-promised findings on C-5A cost overruns."[55]

At the same time that it was rushing to exercise its option on Run B, the Air Force modified the contract to allow "repricing" of the planes in Run A. While Air Force officials claimed that this was just a matter of "spreading out" the repricing payments over the two batches, the service's own Office of Financial Management estimated that this move would add at least another $300 million to the total cost of the C-5A program.

It further emerged that Robert Charles, the "godfather" of the C-5A contract, had not considered any alternatives before rewarding Lockheed with an additional order. Boeing had made a presentation on how it could adapt its 747 transport to do the C-5A's mission for half the price—for $23 million per plane versus $45 million per plane for the C-5A.

When asked by Representative Robert Leggett of California why he had failed to seek competition for the second batch of transport planes, Charles gave the classic bureaucratic answer: "It was not my responsibility."[56]

Among the many questions raised by the Air Force's rush to judgment on more C-5As, one of the most troubling was: Why now? Other than shoveling cash to Lockheed, there should have been no rush. Only four of the planes from Run A had been completed; seventeen others were in "bits and pieces," according to Lockheed. If the needs of the taxpayer and the military personnel who would have to operate the planes were taken into account, the Air Force would have weighed its options much more carefully before giving the go-ahead for Run B.

As we will see in a moment, the Air Force's best efforts to bail out one of its favorite contractors by bending over backwards to cover its cost overruns was not enough by itself to save Lockheed. The first big challenge for the company came from congressional efforts to stop the program at 81 planes, rather than the 120 that had originally been planned. The first step was a Senate amendment calling for a ninety-day delay in approving the final 24 planes, during which time the need for the plane in the light of its cost and performance problems could be more carefully assessed. Senator John Stennis of Mississippi denounced the amendment as part of an effort to "cut the bone and muscle out of our 1975 military capability," rendering America a "second rate nation" that would be "second best to the Russians."[57] Senator Proxmire responded that the C-5A "has little if anything to do with the real defense of this nation," further noting that the alleged "rapid deployment" capability of the plane had not even been adopted as official policy yet. He also noted that the $2 billion overrun on the C-5A was no small matter, equaling as it did over twice what the federal government was then spending on low- and moderate-income housing and almost as much as Washington spent annually on elementary and secondary education. Given this reality, Proxmire felt that "at least we should have a study by the GAO to find out what they say as to cost effectiveness."[58]

Arguments to the contrary revolved around the notion that the Air Force should know what it needs and Congress should provide it, asking few questions. A related point was that, despite the cost overruns, the nation was basically stuck with the C-5A. Senator Margaret Chase Smith (R-ME) made precisely this point, asserting that, "if we are to make the best of a bad situation, it is better to recoup as much money on the C-5A investment as possible rather than to kill the program."[59] Proxmire's protestations that his amendment was about *reviewing* the program, not killing it, fell on deaf ears, and his amendment lost by a vote of 64–23. The House concurred, after a farcical debate in which C-5A supporter Mendel Rivers limited some C-5A critics to as little as forty-five seconds to make their case.[60]

But what the Congress gave, the Pentagon decided to take away. Worried about the public controversy surrounding the C-5A—and the prospect that it might turn into a campaign to lower the military budget in general—in November 1969 the Pentagon announced that it had decided to limit the program to eighty-one aircraft. Lockheed tried to rescue the order for additional planes by coming up with all manner of schemes to justify its existence, proposing that it could be used as a nuclear bomber, a seaplane, or a radar aircraft. The gambit failed, however, and the company had to accept the fact that it would lose money on the C-5A program, albeit not nearly as much as would have been the case if the Air Force had held it to its original contract.[61]

Lockheed's parallel troubles with its L-1011 airliner combined with the C-5A problem to put the company on the ropes financially. In the lucrative market for passenger planes, Lockheed had fallen behind its rivals, Boeing and Douglas Aircraft, in the early 1960s and had never caught up. This problem was exacerbated in the case of the L-1011, which came out during a slump in the airliner market and was able to land only one hundred firm orders—not nearly enough to recoup its development costs, much less provide Lockheed with a profit on the project.[62] Both Ernest Fitzgerald and Senator Proxmire suspected that the L-1101's problems were the biggest fiscal drain on the company. Even worse, Fitzgerald was finding evidence to suggest that the overruns on the C-5A were in part due to efforts to use funds from that program to directly and indirectly finance the L-1011.

Senator Proxmire was on the case, as usual, pointing out that "it is bad enough that the C-5A is being built in a government-owned plant, with government-owned machinery, and with government progress payments up to 90 per cent of the actual costs. Now we find that Lockheed's commercial ventures are being produced in a government-owned plant under a rental arrangement that is a 'sweetheart contract.'"[63] Proxmire uncovered Pentagon estimates suggesting that Lockheed could lose $700 million or more on the L-1011. This was occurring during the same year (1970) when the company was seeking $344 million from Congress to cover cost overruns on the C-5A, plus a $200 million "contingency fund"—described by Fitzgerald as a "slush fund"—to deal with future cost problems. Fitzgerald noted that the proposed appropriations would buy no aircraft at all, "just overruns." Although there was no question that the C-5A itself had experienced major cost overruns, annual appropriations on this scale reinforced Fitzgerald's suggestion that some of these hundreds of millions of dollars were being used to directly or indirectly prop up the L-1011 program.[64]

Senator Proxmire and his colleague Richard Schweiker of Pennsylvania pushed an amendment that would at least require the Air Force to prove that none of the $200 million "slush fund" would be used to subsidize the L-1011. It failed by a vote of 40–30, and the full $544 million payment for Lockheed was cleared to move forward. Opponents made it sound like the Proxmire amendment would end life as we know it. As Ernest Fitzgerald put it, "Advocates of infinite contributions to Lockheed reacted as if the pallid little amendment would have wrecked the national economy and ensconced Bolsheviks in the Pentagon in one fell swoop."[65] As often happens when a major weapon system is perceived to face a budgetary threat, senators from states where the C-5A was built used the jobs argument as a refuge of last resort. Senator Herman Talmadge of Georgia asserted that "I make no apology for not wanting to throw 40,000 people out of work at one fell swoop." The otherwise liberal Senator Alan Cranston of California hit even harder on the economic argument, suggesting that "at a time like this, when the Nation is in an economic recession with high unemployment, the Government dare not risk deliberately sinking a giant corporation which would take thousands of jobs down with it." The same argument was heard forty years later in the battle over the F-22 fighter plane. How an amendment requiring disclosure of how taxpayer funds would be spent could drive Lockheed out of business was never explained.

This was not to suggest that the company wasn't in deep financial trouble. Even with mounting government support, Lockheed's fortunes were sinking. With losses on the L-1011 adding up and no prospect of making up for them with profits from the C-5A, the company seemed headed for bankruptcy.

Chapter 5

BAILOUT

Too Big to Fail?

By today's standards, with hundreds of billions of dollars going to banks with few strings attached and tens of billions more in taxpayer money going to rescue the auto industry, the political battle over a $250 million government loan guarantee that Lockheed received in 1971 seems almost quaint. But in the words of Richard Kaufman, an aide to Senator William Proxmire at the time of the Lockheed bailout, "There are eerie similarities between now and then . . . the amounts of money are different but the arguments are the same—that they're too big to fail."[1]

Companies had been helped by the government before, but the Lockheed deal was unique. Never before had so much money been offered to a single company, and never had the company in question been as large as Lockheed. The decision over whether to help Lockheed sparked a thorough and at times bitter debate in Congress that revolved around basic issues like the appropriate role of government in the economy and the very meaning of capitalism.

At the center of that debate was William Proxmire, the senior senator from Wisconsin who had already established a reputation as a fierce protector of the federal treasury against waste, fraud, and abuse.

Proxmire was no one to mess with. Fresh from his victory as the leader of a coalition that defeated the federal government's plan to subsidize a new kind of commercial airliner, the supersonic transport plane (SST), he was ready to take on Lockheed and its powerful allies in the battle of the bailout. He had already caused the company headaches by exposing its cost overruns on the C-5A fighter. The last thing Lockheed CEO Dan Haughton and his colleagues wanted was another round with the senator from Wisconsin.

Proxmire had come into the Senate in 1957 when he won a special election to fill the seat of the late Joseph McCarthy, the head of the anti-Communist witch hunts of that decade. When then–Vice President Richard Nixon came to Wisconsin to campaign against Proxmire's reelection to a full Senate term, he warned the voters that if Proxmire won, "you will be in for a wild spending binge by radical Democrats drunk with visions of votes."[2]

Nothing could have been further from the truth.

The bottom line was that Proxmire was cheap. He wore inexpensive suits, ran five miles to work every morning (even as he opposed a proposal for an expensive new gym for members of Congress), ate lunch at his desk, and refused to accept campaign contributions. While his colleagues were raising hundreds of thousands, and then millions, to run for reelection, Proxmire would take in a few hundred dollars at most, much of which was used to buy stamps to send back contributions. Much to his staff's dismay, he routinely gave back about one-third of his annual Senate office allowance.[3]

Luckily for the taxpayers, Proxmire took the same approach to his official business as he did to his personal life, even to the point of turning down several large projects for his own state on the grounds that he viewed them as a waste of money. With this attitude, he relentlessly asked questions about why and how money was being spent, whether it was a few thousand dollars for an odd-seeming research project or hundreds of millions for Lockheed and other large corporations. Since he didn't need money, for reelection or otherwise, he could not be bought. And since he wasn't running any kind of contest to be the most popular man in the Senate, he was willing to take courageous stands alone if necessary, with allies when possible.

The Lockheed bailout fight was tailor-made for Proxmire. It played to his strengths at a time when there was growing public skepticism about the role of major corporations and the integrity of the federal government.

But before the debate over the Lockheed loan guarantees came another, larger bailout that received less attention—and less congressional opposition. Under pressure from Lockheed, the Pentagon agreed to reimburse the company for over $757 million in cost overruns for four key programs: the C-5A, the Cheyenne helicopter, the short-range attack missile (SRAM), and several shipbuilding projects.[4] Ernie Fitzgerald rejected these official numbers, calculating the giveback at over $1 billion once budgetary tricks were taken into account. He called it "the great plane robbery" and claimed, perhaps with a bit of hyperbole, that it was the greatest theft of taxpayer money ever undertaken.[5] The arguments Lockheed used to get these hundreds of millions in "relief" from the Pentagon helped set the stage for the debate on the $250 million in loan guarantees for its L-1011 airliner.

Lockheed's opening gambit in its fight for more funding for its four major programs was to ask the Pentagon to pay it up front for the more than half a billion dollars at stake in the contract disputes. In other words, Lockheed wanted to get the money it sought without proving that it deserved it. Then the company could worry about paying the money back later if it lost one or more of its contract appeals. Lockheed described its demands as "interim financing actions" meant to head off "impairment of continued performance."[6] But it was clear what underlay the company's position: blackmail.

In a letter to the Pentagon, Lockheed argued that failure to grant the funds could have "disastrous potential for our company" as well as "grave consequences on the Department of Defense's ability to maintain industrial support, which it traditionally has required regardless of who ultimately wins [contract disputes like the one at issue]." This ominous language was interpreted by some as a threat to stop work on the four systems in question or even to commit "corporate suicide" by going bankrupt, disrupting the Pentagon's procurement system and the economy as a whole in the process. Company spokesman William

R. Wilson highlighted one aspect of this argument during the bargaining over the Pentagon's bailout of Lockheed when he asserted that if Lockheed didn't get the money it was requesting, "we'll stop the [C-5A] program . . . [then] we don't have a financial drain, then we don't go bankrupt."[7]

Representative William Moorhead (D-PA) described Lockheed's threats in the following terms: "This is like an 80-ton dinosaur who comes to the door and says, 'If you don't feed me I will die and what will you do with 80 tons of dead stinking dinosaur in your yard?'"[8]

Despite protestations from members of Congress like Moorhead and Proxmire, Lockheed's arguments were surprisingly effective. In announcing the outlines of a bailout deal, Deputy Secretary of Defense David Packard—the founder of Hewlett-Packard, at that time a major defense contractor—hit all of the same notes raised by Lockheed officials in demanding payment up front. He asserted that Lockheed's "operations are so intertwined with other companies which also contribute to our national defense that it was necessary to consider a chain reaction upon other companies as well." And without a settlement, Packard suggested, Lockheed would be left "in such a precarious financial condition that their capability for future operations would be jeopardized."[9] Lockheed's threat to commit corporate suicide had worked.

The terms were generous. Lockheed was left to cover just $200 million of its massive overrun on the C-5A, and only half of that would come up front. The other $100 million wouldn't kick in for another three years, and even then it would be paid back over a multiyear period. Of the more than $1.3 billion in additional funds Lockheed was seeking, the government agreed to pick up nearly two-thirds of the tab, $757 million. Lockheed claimed that it would still be responsible for $484 million of its own cost overruns, a figure that some critics viewed as an exaggeration.

As it turned out, this wasn't the end for Lockheed. Within a few months of the settlement, the company was citing the remaining $484 million in costs on mismanaged defense programs as a reason it should receive an additional subsidy—a $250 million loan guarantee to keep its troubled L-1011 Tristar airliner project going. The L-1011 was a wide-bodied, long-range aircraft designed primarily for use as a commercial airliner.

Lockheed officials asserted from the outset that the enormous cost overruns stemmed not from any mistakes on their part but from the unfair policies of the Pentagon. Therefore, they deserved the $250 million loan guarantee. It was the least the government could do after the Pentagon had treated them so badly. They were *victims*, or so they claimed. As Lockheed CEO Daniel Haughton put it in June 1971 testimony before the Senate Banking Committee:

> We believe that the circumstances are unusual . . . and are largely the result of forces not within Lockheed's control. The major part of our $484 million in losses on our defense programs was caused by the use of the total package procurement type of contract, a form never used before and since abandoned as unworkable.[10]

So there it was: Robert McNamara's beloved TPP approach—the "damned good contract" he and his associates had spoken so proudly of when it was introduced in the mid-1960s—was now being cited by Lockheed as the source of all of its difficulties.

It was the TPP contract, with its "stringent set of guarantees, requirements, and specifications" that were "rigidly enforced," that had caused the problems, claimed Haughton. After all, how could the company know at the outset that it would have to "stretch the state of design, engineering, and manufacturing" to build the C-5A?[11]

Haughton's argument overlooked the C-5A's performance problems, from a much lower carrying capacity than advertised to cracked wings to an inability to land on unimproved airstrips at the forward edge of battle (FEBA). In fact, when Lockheed offered to give Representative Moorhead and his staffer Pete Stockton a test ride in the plane, they ended up doing the flight in Georgia because the company was afraid that the plane might be damaged if it landed at the Pittsburgh airport, as Moorhead had originally suggested. Stockton described flying the plane as akin to "flying a barn"; Ernie Fitzgerald's nickname for the C-5A was less generous: "the tin balloon."[12]

Contrary to Haughton's claims, the TPP approach was far from being the rigorous approach that McNamara and his Whiz Kids claimed it would be. In 1970 Nixon administration Secretary of Defense Melvin Laird put it aside in favor of "fly-before-you-buy" contracts that appeared to be a variation on the approach that had prevailed prior to the TPP. Companies would bid first on the research and development of a weapon system, to the point of building prototypes. Then a production contract would be awarded once an acceptable prototype had been built, as measured by cost and performance characteristics. As Laird put it himself, "Before going forward with a major contract, we will be doing more test and evaluation. We will be checking out the systems well in advance, and we will be flying aircraft before we buy the aircraft."[13] A related benefit, in Laird's view, was the ability to avoid long-term commitments to one company that might be hard to back out of down the road.

But while Laird was suggesting that a new contracting approach might be better for the government as a purchaser, he did not go so far as to say that total package procurement was particularly onerous for the contractor, as Lockheed's Haughton was contending. In fact, as noted in chapter 4, there was a "repricing" provision in the C-5A contract—the infamous "golden handshake"—that allowed Lockheed to overcharge on the second batch of planes to cover any losses it might incur for overruns on the first batch. The problem had arisen when the *performance* of the aircraft and a more realistic assessment of the military's need for air transport planes had prevented Lockheed from fully benefiting from the repricing formula: Once the Pentagon decided to limit its purchase to 81 planes rather than the original projected buy of 120 planes, there simply weren't enough planes in the second batch to allow the company to recoup all of its losses on the first batch. As a result, Lockheed did not get paid for all of the $2 billion in overruns it rang up on the C-5A program as a whole.

In short, Lockheed's TPP-based contract had been generous, just not generous enough to reward it for one of the largest cost overruns in the history of military procurement.

While the (largely self-generated) financial woes of Lockheed made headlines, the poor quality of the weapons it was being bailed out on drew far less attention. The problems of the C-5A had become reasonably well known, but another of the "big four" troubled programs—the Cheyenne helicopter—was in some ways an even greater disaster.

Meant to operate as part plane, part helicopter, the Cheyenne was touted as a technical marvel from the start. In a December 1967 article prompted by its first test flight, *New York Times* reporter Gene Smith described the Cheyenne as an aircraft that "can take off and land vertically like a helicopter and yet fly forward with the speed and maneuverability of a small airplane." Lockheed Aircraft Division President A. Carl Kotchian praised the Cheyenne as "a new kind of achievement in the whole field of aircraft." Dr. Finn J. Larsen, head of defense research and engineering at the Pentagon, shared Kotchian's enthusiasm: "There is no question that this aircraft is better than any in the Army at this time."[14]

Before a full production model was even built, the Cheyenne was alleged to fly faster, go farther, hover longer, and carry far more armaments than the Cobra helicopter, which had become a staple of Army air support operations in Vietnam. An Army official noted that the plane was being funded at the expense of cutting funds for tanks and artillery, but that "we think it is worth it."

If only the Cheyenne had lived up to the hype, it might have been one of the most impressive aircraft in aviation history. But its reputation was in inverse relationship to its actual performance. Over a two-year period, costs ballooned from $1 million to $3 million per helicopter, and the Pentagon became increasingly concerned about the Cheyenne's growing roster of technical problems. The issues cited by the Pentagon included a poorly designed rotor, engine problems that prevented it from carrying out certain maneuvers, and a series of other structural problems that caused "excessive roll"—which increased the possibility of a crash. These problems were underscored on March 12, 1969, when a prototype crashed over the Pacific Ocean, killing the pilot.

A month later, Lockheed was given a "cure notice" from the Pentagon, which called on it to fix the problems within a reasonable time frame or risk cancellation of the project. The company could not meet the deadline, and in May 1969, a year and a half after its initial test flight, the production contract for the Cheyenne helicopter was canceled. The Army's official notice of the cancellation cited "problems of rotor stability and control, for which the contractor has developed no adequate solution, [that] have limited the safe speed and maneuverability of the aircraft." What was supposed to be a 375-helicopter program ended up producing just 10 prototypes. Representative Otis Pike (D-NY) asserted that "nearly a half-billion dollars in government money has gone down the drain."

But even as production was canceled, the Army continued to provide development money for the Cheyenne. The program limped along for another three years before the development contract was terminated as well. Major supporters of the program had included Vietnam chief commander General William Westmoreland and Representative Barry Goldwater Jr. (R-CA)—the son of 1964 Republican presidential candidate Barry Goldwater Sr. The younger Goldwater had the Cheyenne plant located in his district.

The Cheyenne episode was made even worse by the fact that the original choice of Lockheed to develop the helicopter was the result of an apparent conflict of interest. Willis Hawkins, the Army official whose office awarded the contract to Lockheed, had come to the Pentagon just two years earlier after a stint as an executive at Lockheed. In shades of what happened forty years later with Vice President Dick Cheney and his former company Halliburton, Hawkins sold his Lockheed stock when he joined the government but continued to receive deferred compensation from the company while in government. The award to Lockheed raised additional eyebrows because the company had never built a helicopter before, much less one as complicated as the Cheyenne. To complete the circle, as the Cheyenne program was imploding, Hawkins went back to Lockheed with his assistant, General William W. Dick Jr.[15]

The case of Willis Hawkins and the Cheyenne was a prime example of the revolving door—the movement of personnel back and forth between major corporations and the government agencies charged with regulating them. The Hawkins case was just the tip of the iceberg. A 1969 report released by William Proxmire's office found that over

2,000 military officers had gone to work for major defense contractors as of that year, a threefold increase over a decade earlier. The biggest practitioner of revolving-door hiring was Lockheed, with 210 former military officers on its payroll. Proxmire had a clear explanation of why this was a serious problem:

> The easy movement of high ranking military officers into jobs with major defense contractors and the reverse movement of top executives in major defense contractors into high Pentagon jobs is solid evidence of the military-industrial complex in operation. It is a real threat to the public interest because it increases the chances of abuse. . . . How hard a bargain will officers involved in procurement planning or specifications drive when they are one or two years from retirement and have the example to look at of over 2,000 fellow officers doing well on the outside after retirement?[16]

During the lifetime of the Cheyenne program, the most outspoken critic of the Hawkins-Lockheed connection was Representative Otis Pike, who attempted to block a $138 million appropriation for the program in part because it had been awarded "in very peculiar circumstances." His reference to the Hawkins-Lockheed tie was not enough to stop the flow of money for the Cheyenne. House Armed Services Committee Chairman Mendel Rivers (D-SC) defended Hawkins, saying that the Congress should not find "guilty every businessman who comes down here." Hawkins denied any wrongdoing, saying that he had excluded himself from the evaluation process for the Cheyenne. And Lockheed CEO Daniel Haughton wrote an open letter to the media in which he claimed to have issued instructions to "all Lockheed employees" to "meticulously avoid any business contacts" with Hawkins. Whether these protestations of innocence were accurate was almost impossible to determine. Unless there had been a whistle-blower inside the Pentagon who witnessed Hawkins weighing in on his former employer's behalf, Lockheed's claims could not be verified. But even the *possibility* of this kind of conflict should have been ruled out by a consistent policy of not appointing former arms industry employees to jobs in which they would be in a position to make decisions that might help their former employer.

Not only had William Proxmire followed Lockheed's machinations in its efforts to get reimbursed for cost overruns on military contracts, but he had challenged the company and its allies in the Pentagon at every turn. So he wasn't buying Lockheed's argument that it was the government's fault that they were in need of cash flow and that therefore the U.S. government should come to the rescue once again, this time on behalf of a civilian project, the L-1011 Tristar airliner.

Lockheed wasn't the only player in the bailout drama. The situation was complicated by the financial problems of Lockheed's partner in the L-1011 venture, the Rolls-Royce Corporation. Over protests by U.S. engine makers like General Electric, Lockheed had chosen the British firm to provide the engines for its new aircraft. The win for Rolls-Royce was celebrated in one British newspaper as "the most succulent plum in commercial aviation history."[17] But the "plum" soon went bad, as the engine costs jumped from the guaranteed price of $840,000 each to a cost of $1.1 million per copy, meaning that Rolls-Royce would lose over a quarter of a million dollars on every engine it delivered. With 540 engines pledged, Rolls-Royce stood to lose nearly $150 million unless Lockheed agreed to renegotiate the contract (or the British government agreed to bail it out).[18] Neither happened, at least not at levels that made a difference. The British government had pumped in $160 million in development costs for the engine project and was willing to offer loan guarantees to any banks lending to Rolls-Royce. Lockheed had its own financial problems and wasn't in any position to share the losses on the engine unless it too got help paying its bills.

In February 1971, Rolls-Royce declared bankruptcy, taking with it any prospect that Lockheed would get the engines for its L-1011, barring extraordinary measures. The bankruptcy triggered frantic rounds of shuttle diplomacy between Los Angeles, London, and New York, involving not only Lockheed executives but also Deputy Secretary of Defense David Packard and officials from the Civil Aeronautics Board and the Federal Reserve Bank.

A tense, multi-sided negotiation resulted in Lockheed offering to pay more for the engines: The price of each L-1011 rose by $1 million.[19] The extra costs were to be split between Lockheed and the airlines that already had L-1011s on order. Lockheed's banks—which had already put up $400 million for the L-1011 project—offered additional credit, *provided* that the loans were guaranteed by the U.S. government. And the British government, which now owned Rolls-Royce after taking it over when the firm went bankrupt, agreed to keep Rolls-Royce in business if the banks and Washington did their parts—sooner rather than later. The British government was losing an estimated $1.5 million per week keeping Rolls-Royce afloat, a position that it could not continue indefinitely.[20]

All of this provided a backdrop for a bitter struggle over U.S. government loan guarantees for Lockheed, in the amount of $250 million.

The Nixon administration moved quickly, appointing perhaps its most skilled negotiator, Treasury Secretary John Connally, as its point man on the deal. Connally was probably best known as the man who had sat in the motorcade alongside John F. Kennedy on November 22, 1963, the day he was assassinated in Dallas. Connally, who was then the governor of Texas, suffered severe gunshot wounds from which he fully recovered.

Connally was Richard Nixon's favorite Democrat, a hard-liner who egged the President on to take ever harsher measures in Vietnam, a move that earned him "admiration . . . to the point of adulation," according to historian Stephen E. Ambrose.[21] The *New York Times* described Connally as "tall, gray-haired, handsome, personable and articulate, and his manners and bearing [reminiscent] of Lyndon Johnson. Yet he is suave and has a touch of the Eastern establishment."[22]

Connally may have been personable, but he could also go for the jugular. Lyndon Johnson, who owed Connally a political debt for running his first successful campaign for the Senate, said that Connally "could leave more dead bodies on the field with less remorse than any politician I ever knew."[23]

Had Proxmire met his match?

Connally was appointed Secretary of the Treasury by Nixon in January 1971. The Lockheed bailout initiative was his first major assignment. By mid-April, he had become a key player in the fight to secure the loan guarantees and the negotiations between Lockheed, the banks, the airlines, and the U.S. and British governments on how to save the L-1011 project. By the end of the month, Connally was testifying to Congress on behalf of the loan guarantee concept. He deflected a criticism by New Mexico Senator Joseph Montoya that any loan guarantee scheme would simply be a subsidy for Rolls-Royce, a competitor of U.S. engine makers General Electric and Pratt & Whitney. Connally argued that it would take too long to develop a U.S.-origin engine and that "I don't think the airlines are going to wait around for re-designing." Connally also hit hard on the economic arguments that were to be central to Lockheed's case, arguing that 25,000 to 30,000 jobs and Lockheed's "survivability" were at stake unless there was "a Government guarantee of about a quarter billion."[24]

Connally's first major "catch" in the drive to build support for the loan guarantee was Senator Hubert Humphrey (D-MN), who asserted that a loan guarantee would be a "feasible way" to help the company and argued that "the Lockheed complex has served this country well, and I don't think we should let it go down the drain."[25] Given that Humphrey had been an important player in the successful effort to end federal subsidies for another commercial airliner, the SST, his position on the L-1011 was viewed as a promising sign by Lockheed supporters.

By June 1971, the preliminary sparring over the L-1011 was followed by an intensive round of congressional hearings. Between June and August, six separate sets of hearings were held on the bailout plan, with the longest involving a full eight days of testimony. By the standards that prevailed decades later, when a major issue might be disposed of in one perfunctory hearing in which most of the members of the committee were absent, the $250 million loan guarantee was being subjected to extraordinary scrutiny.

There probably would have been even more deliberation over the loan guarantees if the Nixon administration had not successfully established an August deadline for a congressional decision. The date was set because of fears that Lockheed wouldn't have the cash flow to survive much beyond that. In June 7 hearings, Connally asked that Congress move within forty days (and, presumably, forty nights if needed). The next day Connally upped that ante by saying that the

British government might pull its support for Rolls-Royce if the U.S. bailout plan wasn't resolved by August 8.

One early gambit by Lockheed supporter Senator Alan Cranston (D-CA)—whose state had thousands of jobs tied up in the L-1011 program—was to separate the issue of Lockheed management from the issue of whether to help the company. Cranston introduced an amendment that called for company CEO Daniel Haughton and Lockheed's entire board to resign as a condition for receiving the loan guarantees. In his testimony, Haughton claimed that he would resign if it yielded the votes needed to secure the loan guarantees, but he was quick to point out that he didn't want to resign. He defended his role, saying, "I don't know why everyone thinks that Lockheed is managed so bad. Because I tell you it is not." Haughton asserted that the real problem was that the company was "always trying to do things that have never been done before." And despite the problems with the C-5A program (as discussed in chapter 4), Haughton described that program as an unqualified success that had resulted in "the greatest airplane that's ever been built, without question."[26]

Cranston's maneuver did not result in Haughton's ouster, but the senator from California supported the loan guarantees to the end. Apparently he was willing to throw money at a company that he viewed as grossly mismanaged.

The appeal to jobs was carried into the hearing process, by both Lockheed and the Nixon administration. At hearings before the House Banking Committee in June 1971, Dan Haughton submitted a statement claiming that the L-1011 employed "more than 34,000 workers in 35 states," including over 17,000 at Lockheed and the rest at supplier firms.[27] He reiterated the company's complaint about its alleged losses of $484 million on four major weapons programs as the main reason for its troubles. In what may not have been the wisest move, Haughton noted that Lockheed's net worth had declined from $371 million to $235 million during its financial troubles—meaning that its net worth was now less than the value of the loan guarantees it was seeking. He also bemoaned the "$1.4 billion in U.S. investment" that "hangs on the outcome of the Tristar program." What his argument boiled down to was that we've spent this much so far, so we must spend more. Haughton further noted that the equipment for the L-1011 was so specialized that its use for any other purpose would be "negligible." Finally, he appealed to Main Street, USA, noting that many of the L-1011's suppliers were "small firms . . . located in smaller towns or cities where the loss of any income has a disproportionate effect."[28]

All of this set the stage for the main event—the Senate debate and vote over whether to grant loan guarantees to Lockheed. After a close House vote in which the Lockheed position won by the thinnest of margins—192–189—it was now up to the Senate to determine the fate of the Nixon administration's bailout scheme. In the run-up to the vote, the Proxmire forces won an unlikely ally—conservative Senator James Buckley of New York. Just as Hubert Humphrey's decision to support the loan guarantees had been a huge plus for the Nixon administration, Buckley's position created political cover for Republicans who were skeptical of the plan. Buckley's opposition was based on the notion that saving poorly managed companies would undermine the proper workings of a capitalist economy: "If the inefficient or mismanaged firm is insulated from the free-market pressures that other business firms must face . . . the result will be that scarce economic resources will be squandered on enterprises whose activities do not meet the standards imposed by the marketplace—standards which have assured us of the efficiency on which our industrial supremacy has been built."[29]

The Senate debate was held on August 2, 1971, just six days before the deadline the Nixon administration was attempting to impose. The first substantive points were made by Senator Hugh Scott (R-PA), a supporter of the bailout. Surprisingly, the Pennsylvania Republican suggested that Lockheed's dilemma was tied in part to "the inadequacies of the capital markets where large amounts of risk capital are required." Rather than letting the market take its course, Scott favored government action aimed at "facilitating the capital markets and extending worthwhile credit" to allow a "fundamentally sound company" to "regain their strength and continue to be productive members of our economy and our society."[30] Scott's plea was the antithesis of Buckley's argument that markets enforce efficiency and that interfering with them would reward inefficiency and undermine the greatest strength of our capitalist economy—its ability to weed out bad companies and reward good ones.

Scott's Republican colleague Henry Bellmon of Oklahoma followed with one of the most frequently cited arguments of the anti-bailout forces: Why Lockheed? Thousands of other companies large and small went bankrupt every year without the benefit of a government rescue plan. He noted that not only had 37 Oklahoma firms declared bankruptcy in the first five months of 1971, but over 4,700 companies had done so nationwide over the same time period. He further noted that "the total economic impact of these closings would exceed the effect of the end of the L-1011 project."[31]

Maverick Connecticut Republican Lowell Weicker joined the charge against the loan guarantee bill by questioning the veracity of Lockheed's figures on the economic impacts of the L-1011 project. He asserted that "this little poop sheet that has been placed on the desks of Senators is inaccurate."[32] He backed up his statement with data on Hamilton Standard, a Connecticut-based firm, that indicated that Lockheed had claimed over twice as much revenue as could be justified based on firm orders and options for the plane, "not on some fictitious figure of what Lockheed thinks it can get in the airline market."

Weicker went on to denounce the whole loan guarantee effort as a special interest project through and through: "The only people that I meet or that I hear from that are in favor of this legislation are either in Lockheed, or the airlines, or some subcontractor of Lockheed, or the banks. That is it. No disinterested party wants anything to do with this legislation."[33] The proponents of the bailout bill were to do little to disprove Weicker's assertion.

The anti–loan guarantee faction—a complicated mix of free-market Republicans and anti–big business Democrats—continued to chip away at Lockheed's economic arguments in favor of the L-1011. Illinois Democrat Adlai Stevenson III (the son of the liberal icon and 1950s presidential candidate) pointed out that spending on water and sewer systems, mass transit, and other infrastructure projects under discussion would create substantial numbers of jobs that could offset any losses attributable to the failure of the L-1011. He further noted that even Lockheed CEO Daniel Haughton had acknowledged that "many of the jobs lost at Lockheed and at its suppliers will be filled at McDonnell Douglas and its suppliers, including an American engine manufacturer." Because the L-1011 had a British-built Rolls-Royce engine and the McDonnell Douglas DC-10 had an American-built GE engine, Stevenson suggested that "it is doubtful that it would cause a net loss of jobs in this country" if L-1011 production were to end.[34]

For his part, Republican James Buckley of New York reiterated the point he had made in statements prior to the floor debate on the bill: "If the bill is enacted, a precedent will in fact have been created that will come back to haunt us."[35]

As if to further underscore the fact that the L-1011 debate was driven as much by pork barrel politics as it was by ideology or arguments on the merits, liberal Democrat Alan Cranston of California—the center of L-1011 production—sang the praises of Lockheed, suggesting that the company was an irreplaceable national resource that had produced such essential defense products as the Poseidon and Polaris missiles, submarine-launched ballistic missiles that were fundamental building blocks of the U.S. nuclear arsenal. He then proceeded to trot out the whole series of "Lockheed as victim" arguments that the company had developed in its own promotion of the loan guarantee program: that the company's woes were due to the unfair imposition of the total package procurement contract; that the downturn in orders for the Vietnam War placed "considerable responsibility" on the shoulders of the U.S. government to help a company that had heeded "a call to arms to help equip the nation for national defense"; and that the U.S. government could suffer a loss of tax revenues of up to $500 million if the L-1011 went down, twice the level of the loan guarantees being sought. Cranston's closing argument cited the symbiotic relationship between the Pentagon and mega-contractors like Lockheed, suggesting that these firms were in essence "quasi-governmental companies dependent largely on defense contracts," just as "our country is dependent on them in this world of deadly, sophisticated weapons, for national defense and security."[36]

Of course, the Senate vote was not occurring in a vacuum. Individuals and institutions on both sides of the debate had put on a full-court press in the run-up to the vote. These efforts were intensified at the last minute after the razor-thin margin of the late Friday night vote in the House—192–189 for the loan guarantees, with 54 members absent. Lockheed—whose top dozen executives had spoken to virtually every member of Congress before the House and Senate votes—was not alone. The International Association of Machinists, representing the majority of the workers on the L-1011 project, spent $55,000 lobbying for the loan guarantees and generated (by its own count) over half a million pieces of mail to Congress. The banks and the airlines with a stake in the deal also weighed in, while the anti-bailout side had the quiet but important assistance of McDonnell Douglas, General Electric, and the United Auto Workers, the most likely beneficiaries of an end to the L-1011 program (on the theory that it would boost sales of the McDonnell Douglas DC-10, built by UAW members using GE engines). But the role of McDonnell Douglas was circumscribed: It had received warnings from the banks it depended on for its own financing that they too stood to benefit from the loan guarantees. Depending on which senators one believed, McDonnell Douglas had either been "persuaded" or "ordered" to back off.[37]

Up to the day of the vote, President Nixon called wavering Republican senators while John Connally worked on his fellow southern Democrats. Senator Alan Cranston of California, the representative of the state with the most jobs at stake, took charge of counting the votes and pressuring any last-minute "undecideds." The Proxmire forces reached out as well, focusing on the swing votes of members who had neither Lockheed nor McDonnell Douglas suppliers in their districts.

A conversation between Nixon and Arizona Senator Barry Goldwater captured the dilemma faced by conservatives who were being asked to support the bailout. Even though Goldwater's son, Barry Goldwater Jr., represented the California district where many of the L-1011-related jobs were located, the father was uncertain as to how he would vote:

PRESIDENT NIXON: I know how you feel about it. Here's basically the political problem. The political problem is that having gotten sunk on SST, to lose this one would have a very depressing effect, you see? As you know, southern California's unemployment, and even in Orange County, is 9 percent.

GOLDWATER: Oh my goodness—

PRESIDENT NIXON: And it's a real hell of a problem for us.

GOLDWATER: I know it. Barry's district has Lockheed in it.

PRESIDENT NIXON: I know.

GOLDWATER: You think this isn't a tough decision for me to take—

PRESIDENT NIXON: Sure is. Yeah.

GOLDWATER:—with some of my dearest, closest friends—

PRESIDENT NIXON: Yeah.

GOLDWATER:—working at Lockheed.

PRESIDENT NIXON: Right.

GOLDWATER: But . . . I mean, Mr. President, just to—it's a matter of principle that I just—you couldn't—

PRESIDENT NIXON: You feel you—

GOLDWATER: If we do it for Lockheed, we're going to have to do it for everybody.

PRESIDENT NIXON: Yeah, well, they—the thing is, you know—the bill is now limited to the—

GOLDWATER: I know it . . .

PRESIDENT NIXON:—to Lockheed and—

GOLDWATER: But you just can't justify that I have Ed Uhl up here, with Fairchild, he said, "You okay and by God [unclear] thirty million dollars when I lost last year, I want some of my money back."

PRESIDENT NIXON: Yeah, yeah.

GOLDWATER: And I hear there's over four hundred such cases in the Pentagon.[38]

When push came to shove, Goldwater was one of the few senators who voted against his personal or economic interests—the Lockheed connection to his son and his "dear friends"—and rejected the loan guarantees.

During the final debate itself, Proxmire batted cleanup for the anti-bailout forces, forcefully summarizing their key points: that the bailout would reward Lockheed's mismanagement; that other firms that performed poorly would seek similar treatment; that the job loss figures cited by Lockheed and its allies didn't stand scrutiny once one accounted for the fact that many of the "lost" jobs would just go to McDonnell Douglas to buy DC-10s; and that, ultimately, "the Lockheed bailout does far more than undermine economic efficiency. It undermines the basic morality of American life."[39]

A few more points were made before the final vote, but no one added anything of substance to Proxmire's arguments. It was of interest, however, that one of his major supporters was the conservative Republican senator from Ohio, Robert Taft IV. This merely underscored the unique coalitions that had been built on both sides of the issue.

Among the last speakers in the debate were Senator Herman Talmadge (D-GA) and Senator Robert Byrd (D-WV). Talmadge made no secret of his special interest in the deal, asserting that "I may be somewhat parochial, but some of those jobs are in Georgia. I make no apologies for trying to protect the citizens in my State. I think all Senators should do likewise."[40] Byrd tried to compare the Lockheed bailout to other kinds of loans made by the federal government: "All manner of loans are guaranteed by the federal government—business loans, home loans, educational loans, the list could go on. Only recently, for example, the Federal government awarded almost $7.6 million in loans and grants to build a black-owned hotel in the District of Columbia. . . . This is a small figure, to be sure, compared with the $250 million loan guarantee to Lockheed. But the principle seems to me to be the same."[41]

Principles versus profits. Which was to carry the day? As the final vote was being taken, one side would pull ahead, then the other would catch up. The process continued as the votes mounted past forty on each side. Based on his vote count, Alan Cranston felt certain that the pro–loan guarantee faction was going down to a one-vote defeat. Fearing the worst, he had been working on Senator Lee Metcalf, Democrat of Montana, to see if he could get him to make a last-minute switch. Once Cranston convinced Metcalf that his vote would make the difference, he swung over to Lockheed's side, telling Cranston that "I'm not going to be the one to put those thousands of people out of work."[42] And so Lockheed carried the day, 49–48.

A post-vote analysis by the *New York Times* found that all of the senators with Lockheed-related plants in their state voted in favor of the loan guarantees, while all of those in states with McDonnell Douglas or GE plants in their states voted against. The exception that proved the rule was Missouri Democrat Richard Bolling. Despite the fact that his state was home to McDonnell Douglas, he voted for the loan guarantees. However, his Kansas City–area district included the headquarters of TWA, one of the airlines that would be left holding the bag if the L-1011 project went down.

The vote outcome wasn't simply a matter of pork barrel politics. Seventeen Republicans, many of them moved by free-market arguments, voted against their own president to stop the loan guarantees. And twenty-two Democrats, most moved by the jobs argument—but many, like Hubert Humphrey and Lee Metcalf, not having significant numbers of Lockheed jobs in their own states—voted with the Nixon administration to approve the guarantees.[43]

BRIBERY

With its government loan guarantees in hand, Lockheed still faced a major challenge: how to sell enough L-1011 TriStar airliners to allow it to pay back hundreds of millions in bank loans within a reasonable time frame. The company had deals with several U.S. airlines and British Aerospace but needed a few other big deals to ensure that it wasn't back on the brink of bankruptcy. Japan was the biggest and most important market available for pumping up L-1011 sales quickly. The question was how best to sway the Japanese government and airlines to Lockheed's side in the face of vigorous lobbying campaigns on behalf of the Boeing 747 and the McDonnell Douglas DC-10.

Lockheed needed to buy some influence, fast. Rather than rely on its usual marketing force to make it happen, the company sent its president, A. Carl Kotchian, to do the job. He ended up staking the Japanese deal—and possibly Lockheed's future—on one of the most fascinating and corrupt figures in the annals of Japanese politics.

By any standard, Yoshio Kodama was a shady character. After spending three years in prison on war crimes charges after World War II, he was set free without a trial by the U.S. occupying authority on the grounds that he would make a good ally in the Cold War fight against communism. Kodama then took his fortune—apparently earned by a combination of supplying Japanese troops during World War II and looting diamond and platinum from areas conquered by Japan—and put it to work in Japanese politics. Variously described as an organized crime boss and a CIA asset, Kodama helped found and fund the Liberal Democratic Party, the dominant political party in post–World War II Japan.[1]

So when Kotchian was desperately searching for someone who could help secure a $130 million contract for L-1101s with Japan's All Nippon Airlines (ANA), he decided to look beyond the company's official agent in the country—the Marubeni trading company—and use Kodama instead.

It wasn't as if Lockheed's contacts at Marubeni were sitting idly. The company—whose slogan was "Man, Materials, and Money"— had done a creditable job of reaching out to the Japanese political and business elite on Lockheed's behalf. It was the president of Marubeni, Hiro Hiyama, who was the first to urge Kotchian to go straight to the top by providing a bribe of 500 million yen ($1.7 million) to Japan's new prime minister, Kakuei Tanaka. Kotchian agreed to the payment, but he viewed it as only a first step—the price of admission to a game that was also being played hard and well by Lockheed's rivals Boeing and McDonnell Douglas.[2]

Hence the perceived need to secure the aid of Kodama. The Kodama connection was made with the help of Taro Fukuda, a Japanese American from Salt Lake City, Utah. Fukuda became friends with Kodama when the latter was in jail. After he was released, Kodama helped set up Fukuda in the public relations business. Ken Hull, the head of Lockheed's international business operations, hired Fukuda in the late 1950s, and Fukuda immediately put the company in touch with Kodama. Fukuda's history as an interpreter for U.S. forces in Japan during World War II was also useful to Lockheed: Among other things, he could serve as a go-between with Kodama, who spoke no English.[3]

The L-1011 deal wouldn't be the first time Lockheed had turned to Kodama for help. In 1959 he prevailed upon the government of Prime Minister Nobusuke Kishi—a Kodama protégé—to put aside the plane it had originally planned to buy for its air force, the Grumman F11F Super Tiger, for Lockheed's F-104 Starfighter. It was a huge order: 230 planes. And it had been concluded with "only" a little over $2 million in bribes and commissions—a real bargain compared to what it would take to secure the L-1011 deal.[4]

The sale to Japan may have marked the high point of the F-104 program. The plane went on to generate great controversy after it was sold to the German Air Force just two years later, in 1961. Over a ten-year period, the plane crashed 178 times, killing a total of eighty-five German pilots. The plane's abominable safety record prompted Germans to nickname it "the flying coffin" and "the widow-maker," and a group of fifty widows of the pilots who died flying the plane sued the company for damages.[5] The case, conducted by the well-known U.S.-based lawyer Melvin Belli, was settled out of court for about $1.2 million, less than half the cost of one Starfighter. One point at issue was whether the modifications that the German air force made to some of the planes were a major contributor to the crashes, or whether the problem was simply design flaws that would have been the responsibility of Lockheed. Regardless of which factor was dominant, the F-104's reputation took a huge hit, but Lockheed still managed to sell about three thousand copies of the plane. None of them were ever used in combat, which was probably a good thing. The controversy over the plane's performance was never fully resolved.

The prior F-104 deal with Japan had hardened the belief of Lockheed executives like Kotchian that buying Japanese politicians was the best way to get them to buy the L-1011. But Kodama had a problem: He wasn't as close to the newly elected Tanaka as he had been to prior prime ministers. Luckily for Lockheed, he had a solution—Kodama decided to work through his friend the billionaire Kenji Osano. Not only was Osano a major financial supporter of Tanaka, but he was also the top shareholder in Japan's two largest airlines. Kodama indicated that enlisting Osano's help would cost another $1.7 million, Kotchian's second such payment in one day.[6]

Kotchian's bribes seemed to be paying off. In late August, Prime Minister Tanaka told Hiroshi Hiyama of Marubeni that he would help Lockheed get the L-1011 deal in exchange for the funds it had provided for him. Tanaka's resolve was apparently strengthened by a visit from British Prime Minister Edward Heath, who had come to Japan in part to address the question of the uneven balance of trade between the two nations—Japan was exporting far more to Britain than it was buying in return. Marubeni's Hiyama reminded Tanaka that the L-1011 had British engines manufactured by Rolls-Royce, so that buying the planes would generate goodwill in London as well as Washington.[7] There was even talk that U.S. President Richard Nixon was favoring the Lockheed plane over the other U.S. aircraft that were in the running for the Japanese purchase. Nixon's role was never confirmed, but the perception of his interest seemed to play into the Japanese decision.

Things were looking good for Lockheed, but there would be more money to spread around before the sale was finalized. Kodama himself had received over $7 million, and it was never clear how much of it he pocketed for his own use and how much he gave to Japanese politicians and executives to seal the deal. Lockheed executives claimed not to know or care where their money ended up, as long as they won the contract. For example, in questioning by Senator William Proxmire several years later, after the bribery had been revealed, the following exchange occurred between Proxmire and Lockheed CEO Daniel Haughton:

> THE CHAIRMAN: . . . Do you or don't you have accurate information as to payments that have been made, where your money goes, the officials who receive it? . . .
>
> MR. HAUGHTON: We have accurate information that we paid the commissions. We do not have accurate information to the point as to where the money finally went.
>
> THE CHAIRMAN: You pay out millions of dollars from your corporation without knowing where it goes?
>
> MR. HAUGHTON: We know where it goes. Insofar as the contracts with the consultants are concerned. Where it winds up finally, we do not know.
>
> . . .
>
> MR. HAUGHTON: . . . If payments have to be made and you are doing it to get a contract and payments are made and you get the contract, it is good evidence that you needed to make the payment, I think.[8]

As the competition for the All Nippon Airlines contract went down to the wire, Kotchian suffered debilitating anxiety. As described by Anthony Sampson in his classic work *The Arms Bazaar*, Kotchian ran a high fever, experienced stomach pains, and even became suicidal.[9] After three days in bed, his spirits improved radically when his Marubeni contact indicated that Lockheed would win the contract—but only after making one final round of payoffs: $50,000 per plane to ANA's president and $100,000 to be split among six politicians, including the former minister of transport. Lockheed sales rep Jack Clutter had to run around raising cash at the last minute to complete the cycle of bribery.[10] On the day before Halloween, the deal went through. Kotchian described himself as if he were a victorious general—"the head of the Lockheed forces" prevailed after "70 straight days of battle." He was later to write a book about his experiences in selling the L-1011 in Japan entitled *Lockheed Sales Mission: 70 Days in Tokyo.*[11]

Japan may have been the costliest front in Lockheed's bribery operation, but it was far from the first. Going back to the late 1950s, when the company tried to make its F-104 "the NATO fighter," the use of well-connected agents who could sway the decisions of key government officials was already a common practice. Lockheed's efforts to grease the wheels on behalf of its fighter plane were bolstered by two key arguments: (1) that a common plane would make it much easier for NATO members to cooperate should joint military missions be necessary; and (2) that the United States would be less inclined to defend European countries if they chose the French Mirage III over the Starfighter. While the first argument was made openly, the second was used behind the scenes to scare European officials into buying American. The threat to abandon key allies based on what weapons they chose to buy may not have been accurate, but even the remotest possibility that it might prove to be the case helped tilt the scales toward Lockheed.

The German deal came first, not only because Germany was a larger market, but also because it was assumed that if Germany chose the F-104, the smaller European nations would fall into line. Toward that end, Lockheed deployed a huge lobbying force, far larger than any lobbying effort by its European rivals. The aim was to win over the German defense minister, Franz-Josef Strauss. Strauss was in a quandary over whether to enhance the Franco-German alliance by buying the Mirage or to please Washington by going with the F-104. When journalist Anthony Sampson later asked Strauss which side he would choose, he said, "Do you choose between your shirt or your underpants?"[12]

Strauss did make a choice: In the fall of 1958 he recommended the F-104 Starfighter to the German parliament, the Bundestag. The deal was approved in December, and Lockheed had won an initial order of ninety-six planes.

It was widely assumed that Lockheed had paid off key German officials and/or contributed to their political parties in order to win the deal, but nothing could be proven, in part because Strauss had the good sense to destroy all Defense Ministry documents related to the deal. Not that there weren't allegations. Ernest Hauser, a Lockheed "customer relations" rep who had been hired in part because of pressure from Strauss, claimed that Lockheed contributed $12 million to Strauss's political party in connection with the F-104 sale.[13] But Hauser proved to be an unreliable witness with no credible documentation for his allegations. This is not to say that no money changed hands. Fred Meuser, a naturalized Dutchman and former employee of the Dutch airline KLM who was then serving as Lockheed's Director for Europe, received a commission of nearly $1 million for his help with the Starfighter sale.[14] Whether any of those funds were passed on to German officials may never be known.

More is known about Lockheed's connections in the Netherlands, though in the end it's not clear how helpful they actually proved to be. One of Meuser's first recruits was Hubert Weisbrod, a Swiss lawyer who had been his college roommate. Meuser credited Weisbrod with the major part in Lockheed's lobbying success in Europe, owing to "his expert counseling and behind-the-scenes pulling of strings."[15] The fact that Weisbrod was Swiss was no small matter: He could carry on all manner of questionable activities without being subject to outside scrutiny.

Meuser also brought his Dutch friend Teengs Gerritsen on board. Gerritsen was a minor celebrity in Holland, after a career as an Olympic skier and a member of the Dutch national soccer team. More importantly, he was a hero of the anti-Nazi resistance: Working as a British agent, he had been captured and tortured.[16]

But Meuser's biggest "get"—aided by Weisbrod and Gerritsen—was Prince Bernhard, the husband of Holland's Queen Juliana. To say that Bernhard was well connected would be a vast understatement. Bernhard was active on one level or another in literally hundreds of organizations. Most importantly for Lockheed's purposes, he was the Inspector General of the Armed Forces and a director of KLM Airlines. In late 1959, well after Meuser and his associates had first cultivated the prince, Holland decided to buy the F-104. As in the German case, there was no clear paper trail to indicate whether the deal was sealed with bribes. But it is curious to note that after the sale was made, Lockheed considered making a gift of a JetStar executive aircraft to Bernhard. When they were questioned about the purpose of the proposed gift, Lockheed officials denied that there was any quid pro quo for the F-104 sale, asserting instead that it was meant to ensure a "favorable atmosphere for the sale of Lockheed products in Holland."[17]

When push came to shove, the company decided not to give Prince Bernhard the jet, but Meuser suggested a convenient alternative: Why not give Bernhard $1 million instead?

Whether the money ever made it to Bernhard was unclear, but it wasn't for lack of trying. In September 1960, Lockheed CEO Robert Gross met with Bernhard in Rome, and a few weeks later Lockheed lawyer Roger Smith visited Bernhard at the Dutch royal palace. It was at this meeting that Bernhard indicated that he would like to receive the $1 million via Weisbrod in Switzerland.[18]

A few days later, Smith sat down in Zurich with one Colonel Pantchoulidzew, a Russian national who was on close terms with Prince Bernhard's mother. Pantchoulidzew gave Smith the number of the bank account through which the payments should be made, and a schedule was drawn up that called for disbursing the funds in three installments.

The Lockheed–Prince Bernhard connection continued into the mid-1970s—up until the investigation by Senator Frank Church's (D-ID) Subcommittee on Multinational Corporations—the Church

Committee—put the company's business practices in an international spotlight. From the late 1960s through 1974, Bernhard claimed to be working overtime to convince Dutch officials to pick Lockheed's P-3C Orion antisubmarine warfare (ASW) aircraft over its French rival. Whether through Bernhard's efforts or through other channels, the deal—which appeared to be wrapped up for the French—was delayed, and Lockheed seemed to have a legitimate shot at winning the contract.

At this point Bernhard made the ill-advised move of sending two angry letters to Lockheed's lawyer Roger Smith, seeking compensation for his role in helping the company. One account suggested that he was seeking a commission of $4 million to $6 million, to be disguised as a donation to the World Wildlife Fund, an organization that Bernhard had helped to found. In one of the letters, he indicated that he had done "a hell of a lot of pushing and pulling" on behalf of the Orion and deserved to be paid for his efforts. In the second, he declared that "since 1968 I have in good faith spent a lot of time and effort to push things the right way in critical areas to prevent wrong decisions influenced by political decisions. I have done this based on my old friendship with Lockheed—and based on past actions. So I do feel a little bitter."[19] Presumably the bitterness had to do with the fact that he hadn't received a commission for his valiant efforts.

For all of his complaining, it ended up that Bernhard was the one taking advantage of Lockheed, not the other way around. It later emerged that Prince Bernhard, Fred Meuser, and Meuser's colleague Hubert Weisbrod had all been working for Lockheed and its rival Northrop *simultaneously*. On behalf of Northrop's N156 Tiger aircraft, Bernhard did everything from writing to the American secretary of the Air Force to setting up a meeting between a Northrop official and the Dutch defense minister. He also helped broker a deal in which Northrop bought 20 percent of the Dutch aircraft maker Fokker and placed Bernhard's friend, Northrop CEO Tom Jones, on the Fokker board.[20] The problem with buying influence is you can never be sure if your connection will stay bought.

The last major front in Lockheed's European influence-peddling surge was in Italy, where it was assumed that bribery was a routine part of doing business. After losing out to a French company in its drive to sell the P-3C to Rome, Lockheed put on a full-court press to sell Italy up to fourteen of its C-130 Hercules cargo planes, which had been doing heavy service ferrying troops and matériel in and out of Vietnam. The cost to Italy: $60 million.[21]

An Italian senator told Lockheed President Carl Kotchian that the best way to proceed was to hire a well-connected agent, Olvidio Lefebvre. Shortly after he was brought on, Lefebvre told Kotchian that he was "embarrassed" to say that he would have to "make some payments if you want to sell aircraft in this country." He eventually put a price tag on the bribes, suggesting that they would amount to $120,000 per plane, or over $1.6 million if all fourteen planes were purchased.[22] According to a handwritten letter from Roger Smith that surfaced in later congressional investigations, an Italian contact known as "Antelope Cobbler" would give a final figure on what Italian officials would need to consummate the deal. He advised his correspondent to consult his "little black book"—a code book that Lockheed was using to describe major transactions. It ended up that "Antelope Cobbler" was code for the Italian prime minister.[23] Unfortunately for the later investigations, Italy had three different prime ministers during the two-year period during which the C-130 deal was being arranged. The volatility of the Italian political scene played a role in Lockheed's tactics as well: An internal memo stated that the deal should be hurried up because "the last thing we want is a new government and a new set of players at this stage of the game."[24] A new government could mean a whole new round of bribes.

Bearing that in mind, the company pushed through a final payment of $765,000, which brought the final price in bribes to $2 million—between 3 and 4 percent of the total cost of the C-130 package. A payment of $50,000 went to the Italian defense minister, with the bulk of the rest going to "the minister's political party past and present," according to internal Lockheed documents.[25] Kotchian was happy—the deal was done, the bribes were within the "normal" range, and the company could move on to its next marketing conquest.

Although Japan, German, and Italy received the most attention in Lockheed's bribery binge, they were not the only places involved. Other states where agents' "commissions" were used as conduits to pay off local officials included Turkey, Indonesia, Colombia, and Saudi Arabia.

In the Indonesian case, some memos were uncovered that raised once again the question of who was corrupting whom. In a memo-to-file dated June 7, 1965, Lockheed executive W. G. Myers complained about Indonesia's demand that the fourth of four JetStar executive aircraft being purchased by Jakarta include a commission of $200,000 rather than the $100,000 paid on the first three planes. He noted that similar tactics had been used on other Indonesian purchases from Lockheed, including a buy of C-130 transport aircraft. Myers was clearly fed up. He said as much in the memo:

> D. J. Haughton [Lockheed CEO Daniel Haughton] and I discussed this. I stated I thought we should hold at $1,874,000; that this hanky panky had gone far enough. We discussed the various ethics of it, and agreed that even though it would not be costing the company or the U.S. (ostensibly) any money, it just isn't right, and there's some limit to going along with this. Dan asked me to check with Carl [Kotchian], and if he agreed we three should get back together again.[26]

In the end the company decided to hold the line at a $100,000 payment, not the $200,000 requested. In hearings over a decade later, Senator Charles Percy (R-IL) suggested that this was a case in which Lockheed had tried to do the right thing and wondered why the company couldn't have done so in other instances as well. Of course, W. G. Myers's sense of what was "ethical" was somewhat nuanced. He was really arguing about the price of the bribe, not whether it should be offered at all.

The Indonesian case offered other insights into the complications that can arise when bribery and influence-peddling become a standard way of doing business. For example, what happens if there is a coup, as happened in Indonesia in 1965 when the CIA helped the right-wing general Suharto overthrow the nationalist regime of Sukarno? How do you know the new players without a scorecard?

Of particular concern to Lockheed was whether its Indonesian agent, Isaak Dasaad, would still be of use. In a November 1965 memo-to-file, written less than two months after the coup, Lockheed marketing executive D. D. Stone noted that a company official "went to the U.S. Embassy in Jakarta and asked them specifically whether Dasaad could continue, under the new regime, to be of value to Lockheed." The embassy's answer was yes, and Stone wrote that "apparently Dasaad has made the transition from Sukarno to Suharto in good shape." But Stone clearly had some misgivings, noting that "there is always the possibility that the present government is merely using Dasaad and may have him on the list for liquidation somewhere down the road." The company continued to use Dasaad for another few years, at which point the Indonesian Air Force told Lockheed that going forward, it wanted to be paid directly, dispensing with any middlemen.[27]

The notion of direct payments raised no ethical concerns with Lockheed, but there were practical considerations. Among the objections cited by the company was the need to use a third party to transmit the payments so as to establish "at least a nominal buffer." Another concern was the fact that, without an agent to launder the payments, "we have no legal means of charging off these 'commissions.' Thus, they may not be considered allowable deductions by the Internal Revenue Service." And in a comment that proved prescient, the author of the memo suggested that, "if such payments should someday become public knowledge, the repercussions could be damaging to Lockheed's name and reputation."[28]

Not surprisingly, the biggest commissions were paid on sales to Saudi Arabia, which was at the center of the early 1970s arms-buying boom in the Middle East that was driven by the increased revenues available to oil-producing states in the wake of the creation of the OPEC (Organization of Petroleum-Exporting Countries) oil cartel. Lockheed's man in Saudi Arabia was Adnan Khashoggi, a jet-setting playboy and international businessman who made the bulk of his fortune serving as a middleman between the Saudi royal family and Western companies seeking to do business there.

Among its rivals in the arms business, Lockheed got to Khashoggi first, hiring him to represent them in 1964 when he was only twenty-six years old and had yet to make himself rich. In spite of his youth, he was slick and already had good connections with key Saudi officials. His father had been one of the personal physicians of the Saudi King Ibn Saud, and Khashoggi himself had gone to school in Egypt with King Hussein of Jordan. In addition to Ibn Saud's son, Khashoggi's most important friends among the many Saudi princes were Prince Fahd, who would go on to rule the country, and Prince Sultan, who later became the Saudi defense minister.[29]

Khashoggi cultivated connections with key American officials as well, cozying up to Richard Nixon during his period in political exile by wining and dining him in Paris and smoothing the way for him to be received in style in major Arab capitals. Khashoggi's "generosity" paid off when Nixon was elected president in 1968. Although it was never made clear what the American president did for his Saudi friend, the two men had several private meetings during the Nixon presidency, suggesting a level of access and influence that could only help Khashoggi rack up new clients, whether or not Nixon lifted a finger on his behalf. Khashoggi was suspected of funneling millions of dollars to Nixon's 1972 reelection campaign, but the only donation that could be identified was $50,000 that was allegedly used to finance a record album to promote candidate Nixon.[30]

Khashoggi wasn't employed to do a deal here or a deal there, but to represent Lockheed in multiple sales worth billions of dollars. To give some sense of the size of the business, the company acknowledged in the mid-1970s that it had provided $106 million in commissions to Khashoggi between 1970 and 1975, more than ten times the level of payments made to the next most important connection, Yoshi Kodama of Japan.[31] Max Helzel, then Lockheed's Vice President for International Marketing, said that Khashoggi "became for all practical purposes a marketing arm of Lockheed. Adnan would provide not only an entree but strategy, constant advice, and analysis."[32]

Whatever the value of his services, Khashoggi could be extremely difficult to work with. At one point he pushed to change his commission on a sale of C-130 aircraft from 2 percent to 8 percent, claiming that he needed the extra funds "due to more players getting involved, and the necessity to meet their requirements." A Lockheed executive noted that, with respect to an additional $200,000 per plane that Khashoggi demanded as a contingency fee, the funds appeared to be for paying off Saudi officials, but "we have no way of knowing if the so-called 'under the table' compensation is ever disbursed to Saudi officials, or stops at our consultant's bank account."[33] A similar theme was struck in an August 1968 memo-to-file written by Lockheed's A. H. Kaplan, who cited a Saudi official (name blacked out in available copy) who was "completely disenchanted with Adnan Khashoggi. He indicated that he never received the $150,000 that was agreed to . . . during their Paris meeting last year."[34] This was the same problem Lockheed CEO Dan Haughton had described to Senator William Proxmire with respect to payments in Europe, just on a much larger scale.

As was the case in Holland, Northrop followed in Lockheed's footsteps when it came to hiring an agent in Saudi Arabia, coming to an arrangement with Khashoggi in 1970. Northrop approached Khashoggi at the suggestion of its original agent in Saudi Arabia, Kermit Roosevelt, the grandson of Theodore Roosevelt and a key player in the 1953 U.S.-British coup that brought the Shah of Iran to power. Roosevelt represented Northrop in a successful effort to sell twenty of its F-5 Tiger aircraft to the Saudis, and he was intimately involved in efforts to seek a follow-on deal.[35] Both companies knew that Khashoggi was working for the other, but there was enough business to be had in the oil-rich Saudi kingdom that Lockheed and Northrop quietly accepted this unusual arrangement.

Far from coming to light as a result of the mid-1970s bribery investigations undertaken by Senator Frank Church and his Subcommittee on Multinational Corporations, the Saudi commissions—and the payoffs that flowed from them—were well known to the Pentagon at the time, as they were being carried out. In August 1973, Northrop arranged for Khashoggi to meet at the Pentagon with key officials involved in brokering and monitoring major U.S. arms sales, including David Alne, the Department of Defense's Director of International Sales Negotiations. Khashoggi explained the commission system in some depth, all the while giving it the most positive spin possible. Payments were meant to help build up Saudi Arabia's limited economic infrastructure and to meet the needs of the Bedouins. Money for the princes was not given for material gain, but as a sign of loyalty. By the end of the meeting, Alne suggested that far from being some seedy influence-peddler, Khashoggi was in essence running "an inexpensive economic aid program," and Alne described him further as "an honest and astute businessman."[36]

A less euphemistic gloss on the same set of facts was provided by Joe Hoenig, the assistant director of the Pentagon's international sales office, in a 1974 speech to the Electronics Industries Association. He noted the benefits of using agents like Khashoggi to buy influence, ranging from "normal friendships or family ties to the payments of substantial sums of money to individuals in high government positions."[37] While Hoenig claimed that the Pentagon was trying to limit the role of agents by moving toward government-to-government negotiated deals, the meeting with Khashoggi the prior August made it clear that his department was perfectly willing to turn a blind eye to these transactions when they did occur.

With a few exceptions, the Lockheed executives involved in using agents to pass bribes on to influential political and business figures assumed that the practice would go on indefinitely, with no negative legal, political, or financial consequences. It was just a cost of doing business, and everybody did it, so people like Carl Kotchian and Dan Haughton saw no particular problem in continuing to facilitate bribery in the name of higher sales numbers. It never occurred to them that they would lose their jobs in the firestorm that resulted from the revelations of the investigations by the Securities and Exchange Commission and the Church Committee.

Lockheed's first reaction to the bribery charges was to provide as little information as possible. Under pressure from the SEC, the company acknowledged paying $22 million in bribes as pass-throughs to foreign officials and political parties, but it refused to name the recipients of the bribes on the grounds that doing so might hurt future business opportunities and unnecessarily damage foreign officials "without any offsetting public benefit."[38] In fact, CEO Dan Haughton refused to even describe the payments as "bribes," preferring to use the word "kickbacks," on the advice of his attorneys. And they were well-connected attorneys indeed. Lockheed's lead representative in making the case for secrecy was William P. Rogers, former Secretary of State *and* Attorney General in the Nixon administration. Rogers urged his former colleague, Secretary of State Henry Kissinger, to intervene on behalf of the company. Kissinger obliged, sending a note to Attorney General Edward Levi in which he argued that the information in the Lockheed documents was "uncorroborated . . . and potentially damaging" and would do severe harm to U.S. relations with the named countries. But Levi refused to be pressured, and the Church Committee proceeded to release all the details it had to the public and the press.[39]

Although the bribery revelations made a stir in the United States and garnered extensive press coverage—including a cover story in *Time* magazine and a long series of articles and commentaries in the *New York Times*—they were by and large treated as just the latest example of corporate malfeasance and institutional corruption to surface since the Watergate scandals.

The reaction overseas was another matter. In Japan, for example, hearings on the bribery scandal were televised nationwide, and people stopped in the street or interrupted their working day to watch them. While in the United States the bribery scandal was a mere coda to Watergate, in Japan the bribery scandal was their equivalent of Watergate. Looking to distance himself from the wrongdoing in his own party and to burnish his image as Japan's "Mr. Clean," Japanese Premier Takeo Miki launched a vigorous investigation. Over three thousand investigators were put to work on the case. More than two dozen homes and offices were searched, including the residence of Yoshio Kodama, who was in bed recovering from a stroke even as law enforcement officials scoured his home for evidence. The homes and offices of Lockheed executives based in Japan were targeted as well. Ultimately, over a dozen public officials and private middlemen were indicted for their roles in one or another of the bribery schemes.[40]

In the furor in Japan over the bribery revelations, both houses of Parliament passed a resolution urging the Ford administration to immediately forward any and all information it had on the case. This directly contradicted claims by Secretary of State Henry Kissinger and Lockheed CEO Dan Haughton that disclosing the details would harm U.S. relations with Japan and other allies. Instead, it was the *failure* to make full disclosure that was sparking anger in Japan. As one Japanese observer put it, "The United States has told us we have a thief in the house but won't tell us who he is."[41]

The most prominent official to face legal consequences for his role in the scandal was former Premier Kakuei Tanaka. In late July 1976, he was arrested on charges of accepting $1.6 million in bribes in connection with the sale of Lockheed L-1011 airliners to All Nippon Airlines. He was indicted three weeks later and released on $700,000 bail. This gave Tanaka the dubious distinction of being the first Japanese prime minister ever to be indicted for bribery that occurred while he was in office.[42]

Tanaka's case took years to resolve, but he was finally found guilty more than seven years later, in October 1983, and sentenced to four years in prison and a $2.1 million fine. He was one of eleven Japanese businessmen and government officials convicted in the scheme. To give a sense of how deep the feelings about the scandal ran among the Japanese public, on the day of his sentencing as many as 350,000 anti-Tanaka demonstrators were expected to hit the streets to protest in the event that the former prime minister failed to be convicted in the case.[43]

Although Japan was by far the most scrupulous in seeking accountability for the bribery scandal, there were consequences in other targeted nations as well, including Italy, where the popular wisdom suggested that nothing serious would be done on the grounds that payoffs were a "way of life." Instead, the Italian parliament voted to lift immunity from two former defense ministers, Luigi Gui and Mario Tanassi, which cleared the way for criminal trials of the two men. It was the first time in the thirty-year history of the procedure for retracting immunity that it had been successfully used against government ministers for activities that happened while they were in office. Former Prime Minister Mariano Rumor was spared prosecution when the move to lift his immunity to bribery charges failed by one vote. Rumor was a Christian Democrat, but the swing votes in forestalling his prosecution came from the Socialist Party. Angered by their leadership's role in saving Rumor from prosecution, the Socialist Party's rank and file held a sit-in at party headquarters to protest the maneuver.

Meanwhile, in the Netherlands, Prince Bernhard faced a threat to his reputation, but not his liberty. A Dutch government inquiry failed to find evidence of criminal wrongdoing in the prince's dealings with Lockheed, but it did engage in harsh criticism, arguing that Bernhard had "allowed himself to be tempted to take initiatives which were bound to place himself and the Netherlands procurement policy in the eyes of Lockheed—and, it must now be added, in the eyes of others—in a dubious light . . . he showed himself open to dishonorable requests and offers." Short of criminal prosecution, it was a hard blow to a man who had styled himself a citizen of the world, associated with everything from the World Wildlife Fund to the Dutch armed forces. He had attempted to brush off the allegations when they first surfaced, preferring to spend his time skiing or at charity balls. "I have no problems," he told one reporter. "But people make problems."[44]

But once the Dutch government inquiry was made public, Bernhard did indeed have problems. He was stripped of virtually all of his scores of business and government posts. His remaining title was impressive—His Royal Highness Bernhard Leopold Frederik Everhard Julius Coert Karel Godfried Pieter, Prince of the Netherlands—but it could hardly make up for the shame he had brought on himself and the Dutch royal family.

In most of the other nations involved in the bribery scandals, there was no accountability of any sort. Adnan Khashoggi continued to make lucrative deals as a middleman between the Saudi government and its major customers, and government officials in Turkey, Indonesia, Colombia, and Singapore faced no apparent consequences for their actions.

And what of Lockheed's own leaders, Daniel Haughton and Carl Kotchian? Both men were forced to resign their posts in an effort to stem the bleeding and hopefully keep the company from losing too many contracts in the wake of the bribery revelations. Both men were offered cozy consulting arrangements with the company after they stepped down, but the offers were rescinded two months later in the face of a public outcry, not to mention disapproval in government and business circles that were trying to put the scandal behind them. Neither man expressed remorse for his actions.[45] In fact, in a July 1977 interview with the *New York Times*, Kotchian described himself as a "scapegoat" in the affair. Reached at his home—where the *Times* said he was "growing alfalfa and trying to raise money for the Salvation Army"—Kotchian compared himself to Richard Nixon:

> My experience has some of the elements of Watergate. I can compare it because a lot of the things that came out in Watergate were things that were going on previously—and all of the sudden there's a different set of standards. I understand how Nixon feels—it's not easy to lose your purpose.[46]

Not only had it gone on before, argued Kotchian, but any reasonable person would have done what he did in the same circumstances: "For any businessman who is dealing with commercial and trade matters, would it be possible to decline a request of certain amounts of money when the money would enable him to, like myself, get the business award?" Kotchian's answer was an emphatic no. He even dismissed the language of bribery itself: "Some call it gratuities. Some call them questionable payments. Some call it extortion. Some call it grease. Some call it bribery. I looked at all these payments as necessary to sell a product. I never felt I was doing anything wrong. I considered them a commission—it was a standard thing."[47]

Chapter 7

REAGAN
TO THE RESCUE

Between the bailout, the bribery scandal, and the post-Vietnam decline in military spending, the 1970s had been a tough decade for Lockheed. The Pentagon budget declined by over one-third (after adjusting for inflation) from the peak of the war in 1968 through 1973, the year the conflict officially ended. Spending went down further under Gerald Ford, then stayed steady through the Carter years. By the end of Jimmy Carter's term, military spending was at its lowest level since 1951, when there had been a much smaller military-industrial complex to feed.[1]

These lower spending levels were consistent with U.S. security needs. The United States was not involved in a major conflict, and the Nixon-era détente between the United States and the Soviet Union had resulted in rough nuclear parity between the superpowers. If anything, the United States was "ahead," if that word had any meaning in an era of massive nuclear overkill. But these realities were not acknowledged by a new organization, the Committee on the Present Danger (CPD). The CPD was modeled on and named after a similar group that was formed after World War II to promote a consensus for permanently high levels of military spending to fight communism. To the members of the CPD, the Soviet Union was ten feet tall while America barely exceeded five feet; there was a huge gap to be made up, they argued, and there was no time to waste. The committee consisted of hawkish Democrats like former Kennedy administration official Eugene Rostow and Republican luminaries such as former Ford administration Defense Secretary James Schlesinger, former Nixon administration Treasury Secretary George Shultz, and California Governor Ronald Reagan. Its goal was to reverse what it saw as the "ominous Soviet military buildup" and the "unfavorable trends in the U.S.-Soviet military balance."[2] The committee spoke alarmingly of "unparalleled buildup" by Moscow that was "in part reminiscent of Nazi Germany's rearmament in the 1930s."[3]

The CPD came armed with its very own treasure trove of data to support its views in the form of the findings of the so-called Team B, a panel appointed in 1976 by then–CIA Director George Herbert Walker Bush. Bush had done so only after concerted pressure from conservative hawks who questioned the CIA's official estimates of Soviet military strength. Members of the Team B panel included conservative Professor Richard Pipes of Harvard; longtime Cold Warrior Paul Nitze; General Daniel O. Graham, a staunch supporter of missile defense; and William Van Cleave, who went on to play a central role in selecting national security officials when Ronald Reagan came to power in 1981. Another Team B member who was to make his mark later, under the administration of George W. Bush, was Paul Wolfowitz.[4]

As expected given its ideological makeup, Team B alleged that there was a growing gap between U.S. and Soviet military capabilities, an assessment that contradicted the CIA's analysis of the same data.

Armed with the CPD's arguments, Ronald Reagan savaged the Carter administration throughout the 1980 presidential campaign for allegedly letting the United States fall behind the Soviet Union in the arms race. As was the case with the missile gap of the 1960 campaign, a more realistic assessment of the military balance between the superpowers continued to give the United States a clear lead. While CPD members harped on Soviet advantages in large, heavy intercontinental ballistic missiles (ICBMs), they neglected to note that the United States dominated virtually every other category of nuclear strength, from missile accuracy to long-range bombers to relatively invulnerable submarine-launched ballistic missiles (SLBMs). In the end, Team B's estimate of Soviet military spending, based on flawed assumptions, proved to be way off the mark. For instance, they assumed that Moscow's four-million-strong military—which included large numbers of "make-work" positions designed to keep unemployment low in the civilian economy—was paid at generous U.S. rates, not at the much lower levels that Soviet soldiers in fact received.[5] To the extent that Soviet spending was high, it had as much to do with the inefficiencies of Soviet military production and staffing as it did with any surge in capabilities.

But in the wake of the 1978 fall of the Shah of Iran, a longtime U.S. ally, and the 1979 Soviet invasion of Afghanistan, these relatively arcane arguments about the reality of the U.S.-Soviet military balance were crowded out by a torrent of anti-Soviet rhetoric. And the most skilled purveyor of the anti-Soviet case was Ronald Reagan himself, who had spent most of the 1950s traveling the country giving anti-Communist speeches in his role as a representative of the General Electric Company.

Unlike many presidents, who say one thing on the campaign trail and do another when they come into office, Reagan kept his word on building up the military. Working through his hard-line Defense Secretary, Caspar Weinberger, Reagan pushed through $75 billion in additional military spending in 1981 and 1982 alone, hitting a top line of $185 billion in fiscal year 1982. This was a 39 percent increase over 1980 levels, and it was only the beginning—military spending would double by the end of Reagan's second term, in the largest peacetime military buildup in U.S. history.[6] This was obviously good news for Lockheed and its cohorts in the military-industrial sector. Lockheed was particularly advantaged by Reagan's across-the-board increases in spending on nuclear weapons, which included billions for the company's latest SLBM, the Trident.

The climb was rapid. From 1980, the last full year of the Carter administration, to 1983, Lockheed's Pentagon contracts doubled, from $2 billion per year to $4 billion per year. The main products accounting for these burgeoning sales included the C-5 and C-130 transport aircraft; the P-3 Orion antisubmarine warfare plane; the Polaris and

Trident SLBMs; space vehicles; and amphibious assault ships. These contracts were supplemented by ample research-and-development funding across the full spectrum of weapons programs, from missiles to communications systems.[7]

Congress seemed relatively docile during the initial years of the Reagan buildup—encouraged in this stance by the fact that Reagan's "get tough" rhetoric and stepped-up spending were supported by a majority of Americans—but by the end of Reagan's first term there was considerable push-back by the Democratic leadership. This resistance came on two fronts. The first involved the sheer size of the buildup. At a time of rising deficits and growing social needs, Weinberger's calls for double-digit increases in military spending seemed excessive. The second was a basic difference of opinion on what would make America safe. As Reagan and his top aides engaged in heated rhetoric on the nuclear issue while throwing billions at weapon systems like the Trident and MX missiles, there was genuine fear that these reckless policies could spark a nuclear war. In particular, the claims of the increased accuracy of the new missiles raised the specter of a disarming U.S. first strike that would destroy Soviet ICBMs in their silos before they could be launched. This fear in turn could drive Moscow to launch its weapons first in a crisis, increasing the odds of a superpower nuclear confrontation.

The concern about spending led to successful efforts to at least slow the growth of the Reagan buildup. The second concern—about a new generation of nuclear weapons—sparked one of the most impressive citizens' movements of the twentieth century—the nuclear freeze campaign.

Among the most effective tools of the critics of the Reagan buildup were two vastly overpriced items, a $600 toilet seat and a $7,662 coffeemaker. At a time when Caspar Weinberger was telling Congress with a straight face that there wasn't "an ounce of waste" in the largest peacetime military budget in the nation's history, the spare parts scandal opened the door to a more objective—and damning—assessment of what the tens of billions in new spending rammed through in the early years of the Reagan administration were actually paying for. It also opened up Weinberger to ridicule, symbolized most enduringly by a series of cartoons by the legendary *Washington Post* cartoonist Herblock in which the defense secretary was routinely shown with a toilet seat around his neck.

Appropriately enough, the coffeemaker was procured for Lockheed's C-5A transport plane, the poster child for cost overruns on a major weapon system. The heroine of the piece was Dina Rasor, a young journalist who went to work for the National Taxpayers' Union, then moved from there to found her own organization, the Military Procurement Project. Rasor was mentored by Ernie Fitzgerald, who—after a decade-long lawsuit—had returned to his rightful position at the Pentagon. In her excellent book on the subject, *The Pentagon Underground*, Rasor credits Fitzgerald with showing her the ropes for the complex tasks of sorting through Pentagon propaganda and finding sources "inside the building." It was from her network of whistleblowers that Rasor first learned of the overpriced spare parts and broke the story to the press and the Congress.

The first round of scandals involved, not Lockheed, but rather its arms industry cohort Pratt & Whitney, a manufacturer of aircraft engines. The issue first surfaced when Rasor and her colleagues dug up a July 12, 1982, memo written by Robert Hancock, a procurement official at Tinker Air Force Base in Oklahoma. He noted in the memo that Pratt & Whitney had thirty-four aircraft engine parts that had all increased in price by more than 300 percent in just one year. He had little confidence that the situation could be fixed without drastic action, noting with some understatement that "Pratt & Whitney has never had to control prices and it will be difficult for them to learn."[8] When Rasor released the memo to the press, the extensive coverage it received put the Air Force on the defensive. The Air Force's initial response was that the prices were justified—hardly reassuring to taxpayers who had to be wondering how the prices could quadruple in just one year and still be "justified." Ernie Fitzgerald had his own take on the Air Force's response: "Generally the public relations people [in the Air Force] lie instinctively, even when the truth would serve them better."[9] Fitzgerald seemed to have a point. Even after its own internal review indicated that Pratt & Whitney had reaped "windfall profits" on the parts, the Air Force continued to describe the prices as "fair and reasonable" as late as March 1983, over six months after it knew otherwise. This foot-dragging merely prolonged the agony and stoked the public and congressional outcry over the issue.[10]

Overpriced as they may have been, engine parts weren't the best example for maintaining public interest in the issue, for the simple reason that the average person knows nothing about aircraft engines. The same was not the case with a simple claw hammer provided to the Navy by the Gould Corporation at a price of $435. When Democratic Representative Berkeley Bedell of Iowa went out and bought essentially the same hammer in a hardware store for $7, the level of outrage at government and contractor abuse rose noticeably.[11] When the pricing formula for the $435 hammer was explained, matters got even worse. There was a $37 charge for "engineering support," $93 for "manufacturing support" (including nearly an hour for "quality control"), and a $56 fee that essentially represented clear profit. In other words, in addition to padding the cost with outrageously large overhead charges, the contractor was pulling out a profit from the deal that was *eight times* the basic cost of the item itself.[12] As had been done with the Pratt & Whitney engine parts, the Navy indicated that the charges were proper.

The Lockheed cases followed a similar pattern. In August 1984, Dina Rasor was contacted by Bob Greenstreet, an Air Force captain who worked at Travis Air Force Base in California. Greenstreet was a mechanic who worked on both the Lockheed C-5A and the Lockheed C-141. He contacted Rasor because of his concerns over the costs of spare parts that were used to maintain and repair the aircraft. The examples Greenstreet showed Rasor included a mechanical aircraft clock for $591 and a cowling door for the sides of the C-5A's engines that came in at $166,000 per unit. Rasor acknowledges in *The Pentagon Underground* that at least at first she had no point of reference to help her decide whether these were major overcharges, as she was not familiar with the equipment in question.[13]

Greenstreet led Rasor to the next whistle-blower on the case, Airman Thomas Jonsson, who also worked on the C-5A and C-141 at Travis. It is important to note that the revelations regarding the spare parts came not from Lockheed employees but from Air Force personnel in charge of maintaining Lockheed planes. In any event, Jonsson's first revelation was to figure prominently in later debates in the spare parts scandal—a ten-cup coffeemaker for the C-5A that cost $7,662. This cost, incurred in 1984, was a substantial jump from the 1980 cost, which was "only" $4,947. To add insult to injury, Jonsson noted that the coffeemakers were poorly made and needed frequent repairs.[14]

Jonsson's second example was an aluminum and foam armrest pad for the seats in the C-5A. He estimated that the Air Force could make the pads itself for somewhere in the area of $5 to $25 per copy, but Lockheed was charging $670.06 for each one. Despite Caspar Weinberger's institution of a "Zero Overpricing Program" in response to the initial information on spare parts overcharges, Jonsson's efforts to get Weinberger's reform implemented were thwarted at every turn by the Air Force bureaucracy.[15]

While Rasor was thrilled to get the information provided by Greenstreet and Jonsson, she was also concerned about the effect that speaking out might have on their careers. Rasor's mentor, Ernie Fitzgerald, had helped her set up the Project on Military Procurement in part to protect whistle-blowers from the fate he and others had suffered—ridicule, loss of their jobs, blacklisting by key firms in the industry, and, in the case of Henry Durham (see chapter 3), even death threats. The model that Fitzgerald and Rasor developed involved keeping whistle-blowers' identities anonymous so they could continue to work at the Pentagon and provide ongoing information on fraud and abuse. This method would not only protect the jobs of whistle-blowers but ensure a steady flow of solid information on Pentagon procurement practices. Fitzgerald went beyond the word "whistle-blower" and labeled these Pentagon insiders "closet patriots."

Despite all of these concerns, Greenstreet and Jonsson decided to testify to the Senate on what they had found. Greenstreet was relatively safe: He had finished his duty with the Air Force just one day before the hearing and was now in the Air Force reserve. Jonsson had no such protection, and he was later subjected to retaliation for his role in exposing the overcharges. In a congressional inquiry on "Harassment of Air Force Employees," Jonsson revealed that although he was not stripped of a well-earned promotion, "they did demote me in my job position and require me to be accompanied most of the time."[16] This occurred even after Senator Charles Grassley, who presided over the hearing—held on September 19, 1984—had publicly warned the Air Force that he would not stand for any harassment of the witnesses after their testimony. In fact, it was against the law to do so, but as Rasor pointed out, the law was rarely enforced.

The two men responded well to all the pressure generated by their appearance—neither of them had ever been to Washington before for any reason, much less to testify to Congress and take center stage in the media spotlight. Joined at the witness table by Representative Barbara Boxer (D-CA), the two men made a clear and graphic case regarding malfeasance by the Air Force and its contractors—Lockheed being a central player. Boxer held up a diagram of the infamous $7,662 coffeemaker, and Jonsson held up the $670 airplane seat armrest that he maintained could have been built instead by the Air Force at a price of at most $25. Greenstreet rounded out the story by taking apart one of the $181 emergency flashlights to show that they were built with 1960s technology and could easily have been procured at a hardware store for a fraction of the cost the Air Force was paying.[17]

The hearing room was blanketed with reporters and TV cameras, and the hearing received front-page coverage in the *Washington Post*. Greenstreet and Jonsson also appeared on NBC's *Today Show*. The Air Force was hard-pressed to continue its efforts to give its overseers what Fitzgerald and others referred to as "the mushroom treatment"— keeping them in the dark and feeding them manure. The story was everywhere now, from editorial pages to the TV news to Johnny Carson's monologues on *The Tonight Show*. It was at this time that one of the most damning satires on the subject, Herblock's series of cartoons showing Weinberger with a toilet seat around his neck, appeared in the *Washington Post*.[18]

While the Air Force took most of the flak for the spare parts fiasco, Lockheed was also in the docket. After all, Lockheed was the company benefiting from charging exorbitant prices on the toilet seat (destined for its P-3 antisubmarine warfare plane for the Navy), along with the now-infamous coffeemaker and other equipment for its already overpriced C-5A transport plane (see chapter 4).

Lockheed's first line of defense—parroted by the Pentagon—was to claim that the toilet seat was not a toilet seat at all, but a toilet seat *cover*. This was technically true, but the charge did not allow for a certain level of artistic license. Would Lockheed and the Pentagon have been happier if Herblock had shown Weinberger wearing a toilet seat cover as a hat?

Putting aside that particular technicality and going further in its own defense, Lockheed asserted that the toilet cover was really a quite sophisticated piece of equipment, designed to be "a lightweight, corrosive resistant, thermo-formed, polycarbonate material, seamless and sufficiently durable to withstand repeated usage and aircraft landings."[19] Republican Senator William Roth of Delaware was not impressed, noting that "you can go into a mobile home and see something not much different."

The company's final argument was that if the Air Force wanted a cheaper part, it would need to buy more of them. This point was summarized by Lockheed spokesperson James Ragsdale as follows: "This is not an off-the-shelf item. They are designed to military specifications. If only 30 or 40 or 50 are ordered in a year's time, of course you're going to pay more for them than if they were built in the thousands."[20]

In the end, Lockheed did admit some responsibility for the enormous cost of the toilet cover, acknowledging that a review of its records indicated that it should have charged the Navy $540 per item rather than $640. In a letter to Secretary of the Navy John Lehman, Lockheed President Lawrence O. Kitchen indicated that a recalculation of labor costs, overhead, and "handling charges, material and pretax 13.4 percent profit rate" accounted for the $100 cut in the price. "This could lead one to believe that all spare parts are overpriced," noted Kitchen, hence the company's "generous" offer to return $4,606.74 for the overcharge on fifty-four toilet covers.[21]

Not surprisingly, Lockheed's $100 giveback was not enough to stem the uproar over the toilet cover's cost. The company finally cut the cost from $640 to $100, claiming that it was taking a loss. In a telegram to Senator William Roth, Kitchen offered the $100 as a "token price" so as to "prevent this from becoming an unnecessary diversion during Congressional discussions of the national defense budget."[22] Finally, in an effort to put the whole scandal behind them, Lockheed offered to give the toilet covers to the government for free.

Maybe a little diversion—albeit perhaps not on the headline-grabbing level of the $640 toilet seat and the $7,662 coffeemaker—would have been a good thing for Lockheed, given what came next: hundreds of millions of dollars of questionable cost increases on the company's C-5A transport plane and a lobbying scandal relating to its successor, the C-5B. But first the company had to dodge several more rounds of criticism on its spare parts practices.

First came the toilet seats—toilet *covers* that is. As part of the hubbub surrounding the original revelations of outrageous overpricing, it was agreed that Lockheed would put the toilet cover contract up for competitive bidding. But according to Lockheed, a solicitation to thirty companies had yielded no bids as of late November 1985. According to Lockheed spokesperson Rich Stadler, no one bid because with so few items involved, "they knew they weren't going to make a buck," thereby proving that Lockheed's adjusted price of $540 per toilet cover was "a very fair price." In a challenge to company critics, Stadler asserted that, "if someone can do better, we'd be very happy for them to take over the job."[23] But given a set profit of 13.4 percent and generous overhead and handling charges, Stadler may well have been bluffing. And given that small companies had come forward when the scandal originally broke offering to provide the same item for one-fifth the price, Senator William Roth questioned whether the failure to find a bidder had more to do with Lockheed's "inflexibility" than a lack of other sources for the toilet covers. Republican Senator William Cohen of Maine—who a decade later went on to serve as Defense Secretary in the Clinton administration—went a step further, suggesting that the Pentagon produce the items in-house if that was the best price Lockheed had to offer.

Lockheed's credibility was further tarnished just a little over two months later, in February 1986, when Rasor and her Project on Military Procurement released a company memo indicating that they had reached out to less than half as many companies for the toilet cover bid as they had claimed—solicitations had gone out to fourteen companies, not thirty. It was also revealed that Lockheed bid out just ten of the devices, not the fifty-four that were needed, providing a further disincentive for other companies to bid on their production.[24]

And even as it was failing to put the toilet cover issue to rest, *another* bathroom-related scandal popped up, this time involving toilet pans for the C-5A—described by UPI reporter Timothy Bannon as "a Fiberglass part that looks like a large cookie sheet."[25] Peter Stockton, then a staffer for Representative John Dingell (D-MI), referred to the parts more colorfully as "piss pans."[26] The pans slid under the toilet in a C-5A to catch any splash or overflow.

The original price charged to the Air Force for the toilet pans was $317, down from the $642 Lockheed had attempted to charge originally. After further haggling, the Air Force got the price down to $286.75 per item. After initial, exaggerated reports that the toilet pans were akin to a simple roasting pan that could be bought for less than $10 (they were not), Jesse Sandoval, an Air Force craftsman employed at Kelly Air Force Base in San Antonio, Texas, stepped forward to assert that he had produced a similar item on-base for under $90, or less than one-third of Lockheed's lowest offer.[27]

The issue then played out the same way it did with the $640 toilet cover. Lockheed protested that the toilet pan was a small-volume specialty item that it had produced only after telling the Air Force it would have preferred to have some other company do the work. And to avoid "collateral damage" to its larger programs, Lockheed agreed to sell the toilet pans to the Air Force for $1 each.

But this routine did not play out until there had been an extraordinary outburst by Robert B. Ormsby, President of Lockheed Aeronautical Systems Group, in the pages of the specialty magazine *Aviation Week and Space Technology*. He started by lamenting his company's situation—the familiar "Lockheed as victim" approach that had been used in connection with other scandals like the C-5A cost overrun fiasco and the $250 million bailout:

> For the past five years, some members of the media and some politicians have . . . [been] feeding the American people and an unwary Congress a diet of horror stories about a perniciously greedy defense industry that makes immense profits delving into the pockets of

taxpayers by charging hundreds of dollars for items like toilet seats and hammers available at hardware stores and local machine shops for a few bucks.[28]

Arguing to the contrary, Ormsby observed that spare parts represented a very small portion of the 15 million transactions entered into between the Pentagon and industry in any given year, amounting to about 1.6 percent of the total defense budget. This argument begged several questions. First, an overcharge is an overcharge, no matter what proportion of the Pentagon budget it represents. And second, as argued by Ernie Fitzgerald and others, many of the same procurement practices used with toilet covers and coffeemakers were applied to a whole aircraft like the C-5A, making the planes a "flying collection of spare parts," as Fitzgerald put it.

Ormsby went on to blame the messenger, arguing that the spare parts claims lacked merit and were the product of "publicity-seeking politicians," "special interest groups" (by which he meant nonprofit groups like Dina Rasor's Project on Military Procurement), and "irresponsible members of the media." After also denouncing "a few zealous government oversight agencies eager for a part of the headline action," Ormsby had completed his sketch of the anti-industry cabal. He asserted that his company was being unfairly criticized for charging what he viewed as a reasonable price for what was not "a common plastic pot," as he claimed the press was describing it as, but "a three-ply, contoured glass fiber unit designed for a unique transport aircraft." He claimed that it took four and a half production hours and fifteen separate steps to produce the toilet pans, during which time they were subjected to three separate government inspections. Far from overcharging the government, Ormsby suggested, Lockheed had come to its price only after performing an "exhaustive" economic analysis. (He failed to note whether the cost of the analysis itself was folded into the price of the toilet pans.)[29]

Just in case these arguments were not persuasive, Ormsby ended by wrapping his company in the flag:

The fundamental issue is the level of defense spending necessary to sustain the security of our nation and its allies. That question has

been rendered moot by the rush of reporters and politicians to generate headlines charging waste, fraud and abuse in the defense industry and the armed forces.

The following all contribute to a climate that demoralizes the
millions of men and women in and out of uniform, and undermine
our country's peace efforts by projecting to our allies and adversaries
the image of America as a divided and quarreling nation whose military forces lack the confidence and trust of its citizens.[30]

In short, Ormsby was suggesting that those who were uncovering
the fraud, waste, and abuse in military spending were the enemies of
peace and freedom and should just shut up in the interests of demonstrating national unity in the face of global adversaries. In its suggestion that no one should question the contractors or the Pentagon for
fear of being labeled unpatriotic, this statement could not have been
more blatantly undemocratic.

There was evidence that the information on spare parts overcharges
was indeed reducing congressional and public support for the Reagan
administration's record peacetime military budget requests, as Ormsby
suggested. But far from weakening the country, the revelations spurred
a healthy debate about how much is enough when it comes to defense
and underscored the fact that massive military budgets that are not
subjected to rigorous scrutiny are a recipe for waste, fraud, and abuse.

The spare parts scandal was just one symptom of a larger problem
in Pentagon procurement. It was a Lockheed system, the C-5A, that
served as the most obvious example. In January 1980—years before
the spare parts scandal broke—Henry Durham told Dina Rasor about
an Air Force plan to pay Lockheed $1.5 billion to fix severe problems
with the wings on the aircraft. Durham was the same man who had
blown the whistle on overcharging on C-5A components in the early
1970s. He was outraged that the company might get a billion-dollar-
plus payday to fix a problem it had created in the first place.[31]

In the meantime, Rasor's background research had uncovered a
1976 General Accounting Office study that revealed numerous performance problems with the C-5A, including but not limited to the
need to fix the wings. At that time the GAO suggested that the Air

Force cost out alternatives to an expensive fix of the C-5A, from prepositioning more equipment overseas to using fast ships to exploring the possibility of utilizing an adaptation of the Boeing 747—an idea that had been raised when the C-5A first ran into trouble in the late 1960s and early 1970s. Rasor learned that in 1980—four years later—the Air Force had still not done a comparative study of this sort, and if Durham's suspicions were correct, it was about to hand $1.5 billion to Lockheed without exploring any alternatives.[32]

When Rasor spoke with Fitzgerald by telephone about the wing fix issue, he assured her that it was well worth looking into. Despite all he had been through in losing his job over the original C-5A scandal, Rasor found that Fitzgerald had a sense of humor about it all, combined with years of experience in dealing with the Pentagon and Air Force bureaucracies. He was the perfect ally if she was going to take on the issue of the C-5A wing fix.

One of Fitzgerald's first lessons for Rasor—one she was unwilling to accept at first—had been that it wasn't just about information. Reminding the Pentagon and the Congress that there might be a cheaper, more effective way to solve the C-5A problem was not in and of itself going to win the day. As Fitzgerald put it in a conversation with Rasor, "This is another make-work and bailout for Lockheed and the Georgia congressional delegation. It is pure pork barrel. They aren't going to care about the facts."[33]

If anything, the Air Force and Lockheed were going to bend the facts to fit their parochial interests. After she started looking into the issue, Rasor heard from a Dr. Paul Paris of St. Louis University. Paris had served with a 1977 study group known as the Structural Information Enhancement Program (SIEP) that was supposed to address the issue of the C-5A's wing problems. Paris noted that he was the *only* member of the group who didn't work for either Lockheed or the Air Force, and that in any case the participants were given limited technical data and were essentially being pushed toward choosing the most expensive fix possible—building entirely new sets of wings for each aircraft.[34]

It was Paris's belief that a fix of the wings in place would be more than sufficient, and that in pushing for more extensive—and expensive—

work, the powers-that-be in the Air Force were just looking for a way to send as much money Lockheed's way as possible. Not only was the Air Force willing to exaggerate the extent of the wing problems if it meant a fatter contract for Lockheed, but it was also intent on hiding other problems with the plane that might suggest the need for a different solution, and perhaps a different aircraft, in lieu of an exorbitantly expensive effort to repair and renovate the C-5A.

The C-5A's performance problems had had serious—and in one case tragic—impacts in times of war. In April 1975, while evacuating a plane full of refugees from Vietnam in the final days of the U.S. intervention there, a C-5A crashed, killing ninety-eight Vietnamese orphans and dozens of U.S. crew members. A rear cargo door fell off, causing the crash. In the course of her researches on the C-5A wing fix, Rasor had found a 1971 Air Force engineering report that raised serious alarm bells about the cargo door mechanism. One engineer described it as a "monster system that was unreliable and unsafe" and recommended grounding the plane until the problem was repaired.[35]

Other serious questions were raised by the C-5A's performance in support of Israel in the 1973 Mideast war. A GAO study revealed that 60 percent of the planes were not usable owing to maintenance or spare parts issues. Those C-5As that did fly were able to deliver only twenty-nine tanks to the battle area, and only four before the ceasefire was signed in the short conflict.[36] The war was just the kind of situation the C-5A was meant to address: a conflict in which heavy equipment needed to be hauled to the battlefield on short notice. Yet the first time the Air Force tried to use it in this role, it failed the test.

The 1976 GAO report cited here identified a number of defects besides the wing problem that were in need of fixing, including "other modifications such as the aft cargo door, installation of a fire suppression system, and a lift distribution control system." All of these changes were deemed essential by the GAO, but as of early 1980 it appeared that none of them had been made.[37]

As for the wing fix itself, matters came to a head at an August 25, 1980, hearing before Senator William Proxmire's Subcommittee on Economy and Efficiency in Government. Proxmire was well acquainted with the history of the C-5A, having served as the leader of the efforts to end production of the plane in the late 1960s. At the hearing, Proxmire managed to get Robert Ormsby, then President of Lockheed-Georgia, to acknowledge that the wing problem stemmed from a decision the company had made in the late 1960s to shave ten thousand pounds off the C-5A to meet the Air Force's weight requirements. The change had been done without accounting for its impact on the technical performance of the aircraft.[38]

Prior to Ormsby's testimony, Paul Paris did serious damage to Lockheed's case when he noted that the panel looking at the cost of fixing the C-5A's wings had been told to consider only the most expensive option, the so-called H-Mod. He further noted that the decision was based on data provided by Lockheed with no independent scrutiny or verification.[39]

Not only was the extent and cost of the needed fix based almost entirely on Lockheed's word, but the Air Force had stacked the deck in such a way as to ensure that Lockheed would get the contract. Although Air Force officials claimed that Lockheed won the contract through a competitive bidding process, in reality no other company put in a bid. Because Lockheed had been given the research-and-development contract for the wing fix, no defense contractor felt that it had a chance of wresting the production contract away from the company that had designed the wing.

Dave Keating, Dina Rasor's boss at the National Taxpayers' Union— where she worked before going on to found the Project on Military Procurement in early 1981—underscored the perversity of the whole situation in his testimony before Proxmire's subcommittee. He noted that giving Lockheed the contract would set up a "terrible incentive system." If Lockheed profited from the wing fix, he argued, "What type of example will we be setting for other defense contractors? The more inefficient you are, the more profit you make. Build failures into the system and you will be rewarded."[40] Keating went on to suggest that the process that had been carried out to determine the cost and the contractor for the C-5A wing fix raised the question of whether it had been intended all along to provide "a multi-billion bailout for Lockheed."[41]

Proxmire had heard enough. Over the objections of Lockheed and the Air Force, he demanded a General Accounting Office study of the costs and necessity of the wing modification. Unfortunately, as Rasor noted at the time, the study took a year, by which time Congress had already funded what she and her colleagues viewed as a $1.4 billion giveaway to Lockheed.

The fight over the wing fix just set the stage for the next battle: Would Lockheed get to build the C-X, the next-generation Air Force transport plane?

Given Lockheed's record on the C-5A, one would have thought that the Air Force would go out of its way to find another option, but this was not the case. In fact, the Air Force was involved in what looked an awful lot like illegal lobbying activities to help Lockheed win the contract.

From the outset, the 1980s C-5B procurement resembled the 1960s decision to pick the C-5A. In August 1981, McDonnell Douglas was selected as the winner of the C-X competition, with an aircraft that later came to be designated the C-17. Initially, both the "airlift community"— a network of Pentagon analysts who were in communication with Rasor and her colleagues—and the Air Force itself clearly favored the McDonnell Douglas plane. The Air Force enthusiastically briefed the Congress on the merits of the aircraft, and as late as January 8, 1982, Secretary of the Air Force Verne Orr briefed Deputy Secretary of Defense Frank Carlucci on the flaws of the C-5, including a bad maintenance record, an inability to land on unimproved runways, and no offer of a warranty as to the reliability and maintainability of the aircraft. For all of these reasons and more, Orr advocated sticking with the C-17 as the choice for the next-generation transport plane.

This made it all the more surprising when the Air Force reversed course less than two weeks later, on January 20, and announced that it was choosing the C-5B. Even critics like Dina Rasor were shocked. She argued that "it didn't seem logical that the Air Force, after heralding the C-17 so widely in the Congress, would want to have an updated version of one of its most embarrassing procurements."[42] Rasor and Fitzgerald concluded that the only sensible explanation was that this was yet another bailout of Lockheed.

Even as the decision was being announced, critics of the C-5B within the Pentagon were leaking information on the liabilities of the C-5. Not only did it cost more per hour to fly than any other plane in the Air Force inventory, but it required inordinate numbers of spare parts—while the C-5 represented only 1 percent of the Air Force's flying capability, it used up 14 percent of the service's spare parts budget. Of equal importance, the plane was so large and clumsy that it routinely clogged the runways at military bases in Europe, even under peacetime conditions.[43]

The potential deficiencies of a next-generation C-5 were further highlighted when Boeing put forward a surprise offer of new or used 747 cargo planes at a lower price, with larger carrying capacity, a demonstrated capability to land on short runways, and a twenty-year price guarantee. The Pentagon and the Air Force weren't about to change their decision, whether or not the purported price and performance characteristics of the 747 proved true. But it wasn't just up to them. Senator Henry Jackson (D-WA), who came to be referred to as "the Senator from Boeing" for his persistent lobbying on behalf of his home-state firm's interests, used his clout as a high-ranking member of the Armed Services Committee to persuade his Senate colleagues to endorse the 747 cargo plane by a margin of 60–30.[44] It was this decision that sparked an intense, coordinated lobbying campaign on the part of the Pentagon, the Air Force, and Lockheed and its subcontractors to overcome congressional resistance and throw the competition to the C-5B.

The full details of the C-5B lobbying campaign might never have seen the light of day if a Pentagon insider hadn't provided a copy of the ninety-six-page lobbying plan to Dina Rasor.[45] A core element of the plan was to deploy high-level validators who could secure the votes of key House and Senate members, ranging from four-star generals to Senate Majority Leader Howard Baker to Secretary of the Air Force Verne Orr and Deputy Secretary of Defense Frank Carlucci to President Reagan himself. For example, Reagan and Baker were solicited to make calls to Representative Robert Michel (R-IL), the House minority leader, while the others were assigned to lobby lower-level members of Congress. The symbiotic relationship between Lockheed and the Pentagon was set out early in the document when it was noted that Lockheed would be responsible for drafting the Defense Secretary's position paper on the C-5B. The idea of putting a contractor in charge of writing an official government brief on behalf of its own aircraft did not seem to trouble the C-5B lobbying team.

A similar "ghostwriting" role was played by the Pentagon with respect to Congress when the Defense Department's congressional liaison office—meant to be an information-providing body only—drafted a "Dear Colleague" letter for use in recruiting support for the C-5B. A "Dear Colleague" letter is a communication sent from one or more members of Congress to their colleagues seeking support for a particular position or a vote on a specific matter.

In parallel to these propaganda efforts, specific C-5B proponents were given their marching orders. Civil rights legend and Atlanta Mayor Andrew Young was assigned to lobby members of the Congressional Black Caucus; moderate Democratic Representative Dave McCurdy of Oklahoma was asked to "work freshmen"; and Republican Representative Newt Gingrich of Georgia was one of three members charged with "working moderates." The Georgia connection was no coincidence. The main assembly plant for the C-5B was to be in Marietta, Georgia, just north of Atlanta. Lockheed told Young that up to 8,500 Atlanta-area jobs were at stake.

The heart of the lobbying effort, however, lay not in the reputations of the advocates or the words on a piece of paper, but in pure pork barrel politics. Lockheed was assigned early on to garner support from key members of the House Appropriations and Armed Services Committees, while the Defense Department and the Air Force searched for a prominent chairman of a non-defense-related committee to endorse the C-5B—"like on the B-1," the lobby memo said. The B-1 reference was important. The campaign to revive the Rockwell International long-range bomber in the early Reagan years—after it had been canceled by President Carter—was viewed as a model worth adopting in other military budget battles.

As was the case with Andrew Young and Newt Gingrich, a standard practice was to match up production sites for the weapon system in question with members of Congress and other public officials who could be recruited as advocates for it. Bearing this in mind, the lobby plan called for Lockheed to mobilize its subcontractor base, including companies like E-Systems, Vought, Northrop, and Pratt & Whitney. The Pentagon went further, encouraging even contractors without a direct stake in the C-5B to lobby on its behalf and suggesting, in a veiled threat, that their other Pentagon programs could suffer if they failed to comply. And last but not least, the Pentagon attempted to neutralize Boeing. An article in *Armed Forces Journal International* reported that Undersecretary of Defense for Research and Engineering Richard DeLauer had told Boeing President T. Wilson that "we will fight you tooth and nail" and "pull the purse strings" on the company's contracts for the Civil Reserve Air Fleet if Boeing opposed the C-5B. When Wilson questioned whether the pro-C5-B campaign would be carried out "legally and ethically," DeLauer responded, "It will certainly be legal. Ethically? I can't comment."

Among the major players enlisted in the cause because of contracts in their states or districts were House Speaker "Tip" O'Neill (D-MA) and Democratic Senator Carl Levin of Michigan. O'Neill was reportedly told that the C-5B would be a big boon to General Electric, a major employer in Massachusetts, because the plane's engines would be built by GE. What was not stressed was that the engines would be built in Ohio, not in Massachusetts. In Senator Levin's case, the lobbying effort recruited General Dynamics (GD) to get him to press liberal members to vote for the C-5B. The company—a major subcontractor for the plane—had leverage over Levin because it built the M-1 tank, a big job supplier in his state. But GD's assignment went beyond just Levin. The plan also called for it to "provide list and work all members (approx. 60) in their plant locations and areas."

Another of the many examples of direct pork barrel appeals was the pitch made to Representative Glenn Anderson (D-CA). As the lobby plan put it, to ensure his support there was a need for "subcontractor calls or wires from Wetzel (Garrett), Puckett (Hughes), Bannum (West. Gear)."

This wasn't just a case of the Pentagon and Lockheed working together toward the same goal, as evidenced by the lobby plan itself, which carefully coordinated assignments among the Defense Department, the Air Force, and Lockheed. To a considerable degree, Lockheed was calling the shots. Congressional hearings held after the lobby plan was made public revealed that the initiative had been the brainchild of Lockheed President Lawrence O. Kitchen, who attended most of the lobby group meetings and took some of the most important assignments in the form of one-on-one meetings with key members of Congress.

The coordination even went so far as having the Air Force provide customized pictures of the C-5 for use in a full-page ad that appeared in the *Washington Post*:

ACTION: 6/04 AF: Provide LOK [Lawrence O. Kitchen]
composite pictures of C-5 with 3 Chinook helicopters and C-5
with 6 Blackhawk helicopters.
STATUS: Will do pictures at Andrews [Air Force Base] this week.

One of the most interesting aspects of the whole affair was how unapologetic the Air Force and Lockheed were once the lobbying scheme hit the press. For example, Air Force Lieutenant General Kelly Burke, who was responsible for overseeing the C-5 program, asserted, "You're just wrong if you think this is a highly unusual happening . . . all you're seeing is democracy in action. This is how the system is supposed to work."

Not everyone agreed. Representative Jack Brooks (D-TX) asked the General Accounting Office to review the lobbying scheme to see if any laws had been broken. The GAO report, issued on September 30, 1982, was surprisingly hard-hitting. It called for investigations of possible criminal violations of the laws restricting lobbying activities on the part of executive branch officials. Suggested targets of the investigation included individuals in the congressional liaison office of the Air Force, the legislative affairs office of the Pentagon, Secretary of the Air Force Verne Orr, and Deputy Secretary of Defense Frank Carlucci, among others. The first point of concern was whether these individuals violated a 1913 statute prohibiting the lobbying of any branch of government by executive branch personnel; the second involved whether the coordination with contractors also violated the law.

The GAO had this to say about the second point: "Since the Air Force is prohibited by appropriation restrictions from directly mounting a grassroots lobbying campaign . . . it follows that it may not engage in a network of defense contractors to do the same thing." The reference to appropriation restrictions reflected the GAO's view that the salaries paid to Air Force and Defense Department officials during the joint lobbying campaign with Lockheed were an improper use of federal funds.[46]

Ernie Fitzgerald, for one, was skeptical as to whether the referral of these matters to the Justice Department would go anywhere, saying that it was like "asking the King's lawyers to prosecute the King's men for doing the King's business."[47] Calls for a special prosecutor to sort out the facts of the case were ignored.

Unfortunately, Fitzgerald's prediction was on target. The Justice Department let the case languish, then closed it in February 1983 without bringing any charges. The perfunctory nature of the investigation was underscored by the fact that the Justice Department officials involved never even called Carl Palmer, the author of the GAO report that had prompted the investigation in the first place. Palmer said as much in an interview with the *St. Louis Post-Dispatch*: "I'm really disappointed that they've decided not to prosecute. I think they should have gone further than they did. . . . Nobody has contacted us."[48]

Dina Rasor observed that, after the dust settled on the C-5B campaign—with Lockheed and the Air Force winning the battle—the only unusual aspect of the whole affair was that it received as much attention as it did. Calling it "a larger illustration of the congressional role in the procurement process," she noted that "it happens every year with other weapons in a similar but much quieter way."[49] All the same elements are present when other weapon systems are up for debate: Industry and Pentagon lobbyists swarm Capitol Hill; pressure is ratcheted up on members of the Armed Services and Defense Appropriations Committees in the House and Senate, many of whom have had key defense production facilities placed in their states or districts; key members receive generous political contributions from the producer of the weapon system and its subcontractors (a process

that the C-5B lobby plan called being "PAC [political action com-
mittee]-wired"); and official reports and testimony are created that
make a one-sided case for the weapon system in question, often with
the aid of the contractors.

A by-product of this process is that liberal members who often denounce waste and abuse in the military budget suddenly become ar-
dent military budget boosters when it comes to the weapons built in
their states and districts. For example, at the time of the C-5B campaign, the Navy was promoting a McDonnell Douglas fighter jet, the
F-18. There was some sentiment in Congress to kill the plane owing
to extreme cost overruns and performance problems, but among its
strongest defenders were prominent liberals Senator Edward Kennedy
(D-MA) and Senator Alan Cranston (D-CA). Cranston had also
played a key role almost a decade earlier in pushing the $250 million
government bailout of Lockheed through the Senate. The C-5B case
underscores the need to break up what analyst Gordon Adams has described as the "Iron Triangle"—the collusion among the military, the
contractors, and Congress that leads to huge defense budgets and
questionable weapons purchases.[50] To this day Lockheed remains the
leading company spearheading the contractor side of the triangle.

The C-5B program wasn't the only one in which Lockheed pushed
the legal and ethical envelope. It also did so with respect to a critical
component of President Reagan's "Star Wars" project, the Homing
Overlay Experiment (HOE). In 1984 an apparently successful test of
the HOE—an interceptor that opened like a web or a giant umbrella
to block incoming missiles—gave a huge boost to Reagan's missile
defense initiative, a program that faced growing questions regarding its
cost and technical feasibility. But there was more to the test than met
the eye.

The missile defense program was Reagan's pet project, and like any
major undertaking of this kind, it had multiple motivations, both
strategic and political. First, Reagan genuinely feared that the United
States had fallen behind the Soviet Union militarily, arguing in a
March 17, 1980, campaign speech at the Chicago Council on Foreign
Relations that "in military strength we are already second to one:
namely, the Soviet Union. . . . And that is a very dangerous place in

which to be." Most of Reagan's rhetoric as a candidate—as well as his resource allocations in the first two years of his presidency—was focused on across-the-board military spending increases and modernization of the U.S. nuclear arsenal. But he and his top advisers were missile defense supporters well before the program took off in the mid-1980s, even if it wasn't initially the number-one priority of the Reagan defense buildup.

All of this changed in March 1983 when Reagan announced an expanded missile defense effort in what came to be known as his "Star Wars speech." The most memorable phrase in the speech was Reagan's pledge to seek technologies that would render nuclear weapons "impotent and obsolete." Top Reagan aides, including Secretary of State George Shultz, were taken off guard by the sheer ambition of the speech, as well as by the fact that it threatened to undermine efforts at reaching accommodations on nuclear weapons reductions with the Soviet Union even as it antagonized allies. Shultz and others feared that NATO partners would think that a defensive system might encourage the United States to "go it alone" in a nuclear conflict rather than fulfill the U.S. promise to attack Moscow in the event of a nuclear attack on Western Europe. And all of this for a program that seemed like a pipe dream, at least in the form implied by Reagan's rhetoric.[51]

Reagan also had political reasons for suddenly putting missile defense front and center in his defense policy. His harsh anti-Soviet rhetoric and seemingly cavalier attitude toward the prospect of a U.S.-Soviet nuclear confrontation had sparked a strong response in the form of the nuclear freeze campaign, an initiative that called for a freeze on the development and production of new nuclear weapons and nuclear delivery vehicles like ICBMs, long-range bombers, and Lockheed's lucrative Trident submarine-launched ballistic missile (SLBM). Scores of localities around the country passed pro-freeze resolutions, and the House of Representatives came within two votes of passing a resolution sponsored by Representative Ed Markey (D-MA) calling for a nuclear freeze.[52] Reagan aide Eugene Rostow wrote a memo expressing concern that the freeze could begin to erode the administration's support not just among liberals and the peace movement but among mainstream, middle-of-the-road Americans:

There is participation on an increasing scale in the U.S. of three groups whose potential impact should be cause for concern. They are the churches, the "loyal opposition," and, perhaps most important, the unpoliticized public.[53]

In her excellent book on the "Star Wars" phenomenon, *Way Out There in the Blue*, Pulitzer Prize–winning author Frances Fitzgerald observed that "pragmatists" in Reagan's inner circle—exemplified by Chief of Staff James Baker—"began to worry about the effect the anti-nuclear movement might have on the defense buildup and even on Reagan's chances for re-election."[54] The thinking of this group was that the President desperately needed to put a viable nuclear arms control proposal on the table to counter the freeze. But this was easier said than done, as hawkish aides like the Pentagon's Richard Perle—who came to be known in some circles as "the Prince of Darkness" for his dire views of the Soviet Union and the nuclear balance—clashed with arms control advocates like the State Department's Richard Burt. The two sides fought to a standstill, thus blocking any practical proposal.

While his aides were deadlocked over arms control, Reagan's image as warmonger-in-chief was furthered by the May 30, 1982, leak of parts of Defense Secretary Caspar Weinberger's five-year defense guidance, which suggested that the United States could "prevail" in a "protracted" nuclear war. This rhetoric made it sound as if, far from trying to head off a nuclear conflict at all costs, there were circumstances under which the Reagan administration might consider fighting one. General David C. Jones, the outgoing chairman of the Joint Chiefs of Staff, suggested that planning for a conflict of this sort would amount to throwing money down a "bottomless pit," noting that "I don't see much of a chance of nuclear war being limited or protracted."[55]

By December 1982, Reagan's approval rating was down to 41 percent, and two-thirds of Americans disagreed with his approach to arms control. Even worse, 57 percent of Americans worried that Reagan might involve the country in a nuclear war.[56]

It was this political situation, more than anything else, that determined the pace and timing of Reagan's rousing public commitment to missile defense. While it is true that "Star Wars" enthusiasts like Edward Teller, the "father" of the hydrogen bomb, were whispering in Reagan's ear about fantastic technologies like a nuclear bomb–pumped, space-based X-ray laser, it appears that the real genesis of the program came from within the administration, in significant part owing to the groundwork laid by Reagan National Security Adviser Robert McFarlane.[57]

By December 1982, McFarlane had become convinced that a new course was essential for U.S. nuclear policy. This conviction arose in part from the administration's difficulties in generating public and congressional support for a new land-based ICBM known as the MX missile, and in part from McFarlane's belief that if it came to an offensive arms race, the Soviet Union could build new missiles and deploy new nuclear warheads more rapidly than the United States could. Why this mattered in a world in which a few hundred of the thousands of nuclear weapons on each side could devastate the other is a question buried deeply in the arcane annals of nuclear strategy. The basic argument was that one side might develop enough accurate missiles to destroy all or most of the other side's nuclear weapons in a "disarming first strike." Why any leader would risk the fate of his own nation on the unproven theory that such a strike might work was a question that went largely unanswered—and too often unasked—by nuclear strategists at the Pentagon.

Given his fears of a potential Soviet buildup and the apparent unraveling of Reagan's pro-military spending coalition, McFarlane was looking for something to change both the political and strategic calculus underlying U.S. nuclear weapons policy. "Star Wars"—or the Strategic Defense Initiative, as it later came to be known—was that answer, in McFarlane's view. The idea of using America's technological edge to develop potential defenses against Soviet nuclear weapons appealed to McFarlane, not because he thought it would lead to a leakproof nuclear "shield," but rather because it might bring the Soviet Union to the bargaining table to agree to reductions in its offensive arsenal. In short, McFarlane saw missile defense as a bargaining chip, not a technological miracle. Whether or not the missile shield ever worked, McFarlane believed that the threat that it might would provide the leverage needed to get Moscow to agree to deep reductions in its nuclear missile forces. McFarlane later referred to this approach as "the greatest sting operation in history."[58]

Whatever McFarlane may have thought, his boss, Ronald Reagan, had ideas of his own. Only a few weeks after being briefed about the possibility of pursuing missile defenses, Reagan was ready to announce a major initiative along these lines to the entire country. McFarlane tried to persuade him not to do so, but Reagan was dreaming of a way to protect the American people from nuclear war. This would solve two problems at once: It would outmaneuver the nuclear freeze movement by offering a technological rather than an arms control "fix" to the nuclear danger, and it would address his own genuine distaste for basing U.S. defenses on the threat of nuclear annihilation.

Reagan demonstrated his ambitious expectations for the missile defense concept in the run-up to his March 23, 1983, "Star Wars" speech. (He never used the term "Star Wars" in the speech, but the missile defense concept came to be routinely referred to as such.) It was Reagan who inserted language in the speech claiming that his new plan would eventually render nuclear weapons "impotent and obsolete," a concept that Secretary of State George Shultz, among others, viewed as ludicrous.[59]

Reagan's full-blown missile defense program, the Strategic Defense Initiative (SDI), wasn't rolled out until 1985, but a number of key projects received additional funding before that. In the early stages of the Reagan missile defense buildup, the initiative financed a wide range of exotic technologies—from space-based lasers to interceptor warheads that would unfurl umbrella-like spokes to increase the chances of hitting an incoming warhead. Lockheed was in charge of the umbrella scheme, known as the Homing Overlay Experiment. The HOE had been in the concept phase since the Carter administration, but the program was accelerated during 1983 and 1984, after Reagan's "Star Wars" speech gave it a higher priority. As one of the few missile defense ideas to score an actual "hit" by intercepting a mock warhead in flight, the HOE was to play a central role in sustaining missile defense funding even after many of the initial ideas had proven impractical.[60] The successful HOE test occurred in June 1984, after three failed tests during 1983 were beginning to spread doubt about the feasibility of the President's missile defense program. To this day Lockheed Martin brags about the test. For example, a press release issued at the 2009 Paris Air Show touted the "25th Anniversary of the World's First Hit-to-Kill Missile Intercept," claiming that the June 10, 1984, test had "proved the ability to destroy enemy missiles with sheer force of impact."

There was only one problem—the test was rigged. Unfortunately, this was not discovered until a decade later, when an investigation by the General Accounting Office determined that the June 1984 HOE test had been crafted to make it easier for the umbrella-like kill vehicle to hit its target.

Original reports by a former missile defense program official had asserted that the mock warhead used in the HOE test literally sent out a signal that allowed the interceptor to find it—the equivalent of saying "come and get me," as the official put it. But the GAO learned that the reality was more complicated. To avoid "risking failure of the entire experiment" and losing funding as a result, "steps were taken to make it easier for the interceptor's sensor to find the target." The steps included heating up the mock warhead to make it easier to detect against the cold background of space and turning it sideways in flight. These measures made the warhead appear more than twice its normal size.[61] Democratic Senator David Pryor of Arkansas, whose office had requested the GAO investigation, was livid: "Whether you call it test-rigging or mere enhancement, it is an outrage that Congress did not find out about it until 10 years had passed and $35 billion was spent."[62] Lockheed, which cooperated with the Army in fixing the test, reaped billions in additional funding as a result—funding that might not have been supplied had there never been a successful test of the HOE system.

Incredibly, it could have been worse. The Pentagon was contemplating a much more heavy-handed approach to rigging the HOE tests, one in which a bomb would be set off in the target vehicle regardless of whether it was hit by the interceptor. According to the GAO, this so-called deception program was abandoned after the first three HOE tests could not even generate a near-miss. The idea behind the plan was that it would give the Soviet Union an exaggerated sense of U.S. capabilities, thereby furthering the "leverage" that Robert McFarlane saw as the main value of the missile defense program. Of course, it would have the additional benefit—at least to Lockheed and the Pentagon, if not to the taxpayer—of making it easier to keep the "Star Wars" gravy train running in the form of generous congressional support.

Despite the HOE deception, waning support for military spending—driven in part by tales of waste like the $7,662 coffeemaker that contributed to public questioning of permanently high military budgets in peacetime—led to diminished support for "Star Wars" spending as well. This trend was reinforced by increasing skepticism about the ability to develop workable systems that could provide the "leakproof shield" implicit in Ronald Reagan's accounts of the program's goal. By the time George Herbert Walker Bush took office in January 1989, investment in missile defense was dropping substantially from its Reagan-era peak. It wasn't until the mid-1990s, after a concerted effort by "Star Wars" boosters—right-wing think tanks and conservative members of Congress aided and abetted by Lockheed and other missile defense contractors—that the program was restored to the funding levels it had received under Ronald Reagan. Lockheed was to ride the funding roller coaster as skillfully as any of its competitors.

Chapter 8

SAINT AUGUSTINE'S LAWS

Norm Augustine didn't set out to be a captain of the defense industry. His original plan was to be a forest ranger.[1]

If he had gone that route, Lockheed Martin might not exist. The company might have been absorbed into another military mega-firm, as happened with McDonnell Douglas, a onetime rival that was bought by Boeing. Or Lockheed and Martin Marietta—the firms that combined to make up Lockheed Martin—might have subsisted as second-tier contractors, lagging far behind larger firms like Boeing and Northrop Grumman in the annual chase for Pentagon dollars.

It was Augustine who engineered and implemented the strategy of mergers and acquisitions that made Lockheed Martin into the world's largest weapons manufacturer. He was not a "Lockheed man" originally—he pushed for the union of the two companies from his position as CEO of Martin Marietta, the smaller of the two firms. Martin Marietta's roots went back to the aviation pioneer Glenn L. Martin at the turn of the twentieth century. The company brought strengths in space launch services and military electronics, among other key areas that complemented Lockheed's existing strengths.

Not only did "Lockmart" (as some critics call it) top the list of Pentagon-financed companies year after year, but it became the number-one recipient of funds from NASA; number two on the

Department of Energy's list of nuclear weapons contractors; and a major supplier of goods and services to the IRS and the U.S. Postal Service. And for a time during the late 1990s the firm secured contracts to provide social services in Florida, Connecticut, and California, as well as in major cities like Washington, D.C., and New York.

Perhaps most importantly, the firm had more lobbying clout than any of its rivals. At the time of the merger, Lockheed Martin accounted for roughly one-third of all political contributions made by the defense-aerospace industry.[2] Lockheed Martin also benefits handsomely from the "revolving door"—the movement of personnel back and forth between the Pentagon and major weapons companies that helps grease the wheels for major contracts.

Norm Augustine did more than any other single individual to make all of this possible. And much of it happened not under effusively promilitary administrations like those of Ronald Reagan or George W. Bush, but during the presidency of Bill Clinton. Clinton's relationship with the military leg of the military-industrial complex was problematic at best, but that was not the case with his relationship with the defense industry—a difference that Augustine exploited to his and his company's benefit.

At the peak of his career in the 1990s, Augustine stood out as the most visible figure in an industry in which executives generally prefer to operate outside the limelight. The military industry has no equivalent of Bill Gates or Warren Buffett. More often than not, when a defense industry executive does get attention, it is the wrong kind of attention.

Since Augustine stepped down as Lockheed Martin's CEO in 1998, the defense company CEO receiving the most media attention has been Phil Condit of Boeing, who was forced to resign in 2003. Although Condit himself never faced criminal charges, he led Boeing while it was being rocked by a major scandal involving insider dealing with the Pentagon on a $26 billion plan to lease aerial refueling tankers to the Air Force—not the kind of thing a corporate leader wants to make headlines over.[3]

By contrast, Augustine was a virtual renaissance man of the military-industrial complex and has largely been viewed in a positive light. He has written a popular book of management maxims, *Augustine's Laws*, as well as a major defense policy tract, *The Defense Revolution*, co-authored with former Reagan Arms Control and Disarmament Agency Director Kenneth Adelman. Adelman's greatest claim to fame is being the one who asserted that the George W. Bush administration's invasion of Iraq would be a "cakewalk." Augustine and Adelman have also teamed up at numerous points over the years to give tips on how to use the plays of William Shakespeare as a management tool. Toward this end, they co-authored a book entitled *Shakespeare in Charge: The Bard's Guide to Leading and Succeeding on the Business Stage*. Augustine's friend Adelman even managed to abuse Shakespeare's writings in his push for war with Iraq. In a March 2003 commentary for National Public Radio, Adelman argued that a passage from *Othello* justified going to war with Iraq without "complete information" on the state of Saddam Hussein's alleged programs for producing nuclear, chemical, and biological weapons. The passage involves a dispute over how many ships Turkey may have launched against Venice, and therefore how to respond. A colleague of Othello's says that although such reports are "oft with difference . . . they do all confirm the main thing." Therefore, said Adelman, "differences" over Saddam Hussein's possession of chemical, biological, or nuclear weapons—like the minor matter of whether he had them or not—should not change the fact that "he is the number one threat facing America and all freedom-loving nations today." Adelman's interpretation of the play—and its relationship to the deliberations over war with Iraq—was questionable, but the larger issue was why he was allowed to get away with citing a work of fiction as a cause to send people off to die in a war in the first place.[4]

Augustine's reign at Lockheed Martin was marked by a hectic speaking schedule, supplemented by a series of glossy pamphlets issued by the company expressing the "world according to Norm," as one colleague described it. Augustine's inspirational tracts addressed big themes such as "Waging Peace," "Engineering Change," and "Managing to Survive." Augustine is not the shy and retiring type, and his hands-on leadership style reflected that.

To hear Augustine tell it, his position at the pinnacle of the aerospace industry was to some degree accidental. When he went to

Princeton in the mid-1950s, he chose to study geological engineering because, he says, it was "the closest thing they had to forestry."[5] He had developed his appreciation of the outdoors while growing up in the Denver, Colorado, area. His office at the company's Bethesda, Maryland, headquarters was always replete with photographs he had taken while hot-air ballooning, backpacking, snorkeling, dog-sledding, or sailing all over the world with his son Greg.

Augustine's shift into the aerospace field came at the time of the Sputnik launch in October 1957. A first-year graduate student at the time, he was at school when he heard the news and recalls being "utterly shocked because I thought we were the leaders in that kind of thing. . . . I couldn't imagine how we could be number two." Within a few months, he had taken a job with Douglas Aircraft (a forerunner of McDonnell Douglas). He stayed in the defense-aerospace field in one form or another for the rest of his working life.[6]

His own description of his career path, contained in *Augustine's Laws*, has a bit of a "Perils of Pauline" quality about it, underscoring his view of himself as a survivor:

> The author has had abundant opportunities to observe the nature of large and small organizations under duress—seemingly possessing an innate sense of timing that resulted in his . . . accepting a position at the Pentagon just as a war broke out; arriving at the giant LTV Corporation the same week that its founder, Jimmy Ling, was relieved of control; joining the federal government as a presidential appointee just in time to see the president and vice-president resign; and assuming the presidency of Martin Marietta's largest operating element just as the Bendix Corporation initiated its widely publicized (and unsuccessful) takeover assault on Martin Marietta.[7]

By the start of the 1990s, Augustine found himself in another tight spot. But this time he was poised to profit by taking risks that few others in the industry were willing to take.

The heady days of the Reagan administration were over, and the collapse of the Soviet Union had created a situation in which the United States, in the words of Colin Powell, then the head of the Joint

Chiefs of Staff, was "running out of enemies." As the CEO of Martin Marietta, Augustine had to decide whether his company should continue to specialize in defense and fight over a shrinking pie or establish a more diversified business base that would make Martin Marietta less dependent on military spending. Although many critics felt that the Clinton administration didn't go nearly far enough in cutting back the military budget in the wake of the dissolution of its only major adversary, the cuts that were implemented were enough to force changes in the structure of the defense industry. Weapons procurement and research—the two areas most important in feeding the bottom lines of major contractors—had fallen to about one-half the levels they attained at the height of the Reagan military buildup in the mid-to-late 1980s. Early in Bill Clinton's first term, his Defense Secretary, William Perry, held a meeting with defense executives that was later dubbed "the last supper." Perry essentially said, *Look to the left of you, and look to the right—one of you is going to be out of business within the next two years.* The only question was whether to diversify or concentrate on defense.[8]

For Augustine, it wasn't even a close call. He had been a longstanding critic of trying to transform military companies into producers of civilian products, arguing that such attempts were "unblemished by success." Furthermore, Augustine had convinced himself that producing weapons (for a profit, of course) was a patriotic duty. He frequently referred to the weapons industry as "the fourth armed service." So, risky or not, it was virtually a foregone conclusion that he would try to keep Martin Marietta firmly grounded in the weapons business.[9]

Never a person to do things halfway, Augustine announced in a 1994 interview that "I want to build a super-company." His strategy was a "big fish, little fish" approach: Martin Marietta would gobble up parts of smaller defense firms cheaply while banking on an upturn in military spending by no later than 1997. By picking an exact year, Augustine seemed to be showing a bit too much confidence in his own powers of prediction, but in the end he wasn't far off.[10]

By 1994 Augustine had already "bulked up" Martin Marietta through a variety of acquisitions. His biggest coup during this period was the company's purchase of the military division of General

Electric. GE had been dogged by a network of activists who were demanding that it get out of weapons production. Toward this end, they ran a boycott that convinced some hospitals and other large institutions to stop buying GE products. Whether the sell-off was done to get rid of the nuisance posed by the boycott—military contracts were a small portion of the company's $50 billion-plus annual revenues in any case—or just to focus on other lines of business, Martin Marietta was the beneficiary of GE's decision to scale back its military portfolio.[11]

In March 1995, Augustine took the final steps toward building his "super-company." Augustine and Lockheed CEO Daniel Tellep consummated what was then supposed to be a "merger of equals." To keep the deal secret until the last possible moment, final arrangements were reportedly made between the two CEOs in a corporate jet on the tarmac of a still-undisclosed airport. However one characterizes the deal, Norman Augustine clearly came out on top. He quickly became the CEO of the new company, which was to be known as Lockheed Martin. Augustine's ascension marked what the *New York Times* suggested was in fact a Martin Marietta takeover of Lockheed rather than a merger of equals. Further evidence of this was that all of the top management posts, not just the CEO's chair, came to be filled by Martin Marietta personnel, and that the new company was to be based in Martin Marietta's Bethesda, Maryland, headquarters. At the press conference announcing the merger, Augustine slipped and called the new company "Martin Lockheed" instead of Lockheed Martin.[12]

In January 1996, the new firm got even bigger when it purchased the defense division of the Loral Corporation—a key player with heavy investments in defense electronics—for $9.1 billion.[13]

Because of Augustine's unparalleled political connections and the sheer force of his personality, he had a greater impact on U.S. defense policy during the Clinton years than might have been expected, even from the CEO of a company of Lockheed Martin's size and scope. To say that Augustine was wired into the Washington policymaking process is an understatement: For much of his career, he had been one of the handful of people drawing up the blueprints for American defense policies and deciding where the wiring should be placed.

In addition to running the world's largest defense contractor, Augustine served on the Defense Policy Advisory Committee on Trade (DPACT), part of the "acronym city" of little-known organizations that often outrank Congress in their influence over the size and shape of the budget. DPACT is described in its charter as a body formed to "provide confidential guidance to the Secretary of Defense on arms export policies." Augustine also served as the Chairman of the Defense Science Board—a Pentagon advisory panel that has the power to approve or reject nascent weapons programs based on their performance characteristics—and as President of the Association of the United States Army, a politically potent interest group made up of retired army personnel and major army contractors.[14]

Augustine's institutional connections have been reinforced over the years by strong personal ties to influential figures on both sides of the political divide. In 1988 he turned down a feeler from the George Herbert Walker Bush administration to serve as Defense Secretary, and up until the early 1990s he was a business associate of William Perry and John Deutch, who went on to become Defense Secretary and CIA Director, respectively, in the administration of Bill Clinton. On the softer side of his résumé, Augustine served as the President of the Boy Scouts of America and as Chairman of the Red Cross. Augustine's affiliation with the Red Cross overlapped with Elizabeth Dole's stint as Executive Director of the organization. His Red Cross connection helped cement his relationship with then–Senate majority leader and presidential candidate Bob Dole. (Elizabeth Dole's successful Senate run came after Augustine's tenure as Lockheed Martin's CEO had ended.)[15]

Augustine proved to be more than the sum of his credentials. It was his skill and persistence in using his connections to help his company that set him apart from other defense industry executives. An engineer by training and a policy wonk by inclination, Augustine was conversant with all of the key technical and policy issues of import to Lockheed Martin. Because of this background, he stood out among many of his peers in his willingness to personally represent the company's interests to key players in Congress and the executive branch. He needed to exploit every connection he had to win new contracts and subsidies for his firm in the constrictive spending environment of the post–Cold War period. Contrary to popular belief, lobbying can be hard work, even for a multi-talented, in-your-face executive like Norman Augustine.

When the Clinton administration came into office in January 1993, Augustine came into his own as a high-stakes lobbyist and unofficial policymaker. In the first three years of Clinton's first term, he successfully advocated a host of major initiatives that yielded billions of dollars in new government funding for his firm. Probably the boldest move in this regard was his role in creating a government policy that subsidized major arms industry mergers with taxpayer dollars, a policy shift that occurred in time to yield hundreds of millions of dollars in government support for the creation of Lockheed Martin. He also spearheaded efforts to create new subsidies for arms merchants and their preferred customers—a $15 billion loan guarantee fund designed to finance U.S. weapons exports and a $200 million-plus tax break for foreign arms purchasers.[16] The loan fund was later allowed to lapse after few interested customers were able to meet the credit requirements set by Congress, but at the time it represented a major victory for Augustine. In addition, Augustine was a key figure in persuading the Newt Gingrich–led, Republican-controlled Congress of that era to add billions in funding to key Lockheed Martin projects, ranging from the F-22 combat aircraft to the "Star Wars" missile defense program. It didn't hurt that large parts of the F-22 were built in a factory adjacent to Gingrich's Georgia district.[17]

Augustine's remarkable batting average in shaping government policies to bolster his company's bottom line earned him both respect and resentment within the defense contracting community. As one former Pentagon official put it, "If you're concerned about corporate welfare, the one you should look out for is Saint Norman Augustine." It is the work of Augustine and his successors in the lobbying arena that has made it so difficult to reduce the military budget to reasonable levels, even in times of reduced threats like the immediate post–Cold War years of the 1990s.

As noted earlier, Augustine's greatest coup during this period was convincing the government to subsidize the Lockheed–Martin Marietta merger itself. His modus operandi was revealed after the deed had been done, in a summer 1994 House Armed Services Committee hearing that scrutinized Clinton's decision to implement a policy that ultimately yielded billions of dollars in Pentagon "restructuring costs" to companies like Lockheed, Martin Marietta, and Boeing. As a result of an obscure policy change contained in a one-page memo from John Deutch, then the Undersecretary of Defense (and a former Augustine business associate), the Pentagon authorized federal funding for closing plants, relocating equipment, paying severance to laid-off workers, and providing "golden parachutes" to board members and executives affected by the merger.

The Deutch memo was approved by Deputy Secretary of Defense William Perry. Because the decision was being made so early in the administration's first term—and because Perry and Deutch had so recently served as paid consultants to Augustine and Martin Marietta—both men had to get special conflict-of-interest waivers in order to make the policy change that had been so vigorously advocated by their old friend Norm Augustine.

The details of the ethical shortcut taken by Augustine, Perry, and Deutch were first exposed by veteran *Newsday* Pentagon reporter Patrick Sloyan. In a series of articles on the subject, he revealed that Perry's firm, Technology Strategies Alliances (TSA), had a contract with Martin Marietta that ran through late 1992, until just a few months before his appointment to the Clinton administration. As for Deutch, he pocketed $42,500 in 1992 as part of a nine-year consulting arrangement with Augustine's firm. In his official letter justifying the lifting of the conflict-of-interest ban on Perry and Deutch vis-à-vis decisions involving Martin Marietta, then–Defense Secretary Les Aspin argued that, "for both Dr. Perry and Mr. Deutch . . . the interest of the government outweighed the concern that a reasonable person would question their impartiality." After all, what are friends for?

As if to underscore the questionable nature of this arrangement, it was rushed through without notifying Congress and without publishing it in the *Federal Register*, the repository of virtually every significant government decision. Once the deal surfaced in Congress—over a year after it had been struck—most members accepted the claims of

Augustine and Deutch that the subsidies would help speed the clo-
sure of excess production capacity, thereby actually *saving* the taxpayers money. As Augustine put it, "It's more efficient to run three full
factories than six half-full factories." But it was also true that contractors can often pad overhead charges to the Department of Defense
even as they shrink the size of their operations.[18]

One of the reasons Congress was reluctant to question the merger
subsidies had to do with the complexity of the deals. Company A
would merge with company B, then lay off employees and reduce factory floor space. In response, the Pentagon would pay their costs for
closing factories, liquidating equipment, and so forth. But in theory,
the Defense Department would also "restructure" the contracts of
company A and company B for given weapon systems to remove some
of the taxpayer-financed overhead contained therein. Then, bingo!
There would be a "win-win" situation in which both contractors and
the public would benefit.

There were a few obvious flaws in this line of reasoning. First, it
implied that without Pentagon subsidies, firms like Lockheed and
Martin Marietta would not have merged. In fact, they already had
ample economic incentives to do so, with or without taxpayer subsidies. Augustine's strategy was to buy up companies cheaply during the
post–Cold War lull in defense spending, then dominate the market
once spending started trending upward again a few years down the
road. His plan was to spend now in the interest of a moderate level of
profits, then make a killing later once military dollars started flowing
in larger amounts and there were fewer competitors to soak up the
funding. This made sense from Augustine's perspective, whether or
not he could squeeze some additional subsidies from the government
along the way.

The second flaw in the "merger savings" argument was that it was
extremely difficult to penetrate the verbiage of Pentagon contracts
to figure out whether overhead costs built into existing contracts
would in fact be reduced. From the taxpayer's perspective, it would be
a case of spending billions now on the faint hope of getting some of
it back from the contractors later. As later data were to prove, it was
a great bet for contractors and a terrible deal for taxpayers. As former

Reagan Pentagon official Lawrence J. Korb has noted, there is no evidence that any weapon system got cheaper as a result of the merger subsidies. If anything, weapons costs *increased* in the aftermath of the subsidies.[19]

But when it counted, Augustine had already won the propaganda war. To make sure it stayed that way, he tried to keep anyone with the relevant expertise from questioning the deal in congressional testimony. Several former officials with expertise in the vagaries of government procurement regulations indicated that they had declined to testify on the merger subsidies issue before the House Armed Services Committee because, as one of them put it, the word was out that "Norm Augustine really wants this" and no one wanted to cross him.

Finally, the committee prevailed on Lawrence Korb, then based at the Brookings Institution, to testify against Augustine's pet project. As suggested earlier, the gist of Korb's argument was that if defense companies wanted to merge, there was no justification for using taxpayer money to help them do it. It was a good Republican, free-market argument, but not one Augustine was inclined to entertain. Living as they do off government contracts, many of which are awarded with little or no competition, defense industry executives aren't exactly raging capitalists.

In light of his aggressive defense of the merger subsidies, few members of Congress attempted to rain on Augustine's parade. One who did so was Representative Bernie Sanders (I-VT). Once it came out that not only would the *company* benefit by as much as $1.8 billion from the new policy, but that *Augustine himself* would reap millions, Sanders had the hook he needed to embarrass his colleagues into taking action. Part of the subsidy policy allowed companies to bill the Pentagon for the costs of severance packages for executives and board members who were dismissed or displaced as a result of a merger. Of $92 million in such "golden parachutes" for Lockheed Martin's leadership, the Clinton administration agreed to pay for about one-third, or $31 million.

And despite the fact that he basically got a promotion—from CEO of Martin Marietta to CEO of Lockheed Martin—Augustine was by far the biggest beneficiary of this windfall, netting $8.2 million in bonuses for "leaving" Martin Marietta to head the merged company. Roughly $2.9 million of Augustine's windfall was paid for with taxpayer dollars. Other beneficiaries of the policy included former Tennessee Senator and presidential hopeful Lamar Alexander. The payments to Alexander—$250,000 to compensate him for being squeezed off the board of the merged company—were particularly ironic in light of his efforts to portray himself as a populist "good old boy" in his presidential campaign, complete with plaid work shirts and down-home phrases. While executives made out like bandits, the more than nineteen thousand workers who were laid off as a result of the Lockheed–Martin Marietta deal received little assistance.[20]

Sanders termed this outrageous policy "payoffs for layoffs" and managed to get the House to pass an amendment to the fiscal year 1996 defense appropriations bill stating that no government monies could be used to pay for bonuses triggered by the Lockheed–Martin Marietta merger. In the meantime, the bad PR generated by the "payoffs for layoffs" stories in the press persuaded Augustine to give the government-funded portion of his bonus to charity, "to avoid the appearance of personal enrichment," according to Lockheed Martin's public relations officer, "Chip" Manor. This gesture still left him with $5.3 million in severance, most of which was indirectly subsidized by taxpayers. For a company like Lockheed Martin, which derived 80 percent of its revenue from military contracts, most of what they spent for any purpose was essentially reimbursed by the government, from three-martini lunches to three-stage rockets.

In the midst of his effort to spin the personal subsidies for Lockheed Martin executives and board members as a benign approach that did not involve "personal enrichment," Augustine tried to kill the Sanders amendment by personally lobbying members of the House-Senate conference committee that would determine its fate. He was partially successful. Lockheed Martin's lawyers argued that since Sanders's amendment applied only to the fiscal year 1996 Pentagon budget, they could still reap subsidies for prior years under an "amended and restated long-term performance compensation plan." Wouldn't it be great if the average person could cook up a phrase like that and end up earning millions of dollars as a result?

In the end, about half of the $31 million in executive subsidies survived. More importantly, the hundreds of millions of subsidies for the company as a whole were left untouched.

The lessons of the "payoffs for layoffs" scandal were twofold. First, a determined member of Congress can stand up to the Pentagon and a major contractor and claw back some money for taxpayers from an ill-conceived subsidy. Unfortunately, however, it is extremely difficult to "win the war" in such disputes, even if there are some tactical victories along the way. A company like Lockheed Martin has too many resources and too influential a network for the average elected official to contend with.

But there was one major battle that even Norm Augustine couldn't win: his effort to buy Northrop Grumman, an $11 billion-plus weapons firm that specialized in defense electronics components ranging from radar to fire-control systems. The merger seemed like a perfect fit to Augustine, as it would allow the company to build not only the airframes for planes like the F-22 but also the most sophisticated parts that went into the plane. As stock analyst Wolfgang Demisch of BT Alex Brown put it, if the merger was approved, "the nervous system of the military of the 21st century is going to be designed, built and maintained by Lockheed Martin."[21] Demisch also noted that such a merger would put the company in a favorable position with respect to its two remaining rivals, Boeing and Raytheon, because it would then be "in the enviable position of having a seat at every table of defense procurement . . . if you wanted aircraft, it would have been Boeing or Lockheed, and if you wanted electronics, it would have been Raytheon or Lockheed." Or as Roger Threlfal of J. P. Morgan Securities put it, "With Northrop, Lockheed Martin would have been a super, super company. Without it, it's just a super company."[22]

The merger was first proposed in July 1997, and it seemed poised to move full speed ahead, as had happened with the more than twenty prior mergers and acquisitions that went into making Lockheed Martin the $28 billion giant it had become under Augustine's leadership. Lockheed Martin shareholders approved the move at the company's February 1998 annual meeting, and no Lockheed Martin official expressed any concern about the deal going through. But two weeks later, the two companies were in discussions with the Justice Department about whether the combination would preserve adequate competition in the defense industry; they issued a joint news release asserting that the Justice Department was "fundamentally opposed" to the merger. The companies made it clear that they wouldn't take that opposition lying down, vowing to "vigorously oppose any attempt to block the transaction."[23] Within two more weeks, the Justice Department had filed suit to stop the deal from taking place. Attorney General Janet Reno asserted that "this merger isn't just about dollars and cents. It's about winning wars and saving lives." She argued that once the two companies joined forces, it would "cost taxpayers more and take the competitive wind out of the sails of innovation in the production of many critical systems that protect our fighting men and women."[24] It was going to prove to be a hard argument for Lockheed Martin to counter.

But first, company executives cried foul play, claiming that the first they had heard of the government's objections was at a meeting at the Pentagon on the weekend of March 6—that is, not until *after* Lockheed Martin shareholders had already signed off on the deal. The Justice Department denied the claim, producing a two-hundred-page Lockheed Martin memo from January 23—over a month prior to the company board meeting—in which all of the objections raised by Justice were dealt with in exquisite detail.[25] As for the meeting itself, Augustine was furious, describing it as "the worst meeting I've been to in this building . . . aside from those meetings where we were deciding whether it was likely people would be killed [referring to his days as a Pentagon official]."[26]

The merits of the case boiled down to what in legal terms is referred to as vertical integration—one company being in a position to make all major elements of a product, from components to final assembly. The downside of such an arrangement is that rather than seek competitive bids for key parts of the system, the vertically integrated company can essentially sell them to itself, generally at a higher price than would have been the case if outside firms were involved. That, combined with diminished competition for airframes and crucial electronics systems, led the Justice Department—backed up by the Pentagon—to oppose the merger absent a major restructuring of the deal. As Defense Secretary William Cohen put it, "Increased vertical integration provides incentives for firms . . . to favor their own in-house systems, even when better or cheaper products are available from the outside." Attorney General Janet Reno was even more specific: "If this merger were to go forward, America could face higher prices and lower quality in advanced tactical and strategic aircraft, airborne early warning radar systems, sonar systems, and several types of countermeasure systems that save our pilots from being shot down when they are flying in hostile skies. We want to ensure that any defense merger protects our soldiers' lives."[27]

The government's proposal was for Lockheed Martin to sell off Northrop Grumman's $4 billion electronics operation in exchange for the right to merge. The company countered with an offer of $1 billion. There was no middle ground, as Lockheed Martin's main interest in Northrop Grumman *was* its electronics unit.

But the two potential merger partners weren't giving up yet. Lockheed CEO Vance Coffman (Augustine had since retired from that position but remained active as Chair of Lockheed Martin's board) and Northrop Grumman CEO Kent Kresa issued a press release contending that it would be a win-win situation for virtually everyone if the merger was approved: "We stand by our conviction that this merger is in the best interests of taxpayers, customers, suppliers, shareholders, employees, and the armed forces of the United States." And contrary to the government's contention, Lockheed Martin and Northrop Grumman claimed they would save $3 billion by merging, presumably by laying off workers and shutting down factories. Lawrence Korb argued otherwise: "Whatever efficiency gains might accrue to the government—and this is by no means assured—will be more than offset by the declining level of competition among these quasi-monopoly suppliers."[28]

Finally, after four months of legal maneuvering, Lockheed Martin decided to give up the fight before the antitrust suit even made it into court. It was widely agreed that the move was made to avoid unduly aggravating the company's main customer, the Pentagon. As Renee Gentry of the Teal Group noted at the time, "Every dollar they have to spend on this merger lessens the attractiveness of the deal. And the nastier it gets with the Pentagon does not help in future competitions [for weapons contracts]."[29] In keeping with this analysis, Vance Coffman was extremely conciliatory in his statement on the end of the company's quest to merge with Northrop Grumman: "I extend my personal thanks to Defense Secretary William Cohen and his team for their good-faith efforts to resolve this complex issue and look forward to continuing our working relationship."[30]

In the postmortems that inevitably followed the failure of the merger, several analysts expressed surprise that the company had not done a better job of reading the prevailing winds with respect to the Clinton administration's shifting policy on defense industry mergers. In fact, the company leadership had been so confident that they didn't even hire a lobbying firm to help promote the deal, as they had in the original merger of Lockheed and Martin Marietta. Factors cited included new personnel at the Justice Department and the Pentagon, from an aggressive antitrust bureau chief, Joel Klein—who went on in a later incarnation to head the New York City school system—to Jacques Gansler, an industry expert and economist who had been brought in as head of acquisition at the Pentagon. The ultimate reason may have simply been that the merger wave in the industry had run its course but Augustine and his cohorts were so enamored of the idea of building a "super, super-company" that they failed to notice. Gansler reiterated the point that allowing the merger to go forward would have given the new firm a stranglehold on the production of key military components; he noted that "going from two to one is a problem" when it comes to weapons purchasing, whereas "five to three isn't a problem, or even three to two." More broadly, Gansler asserted that the denial of the merger "gave out a sign that the tendency of mergers is toward monopoly . . . somebody had to say no."[31]

When a similar battle emerged over a defense industry scheme to increase government subsidies for weapons exports, once again Augustine was on the front lines. Overseas sales are even more lucrative than sales to the Pentagon, for a number of reasons. For one thing, the items being exported, like Lockheed Martin's ubiquitous F-16 combat aircraft, have already had all of their research-and-development costs paid for with taxpayer dollars. The companies have also worked most of the "bugs" out of the production process over years of sales to the Defense Department. And they can charge whatever the market will bear in costly follow-on contracts for maintenance and upgrades of the weapons sold. So why not strike while the iron was hot?

So felt Norman Augustine. Lockheed Martin had set a goal of doubling its arms exports over a five-year period. The biggest problem with doing so was that only a handful of countries could afford to purchase major items like the F-16 in any significant quantities. For example, a blockbuster deal to sell 150 F-16 combat aircraft to Taiwan cost over $6 billion once the associated bombs, missiles, and support systems were taken into account. Not too many countries have that kind of money to burn: perhaps thriving Asian economies like South Korea, oil-rich states like Saudi Arabia, or heavily subsidized buyers like Turkey, Israel, and Egypt. But most of these countries had already bought F-16s. And with Turkey, Israel, and Egypt absorbing 85 to 90 percent of existing U.S. military aid, the foreign market for F-16s and other major Lockheed Martin weapon systems appeared to be on the verge of drying up.

This is where Augustine's advocacy for a new subsidy plan came into play. As Chairman of the Defense Policy Advisory Committee on Trade, Augustine had been leading an effort to create a new form of arms export subsidy. The vehicle for doing so would be a $15 billion fund that would provide low-rate, U.S. government–backed loans to potential arms-purchasing nations. A similar program that had existed in the 1970s and 1980s was closed down after over $10 billion worth of loans were either forgiven or never repaid; in essence, what had started as a loan program ended up being giveaway to U.S. contractors and their foreign clients. Even so, DPACT members were able to argue that this time would be different—the loans would be repaid.

With the advent of Newt Gingrich's "Republican revolution"—in which Republicans seized control of the House after the 1994 midterm elections—the arms industry was finally able to carry the day, after six long years of lobbying for the new loan guarantee fund. With aircraft production factories in Texas and Georgia—right next to Gingrich's district—Lockheed Martin was now well positioned to make its case. The loan guarantee fund was approved by Congress and signed into law by President Clinton in December 1995. It looked like another big win for Augustine and the military-industrial complex.[32]

Armed with this new tool, Augustine and his colleagues, most notably Bruce Jackson, then the company's Vice President for International Operations, looked for the most likely set of customers to match it up with. They quickly determined that their best hope would be to go all out in support of the Clinton administration's campaign to extend the Cold War–era North Atlantic Treaty Organization (NATO) into the former Soviet satellite states of eastern and central Europe. Official arguments for NATO expansion included reassuring the new U.S. allies in the region that Moscow would not be allowed to revert to its imperial past; building new military relationships with these emerging democracies that would groom them as allies in support of future NATO and U.S. security objectives; and helping to promote and sustain democracy by building a bridge to the West. Arguments against NATO expansion included the political backlash it was likely to provoke from Russia. Strained relations with Moscow could put at risk important post–Cold War objectives such as further reducing nuclear arsenals and dismantling "loose nukes" to keep them out of the hands of potential terrorists or "rogue nations."

For the Boeings and Lockheed Martins of the world, NATO expansion spelled one thing: new markets. New NATO entrants would be required to gradually discard their Soviet-era weapons and replace them with systems that were compatible with those of other NATO member states (meaning U.S. or European systems). This requirement—coupled with a new U.S. arms export fund that potential customers could tap into—seemed almost too good to be true to Augustine, Jackson, and the rest of the Lockheed Martin hierarchy.

Augustine quickly moved to capitalize on NATO expansion by scheduling a tour of eastern and central Europe that included stops in potential new member states Romania, Poland, Hungary, and the Czech Republic. In Romania, he pledged that if the government would buy a new radar system from Lockheed Martin, the company would use its influence in Washington to promote Bucharest's NATO candidacy. In other words, a major defense manufacturer expressed a

willingness to reshape U.S. international security policy in order to secure an arms order. Rarely had a defense industry executive so openly
advocated his company's narrow interests.[33] But Norm Augustine was
no ordinary executive.

Although Augustine's tenure was marked by an aggressive push
for more Pentagon contracts, the company also engaged in a parallel
effort to expand its portfolio by providing services to state and local
governments. This was not a new activity for the company, but the
1990s push to privatized government services led Lockheed Martin
to accelerate its activities on this front, with a special emphasis on social services.[34]

At first, the idea of a defense contractor engaging in activities like
collecting parking fines and chasing after "deadbeat dads" raised few
eyebrows.[35] But that changed with the passage in 1996 of landmark
welfare reform legislation, the Personal Responsibility and Work Opportunity Reconciliation Act (PRWORA); with "welfare-to-work"
programs mandated nationwide, states and localities increasingly
looked to private companies like Lockheed Martin to help them fulfill the new requirements. The $17 billion in relevant funds flowing
to states and localities made welfare reform the biggest potential revenue source yet in Lockheed Martin's move into civilian government
markets, but the idea of a weapons contractor becoming a major part
of the public "face" of the social services sector struck more than a few
people as inappropriate.

The biggest prize in the welfare reform sweepstakes was a com-
petition in Texas to screen applicants for food stamps, welfare, and
Medicaid.[36] The bidding was conducted during the governorship of
George W. Bush.

When Lockheed Martin's Information Management Services
(IMS) unit first arrived in Texas in 1996, it occupied an old, window-
less factory on the outskirts of Austin where the company had recently
terminated local production of components for its Trident missile system. Over 760 Austin-area workers had been laid off. Lockheed's
move to Austin was prompted by George W. Bush's campaign promise to privatize welfare services in Texas, a pledge that quickly bore
fruit. In May 1995, Bush's legislative liaison, Dan Shelley, slipped a

provision into the state's welfare reform bill requiring a study on privatizing public assistance.

Six months later, Shelley resigned from government to set up shop as a private lobbyist. One of his first clients was Lockheed Martin. And what started out as an effort to streamline welfare enrollment and upgrade the state's computer systems quickly mushroomed into what Representative Elliott Naishtat, a transplanted New Yorker and then Vice Chairman of the Texas House Committee on Human Services, described as "full-blown privatization"—an initiative worth $2 billion to $3 billion to the winning bidder.

Seeing a bright future ahead for its Texas operations, Lockheed Martin IMS moved from the outskirts of town to plush new offices on Congress Avenue, within view of the Texas Capitol building, a huge pink-domed structure that is larger than the U.S. Capitol building in Washington, D.C. On the day I visited the offices, all the senior staff were out; some had traveled to other parts of the country trying to win similar, albeit smaller, contracts in other states and localities. Even a quick glance at the space made it clear that this was no ordinary social services provider. Lockheed Martin's share price was displayed prominently on a desk on the way in. Posters on the wall touted MISSION SUCCESS—DEEP IN THE HEART OF TEXAS and PUBLIC/PRIVATE PARTNERSHIPS, accompanied by a montage of colorful pictures alternating fighter planes and missile launchers with shots of school-age children smiling for the cameras.

The need to prove that it was a "Texas" company loomed large for Lockheed Martin given that one of its prime competitors for the public assistance contract was Ross Perot's former firm, EDS, which was founded and headquartered in the Lone Star State. One of Lockheed Martin's in-state lobbyists said that part of his pitch was that the company could be trusted "even though they don't talk like us."

The Texas privatization plan, known as TIES (Texas Integrated Enrollment System), marked the first time that a state had sought to allow private companies to bid on both redesigning its major public assistance programs and determining who was eligible for them. Implementing TIES called for a special federal waiver, because the new welfare law signed by President Clinton allowed private companies to determine eligibility for cash assistance but not for food stamps or Medicaid. Governor Bush wanted to hand all three programs over to a commercial enterprise, a move that required a sign-off from Washington.

The TIES contract offered Lockheed Martin its best chance yet to score big in the social services market, this time with a contract in the billions, not the millions or tens of millions, as had been the case with most of its prior ventures into the provision of social services. Even before the Texas contest was decided, company executives were fanning out across the country pitching the "Texas model" of comprehensive privatization to legislators in Florida, Michigan, and Arizona. In the meantime, back in Texas, Lockheed Martin had teamed up with the Texas Workforce Commission, a newly formed agency charged with overseeing the state's job training programs. Rival bidder EDS paired up with the Texas Department of Human Services; the third contender, Arthur Andersen, had no public partner.[37]

For all of Lockheed Martin's experience in lobbying for—and winning—government contracts, trying to land the Texas deal was going to be one of the company's greatest challenges yet.

The first blow to Lockheed's marketing strategy grew out of allegations of improper lobbying brought in October 1996 by the Texas State Employees Union (TSEU), the representative of the civil service workers who could be displaced by full-scale privatization of welfare services. The union cited seven current or former state officials who had lobbying contracts with Lockheed Martin or affiliated companies, including Dan Shelley, the Governor's point man on the welfare privatization bill; Richard Evans, a former Bush aide and Texas Workforce Commission operative who had been directly involved in structuring the state's TIES request for bids; and Steve Bresnen, a former special assistant to the Democratic Lieutenant Governor, the late Bob Bullock. The Bullock connection was particularly important. Bullock was a gravelly-voiced wheeler-dealer known by some as the "other governor of Texas," and his approval of the welfare privatization scheme was critical to its success. Many of these revolving-door hires also had connections to decision-makers on the State Council on Competitive Government, a body authorized by the legislature to award the TIES contract. Its Texas campaign was reminiscent of

Lockheed's familiar practices on the military side of its operations, where the hiring of former Pentagon officials to help steer contract decisions has long been standard practice. Texas State Representative Garnet Coleman was one of many who wondered whether the whole TIES project wasn't "wired for Lockheed Martin" from the outset. In response to the TSEU complaint, Travis County District Attorney Ken Oden—the DA for the Austin area—opened an investigation into Lockheed's activities surrounding the TIES bid. No charges were ever filed, but the investigation cast a cloud over the company's campaign for the Texas contract.[38]

Other problems with Lockheed Martin's bid stemmed from the near-total secrecy surrounding the TIES plan. From April 1996 to May 1997, no member of the legislature or public was allowed to see the revised request for bids on TIES, which meant that even basic questions couldn't be answered: Would Lockheed try to squeeze profits by denying needy Texans welfare? What kind of government oversight was being planned? Would access to public information be denied because a private company considered it "proprietary"? The closed process provided Governor Bush the cover he needed to issue wildly optimistic savings estimates of up to 40 percent from privatization. But as Texas Human Services Commissioner Dr. Michael McKinney admitted in an interview, the purported savings were almost entirely based on "vendor estimates" offered by Lockheed Martin and other bidders.

When details of Lockheed Martin's proposal were finally released, concern arose over the plan's relentless emphasis on "diversion"—a euphemism for steering large numbers of people away from public assistance to job-placement programs that were clearly inadequate to serve them. Marcia Kinsey, formerly of the Austin-based Center on Public Policy Priorities, noted that in a state where the biggest job-training program served thirty thousand, it was ludicrous for Lockheed to assume that two million people on public assistance could be "diverted" so easily. "Diversion simply means making people jump through more hoops," noted Richard Levy, Legal Director of the Texas AFL-CIO. "If they don't jump through them, they lose their benefits."

Determined to halt Lockheed Martin's sweeping privatization plans, the Texas State Employees Union spearheaded a statewide grassroots campaign that included town meetings, public demonstrations, a mass mailing of more than eleven thousand anti-privatization postcards, and a series of radio ads exposing Lockheed's price-gouging at the Pentagon. The ads featured the sound of a toilet flushing with a voice-over that said, "Remember the company that brought us the $3,000 toilet seat? Now they want to run public services in Texas." The 1980s overcharge scandal actually involved Lockheed-supplied toilet covers that cost the taxpayers a mere $640 each, but the basic point of the ad still held true.

This public pressure galvanized a national coalition of unions and public-interest groups to join the anti-privatization battle, and in May 1997 the Clinton administration denied Texas's request for a federal waiver that would have allowed a private firm to determine eligibility for food stamps and Medicaid as well as cash assistance. This made it a much less lucrative, and therefore less attractive, deal. Meanwhile, back in Texas, the legislature scaled back the TIES initiative to a feasibility study while strengthening legislative control over the project.

But Lockheed wasn't ready to give up yet—and neither was a Texas congressional delegation that included such heavy hitters as House majority leader Dick Armey and Senators Phil Gramm and Kay Bailey Hutchison. The Texans immediately sought to pass a "welfare flexibility" bill—also known as "Lockheed Martin's bill"—allowing Texas to proceed with across-the-board privatization. Campaign donations from Lockheed Martin and its employees during the 1995–1996 election cycle included $6,000 to Armey, $12,235 to Gramm, and $20,382 to Hutchison.[39] But the pro-Lockheed amendments were stripped out of Congress's budget reconciliation bill in the summer of 1997, and Texas-based EDS ultimately won the scaled-down contract, which looked far more like an upgrade in computer systems and data management than the all-out privatization plan hoped for by Lockheed Martin and the other corporate bidders.

Edward Gund, a Lockheed Senior Vice President, refused to see the setback in Texas as a defeat for the company's new welfare mission. "A lot of people wanted to pose Texas as a make-or-break thing," says Gund, "but we were never going to be involved unless we felt there were business opportunities throughout the country."[40]

This was partly true, but Gund did some convenient rewriting of history in implying that the Texas contract was not that crucial. As analyst Bill Eggers of the conservative think tank Reason put it, "Everyone is looking to Texas. This is the new frontier." And Lockheed Martin's Vice President for Information Services, Gerald Miller, also the former head of the state of Michigan's welfare-to-work program, acknowledged, "As we show our success [in Texas], you're going to see more states doing this." This was one of the few points upon which the company agreed with the Texas State Employees Union, whose president, Linda Herrera, said, "If this happens in Texas, it will be the big go ahead nationwide—and I don't think this is going to be good for the country." So its loss in Texas was a big blow to Lockheed Martin's welfare services business strategy. Without a Texas contract, it was considerably harder to tout the "Texas model."

After four more years of chasing state and local government contracts, Lockheed Martin pulled the plug on most of its activities in this arena. Under pressure from Wall Street to stick to its "core competencies" in federal government contracting—and no doubt moved to action by its decidedly mixed record in areas like welfare and child support enforcement—the company sold its Information Management Services unit in August 2001 to Affiliated Computer Services Inc. (ACS), a company based in Dallas, Texas, that specialized in providing computer services to government and corporate clients.[41] Lockheed Martin President and Chief Operating Officer Robert Stevens euphemistically referenced the company's difficulties in places like Texas and Connecticut when he said, "As we focused on the systems-integration business at the federal level for large customers like the Department of Defense, the IMS business was devoted to a really quite different market [serving] individual states and localities."[42] Whatever the relative weight of these factors, Wall Street was clearly happy with the move toward going after fewer, larger contracts at the federal level rather than scrambling for relatively smaller deals at the state and local levels, where the politics of winning business could be just as complicated as doing business with the Pentagon, if not more so. At the time of the sell-off, analyst Pierre Chao of Credit Suisse First

Boston praised the sale as part of the company's "get well program . . . to focus on core business and sell non-core businesses to work down a pretty heavy debt load."[43] Lockheed's experiment in being a social services provider had come to an end, just a few months short of the historic boom in military spending that followed closely after the September 11, 2001, terror attacks.

Alongside the failure to merge with Northrop Grumman, the "welfare wars" in Texas marked one of the few major losses of the Augustine era. The company had grown in size by over 50 percent during his roughly three years as CEO. When he stepped down as Lockheed Martin's CEO in April 1998, he had indeed helped create the "super company" he had envisioned.

Augustine carried on as chairman of the board for another six years, during which time he continued to have considerable influence over U.S. foreign and defense policies. He also kept up a busy schedule of activities outside the defense sphere, from teaching mechanical and aerospace engineering at Princeton to heading up a blue-ribbon panel that urged greater attention and resources for science education in the United States to chairing a NASA task force on the future of manned space flight. And in April 2010, Augustine was appointed to a "safety and quality panel" assembled by Toyota to investigate and make recommendations on company production practices in the wake of its problems with unintended acceleration in the majority of its Toyota and Lexus models.[44]

One of Augustine's more intriguing outside projects was his role as an adviser to the CIA in the forming of its own venture capital company, In-Q-Tel, which has invested tens of millions of dollars in over three dozen companies in the United States and Canada. As noted in a profile of the firm by Cox News Service reporter Bob Keefe, "the VC [venture capital] firm's goal is not to make money, but to find high tech products that may someday be used for security or spying."[45] Early In-Q-Tel investments included Language Weaver, Inc., a company that has designed software for translating Arabic radio broadcasts into English. But because of the secrecy surrounding In-Q-Tel, even Language Weaver's CEO, Bryce Benjamin, was not informed of how—or whether—the CIA was actually using his product.[46]

Augustine also kept a hand in at the Pentagon. Shortly after stepping down as Lockheed Martin CEO, he served as an influential member of a panel established by Clinton administration Defense Secretary William Cohen to assess whether the Marine Corps should proceed with production of the troubled V-22 aircraft, a Boeing-produced vehicle designed to land and take off like a helicopter and fly like a traditional aircraft. The concept behind the plane was to use it to quickly drop in and out of remote areas that lacked traditional airstrips, a potentially useful capability for fighting wars of counterinsurgency. In the two years prior to the panel's appointment, the plane had suffered serious cost and performance problems, including two crashes during testing that ended up killing twenty-three Marines. Dick Cheney had tried to cancel the plane when he served as Defense Secretary in the administration of George Herbert Walker Bush, but Congress and the Marines pushed back, and funding for the V-22 was restored. While cautioning that production of the V-22 should be started in low-rate production, Augustine still went to bat for the aircraft. Sounding more like an aircraft enthusiast than an objective observer, Augustine said, "I'd love to fly in one. . . . I think the V-22 will turn out to be a very fine flying machine."[47]

No one raised any questions about the potential conflict of interest entailed in Augustine's role in bailing out Boeing's V-22 project, even though Lockheed Martin and Boeing had been partners on multibillion-dollar projects like the F-22 combat aircraft and the United Space Alliance, a private entity that handled all commercial space launches within the United States.

In an even more controversial arrangement, in March 2006 Augustine was retained as a consultant by the Defense Department to oversee an investigation of potential fraud in missile defense research at the Massachusetts Institute of Technology. The inquiry revolved around allegations by MIT Professor Theodore Postol—a missile technology expert who had debunked exaggerated claims of the effectiveness of the Patriot missile in the 1991 Gulf War—that MIT researchers had "cooked the books" by endorsing a 1997 test of a missile defense sensor that was in fact deeply flawed.

Postol, who had for years been calling for an independent investigation of the incident, was outraged at the plan to let the Pentagon and Augustine oversee the work. "It's hard to believe people can be so clumsy and dishonest. . . . What MIT is in effect doing is turning over responsibilities for oversight of its own academic operations to the Department of Defense." As for Augustine's role, Postol noted that the former Lockheed Martin CEO had been a staunch supporter of the Patriot missile, which had failed to intercept even one enemy missile in the 1991 Gulf War. Lockheed Martin had also been one of the Pentagon's top missile defense contractors, with contracts for, among other projects, the Aegis sea-based missile interceptor system.[48]

In April 2007, the results of the investigation were released. They exonerated MIT of any wrongdoing.

As was the case when he ran Lockheed Martin, Augustine continues to get at least as much attention for his nonmilitary pursuits as for his role as a long-standing leader of the weapons industry. His main public profile is that of an all-around good citizen, as evidenced by his May 2007 receipt of an honorary degree from Princeton.

The fact that Augustine served as a tough behind-the-scenes lobbyist, seeking special treatment for the largest weapons manufacturer in the world, remains a little-known aspect of his public career. If we want to blunt the effects of future Augustines on the public purse, the Congress and the media will have to pay much more attention to the symbiotic connections between industry and government that allowed Norman Augustine—a master of utilizing his alternating government and business connections to yield billions for his own company—to exert such a powerful influence over the distribution of the Pentagon budget.

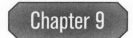

THE ADVOCATE

Bruce Jackson was championing the invasion of Iraq long before it was fashionable. Starting in mid-1997, he served as a director of the Project for the New American Century (PNAC), a hastily assembled group of hawks and neoconservatives who considered the Clinton administration soft on defense. In the founding statement it issued in August of that year, PNAC called for a "Reaganite policy of military strength and moral clarity" that, among other things, would include intervening against recalcitrant regimes like Saddam Hussein's government in Iraq.[1] The organization was even more explicit the following year: In a letter to Senate majority leader Trent Lott (R-MS) and House Speaker Newt Gingrich (R-GA), it called for a "removal of Saddam and his regime from power" because "Iraq has yet to provide a complete account of its programs for developing weapons of mass destruction."[2]

Jackson's cohorts in the PNAC network were a who's who of people who would go on to fill high-level national security jobs in the George W. Bush administration, from Paul Wolfowitz to Donald Rumsfeld to Dick Cheney. Conservative former Congressman Vin Weber—who later became a lobbyist for Lockheed Martin—also signed PNAC's founding statement. George W. Bush himself was not a signatory, but his brother Jeb was. The difference between Jackson and his PNAC cohorts was that he was the only one who worked directly for a major military contractor; his preferred modus operandi was to influence government from the outside rather than make policy from the inside.

While Jackson was working from the outside, a series of Lockheed Martin officials accompanied Cheney and his PNAC cohorts into the Bush administration. Cheney himself had a family tie: His wife Lynne served on Lockheed Martin's board from 1994 to 2001 and stepped down just before Cheney took office as Vice President. Although the $500,000-plus she earned from Lockheed Martin during her tenure on the board pales in comparison with the tens of millions Dick Cheney earned in connection with his role as the CEO of Halliburton, it represented a significant link between the Cheney family and the nation's largest military contractor.[3]

While the Cheney connection was indirect, more than half a dozen important policy posts in the Bush administration were filled by Lockheed Martin executives, lobbyists, or lawyers, including former company Chief Operating Officer Peter B. Teets, who became Under Secretary of the Air Force and Director of the National Reconnaissance Office (NRO), a position responsible for making decisions on everything from surveillance satellites to space-based elements of missile defense; Everet Beckner, who went from running the Lockheed division that operated the United Kingdom's Atomic Weapons Establishment (AWE) to becoming chief administrator of the U.S. nuclear weapons complex in his role as Deputy Administrator for Defense Programs at the National Nuclear Security Administration (NNSA); Otto Reich, who served a stint as Assistant Secretary of State for Latin American Affairs after working as a paid lobbyist promoting the sale of Lockheed Martin F-16 combat aircraft to Chile; Stephen Hadley, who worked at Shea and Gardner, a powerhouse D.C. law firm that represented Lockheed Martin, before becoming Deputy National Security Adviser; and Norman Mineta and Michael Jackson, both of whom served as vice presidents at Lockheed Martin before taking the number-one and number-two spots, respectively, in the Department of Transportation.[4]

Michael Jackson went on to become Deputy Secretary of the Department of Homeland Security (DHS)—a major source of revenue for Lockheed Martin. According to former DHS Inspector General

Clark Kent Ervin, Jackson's industry-friendly approach "set the tone for a laxity in terms of contract oversight" at the agency. Ervin also criticized Jackson's "undue use of no-bid contracts," or "contracts that fail to deliver what's promised even though billions of dollars have been spent." Jackson left DHS in September 2007.[5] During his tenure, Lockheed Martin received over $650 million in DHS contracts.[6] Although there is no evidence that Michael Jackson played a direct role in steering any contracts Lockheed Martin's way, the company presumably benefited from the "lax" overall approach described by Ervin.

All of these appointments ensured that Lockheed Martin would get a sympathetic hearing in the Bush administration for all manner of issues of interest to the firm.

Bruce Jackson, however, may have had more influence than all of the company's "revolving-door" connections combined. He was a Republican Party activist. He was a co-finance chair for Bob Dole's unsuccessful 1996 run for the presidency, and he drafted the foreign policy platform at the 2000 Republican convention that nominated George W. Bush as its candidate for the presidency. Prior to the convention, Jackson was overheard telling several colleagues from other defense firms that they had "nothing to worry about" because "I'll be drafting the platform." Jackson's bragging ignored the fact that platform promises don't always make it into official policy, but his role was a measure of his—and Lockheed Martin's—influence nonetheless.[7]

Perhaps Jackson's most successful foray into politics during the 1990s was his role as Chairman of the U.S. Committee to Expand NATO, a boiler-room operation that shared offices with the conservative American Enterprise Institute (AEI). Although Jackson described his role as president of the committee as a "hobby," his visibility as a spokesperson for NATO expansion makes it hard to avoid the conclusion that he was on loan from Lockheed Martin to the lobbying group as needed.[8] The committee spearheaded the effort to move elite opinion around to the view that bringing Poland, Hungary, and the Czech Republic into the alliance was a plus for U.S. security, even if it undercut relations with Russia. Back in 1989, at the time of the fall of the Berlin Wall, James Baker, then the Secretary of State, had promised Russian President Mikhail Gorbachev that if

Moscow withdrew peacefully from eastern Europe, NATO would not move closer to Russia's borders by bringing former Soviet satellite states into the alliance.[9] The position that Jackson was pushing—in support of the posture taken by the Clinton administration—ran directly counter to this pledge.

The modification of the NATO treaty to admit new members required ratification by the Senate—hence the need for a lobbying campaign.

Jackson's commitment to expanding NATO may have been sincere, but it was also good business for Lockheed Martin. If anything, the arms industry's lobbying efforts in eastern and central Europe were even more blatant and aggressive than their campaigns in the United States. Jeff Gerth and Tim Weiner of the *New York Times* described Norman Augustine's April 1997 tour of Hungary, Poland, the Czech Republic, Romania, and Slovenia (see chapter 8) as having the goal of "drumming up business and supporting the largest possible expansion of NATO."[10] And as noted earlier, in Romania, Augustine even promised to support that nation's bid for NATO membership at the same time that Romania was negotiating the purchase of an $82 million radar system from Lockheed Martin. Bruce Jackson denied that Augustine's pledge had a commercial motive, arguing that "Norm has an emotional commitment to NATO expansion."[11]

In October 1996, six months prior to Augustine's marketing trip, Lockheed Martin engaged in an even more innovative promotional tactic when it prepared a series of free "defense planning seminars" for officials in Poland, Hungary, and the Czech Republic. Gordon Bowen, Lockheed Martin's director of requirements and analysis, described the seminars as a way to provide its potential clients with "a structured way to try to analyze military objectives and a structured process for looking at military alternatives." Bowen claimed that the free seminars were not "marketing operations." "We were not handing out pamphlets explaining why the F-16 is the best fighter in the world," he stressed. But Bowen did admit that the meetings benefited the company because "they allow us to know who the decision makers are, what their value structures are, and what their needs are; to build relationships with these people. . . . It is in line with our own beliefs and objective that we want to be the major defense contractor to supply these countries."[12]

A review of the company's presentation outline for its two-day seminar with Polish officials, obtained by the author, suggests that the sessions, whatever else they may have been, were also a thinly disguised marketing pitch. For example, the presentations included a map entitled "Postulated Military Threats," with menacing arrows itemizing specific numbers of enemy fighter planes (860), attack helicopters (360), and surface-to-air missiles (1,700), all converging on Poland. David Ruppe of *Defense News* reported that a second map displayed during the seminar "shows attacks coming from Russia and the Baltic Sea, and conflict occurring on Poland's Ukrainian, Belarussian, and Czech Republic borders." One of the later presentations included a chart detailing a "Best Acquisition Plan" that proposed a lease of seven fighter aircraft for the period 1996 to 2001 (a reference to the leases of used F-16s that Lockheed Martin had convinced the Air Force to offer to Poland), overlapping with an initial purchase of twenty-four fighter aircraft on a "12 year loan."[13] In one sense, Bowen's description of the seminar was accurate: The goal was not so much to convince the Polish military of the specific virtues of the F-16 as to scare them into buying as many F-16s as possible.

The procurement seminars were just one part of a multi-pronged marketing blitz that Lockheed Martin launched in eastern and central Europe in the fall of 1996. According to a company press release, Dain Hancock, the President of Lockheed Martin Tactical Aircraft Systems, made several pitches for the F-16 in Hungary, Poland, and the Czech Republic in September 1996, several weeks prior to the free procurement seminars. According to Lockheed Martin's own account of these meetings, Hancock "outlined potential F-16 programs, including industrial participation in the production of the aircraft . . . up to 100 percent financing, and an F-16 unit flyaway cost of approximately $24 million per aircraft." In essence, Hancock's offer of 100 percent economic cooperation (investments or contracts equal to the entire cost of the F-16s) plus full financing made it sound like a "no-lose" proposition for the purchasing countries. The potential impacts of such an arrangement on U.S. taxpayers and U.S. workers were another matter.

Hancock's tempting offer was supplemented by opportunities for Polish Air Force pilots to test-ride F-16s at Poland's August 1996 Bydgoszca Air Show. F-16 flights were also provided for "senior Hungarian government officials" at an air show held at the Kecskemet Air Base in Hungary on October 29–30, 1996. The Kecskemet flights were followed up by a weeklong "flight evaluation" of the F-16 by a team of Hungarian pilots and technical experts, held at Lockheed Martin's Fort Worth facilities in November 1996. Lockheed Martin Tactical Systems even appointed an "International Vice President for Hungary," Doug Miller, who described his goal simply as "the successful introduction of the F-16 into the Hungarian Home Defense Forces."[14]

All of this furious marketing activity eventually paid off. It took quite a while, but the end result provided clear evidence of Lockheed Martin's patience and persistence when it came to pursuing a major arms sale. In late 2003 Lockheed Martin succeeded in closing a deal with Poland for $3.8 billion worth of F-16s. The sale was accompanied by a subsidized loan that covered 100 percent of the cost of the jets, with a below-market interest rate and no payments required for the first *eight years*. A Pentagon official told Leslie Wayne of the *New York Times* that the Defense Department didn't expect to ask Congress for another loan this generous. It was sort of a "loss leader" to get a foot in the door so that Lockheed Martin and other U.S. weapons makers could make further sales in eastern and central Europe.

But the costs to the United States went beyond just a subsidized loan. The deal included roughly $3 billion in promised "offsets"— various ways of steering business to Poland to counterbalance the vast sums it was spending on the F-16. The most obvious examples included an agreement to produce the engines for the aircraft in Poland. Other arrangements worked out by Lockheed Martin subcontractors included contracts for Polish firms to make jet trainers; components for business aircraft like the Gulfstream; and the creation of a new technology start-up firm in Lodz. These deals may have been good for Lockheed Martin, but they took away business and jobs that might otherwise have gone to U.S. firms and U.S. workers. Describing the range of offsets involved, Leslie Wayne wrote that "Lockheed went into Poland like Santa Claus."[15]

Well before the Polish deal could be made, however, Congress had to be persuaded to bring it into NATO. Toward that end, Lockheed Martin spent furiously to influence the votes of key senators. In the 1995–96 election cycle alone, the company and its executives distributed $2.3 million in political donations—more than any other military contractor over that time period.[16]

When it came down to it, the vote wasn't even all that close. NATO expansion passed the Senate by a vote of 81–19, a testimony to the sales job done by the Clinton administration and the supporting efforts of individuals like Bruce Jackson and organizations like his U.S. Committee to Expand NATO.

In some respects, Jackson's work on behalf of NATO expansion was just a tune-up for the campaign he helped to run in support of the 2003 Bush administration intervention in Iraq. Although he left his full-time position with Lockheed Martin in 2002, his ten years with the company helped shape his approach to matters of national security, and he continued to take actions that benefited his former employer.

As a co-founder of the Committee for the Liberation of Iraq, a neoconservative network augmented by the membership of a few Democrats like Peter Galbraith and former Nebraska Senator Bob Kerrey, Jackson worked directly with the Bush administration in the marketing of the war. In fact, according to Jackson himself, the White House asked him to "do for Iraq what you did for NATO."[17] Jackson even found a way to link the two efforts. One of his most important contributions was drafting a letter that was signed by the presidents of the "Vilnius Ten"—a bloc of major central and eastern European nations that Jackson and others were pressing to have admitted en masse to NATO in its next round of expansion. The letter essentially endorsed an invasion of Iraq to deal with Saddam Hussein's alleged weapons of mass destruction. The operative sentences of the declaration were as follows: "The clear and present danger posed by the Saddam Hussein's regime requires a united response from the community of democracies. We call upon the U.N. Security Council to take the necessary and appropriate action in response to Iraq's continuing threat to international peace and security."[18]

The letter was critical because it came right after Secretary of State Colin Powell's presentation of the U.S. case for war to the UN Security Council, when the Bush administration was still pushing for a UN vote to legitimize its proposed intervention in Iraq. Jackson reportedly told officials from some of the countries that supporting the Iraq war would increase their chances of being included in NATO in the next round of expansion.

Jackson's points of leverage over defense policy and spending did not end with PNAC or the U.S. Committee to Expand NATO, both organizations that he had helped to found. He also worked closely with existing neoconservative think tanks like Frank Gaffney's Center for Security Policy (CSP). Gaffney, a hard-liner who left the Reagan administration in 1987—in part because of his disagreement with the administration's decision to remove nuclear missiles from Europe under the Intermediate Nuclear Forces agreement (INF)—was an influential advocate for an ambitious missile defense program. This was another area of interest to Lockheed Martin, from its role in the controversial Homing Overlay Experiment (HOE), to serving as the prime contractor role on the Theater High-Altitude Area Defense (THAAD) system to its work on the sea-based Aegis missile defense project. Gaffney's advocacy for the most extensive missile defense system possible served Lockheed Martin's needs quite nicely. So nicely, in fact, that Lockheed Martin helped bankroll Gaffney's operation. Although the amount of money is unclear, it was enough for Gaffney to thank the company in its 1998 annual report. His center received over $3 million in corporate donations from its founding in the Reagan era through the first year of the George W. Bush administration, with the bulk of it coming from defense contractors like Lockheed Martin, Northrop Grumman, and Boeing. Jackson and his fellow Lockheed Martin executives Brian Dailey and Charles Kupperman—the latter the Vice President of Lockheed Martin's Space and Strategic Missiles Sector—served on Gaffney's "National Security Advisory Board." Kupperman also served on CSP's seven-member board of directors.[19]

Jackson's CSP connection allowed him to do "one-stop shopping" to coordinate his efforts with members of Congress who took positions favorable to his company. In addition to Jackson and his Lockheed Martin colleagues, the center's advisory board included influential legislators who were in the forefront of influencing U.S. nuclear and missile defense policies. This group included Senator Jon Kyl (R-AZ), who led the successful 1999 fight in the U.S. Senate against ratification of the Comprehensive Test Ban Treaty (CTBT), which would have ended all testing of nuclear warheads, both above- and underground. The test ban was of particular interest to Lockheed Martin because it had a $2 billion per year contract from the Department of Energy to run the New Mexico–based Sandia National Laboratories, one of the nation's three nuclear weapons labs.

Other CSP advisory board members included Representative Curt Weldon (R-PA), then Chair of the Military Procurement Subcommittee of the House Armed Services Committee and head of the Congressional Missile Defense Caucus; and Senator Robert Smith (R-NH), the sponsor of a bill that created a commission on national security uses of outer space that, under the leadership of Donald Rumsfeld, helped keep the door open for the concept of placing weapons in space.[20] Lockheed Martin had no representation on the panel, but the Center for Security Policy did, as did eight other defense contractors. The CSP representatives included its board members William Graham, retired General Charles Horner, and Senator Malcolm Wallop (R-WY). Military contractor executives included Duane Andrews of Science Applications International Corporation (SAIC), General Howell Estes and General Thomas Moorman of the Aerospace Corporation, and General Jay Garner of SY Technologies, a small missile defense contractor based in Huntsville, Alabama.[21] Garner went on to play a key role in the early months of the U.S. occupation of Iraq.

Weldon was perhaps the most important contact of all, as he was the sponsor of an amendment that created the Commission on the Ballistic Missile Threat to the United States (CABMTUS), another Donald Rumsfeld–chaired body that published an alarmist assessment of the North Korean missile threat that was used to help push a pro–"Star Wars" amendment through Congress in 1998. The amendment—whose meaning is disputed to this day—stated that it was the policy of the United States to deploy a ballistic missile defense system as soon as technologically possible. But the Senate version of the bill called for any system to be funded through the regular budgetary process and to be compatible with continued progress with Russia on arms control. Senator Carl Levin (D-MI) argued that the amendment meant that a deployment decision was not written in stone, since funding for missile defense would be decided on a year-by-year basis. He also contended that the provision about arms control with Russia meant continuing to abide by the Anti-Ballistic Missile (ABM) Treaty, an agreement negotiated during the Nixon administration that put strict curbs on any missile defense deployment. These considerations were cited explicitly in President Bill Clinton's signing statement that accompanied the passage of the bill into law. There is still disagreement on Capitol Hill as to whether an ambitious missile defense system is either workable or affordable.[22]

But at the time that CABMTUS—also known as the Rumsfeld Commission—was meeting, the issue was whether there was a substantial ballistic missile threat to the United States. The commission—which one veteran missile defense watcher described as "something Curt Weldon dreamed up in the shower one morning"—emerged as a critical weapon in the conservative drive to reshape the debate over missile defense and create a sense of urgency for the deployment of a missile defense system. In painting the ultimate worst-case scenario, the report systematically ignored all of the real-world obstacles that a country like North Korea would face in trying to achieve a long-range ballistic missile capability and played up any factors (however remote) that might increase North Korea's chances of getting such missiles in a shorter time frame. As a result, the Rumsfeld Commission gave missile defense advocates in Congress the quasi-official endorsement they needed to effectively move forward on the issue.

Specifically, the commission's July 1998 report asserted that "rogue states" like North Korea and Iraq could acquire workable long-range ballistic missiles within "five years of a decision to do so," not the ten to fifteen years suggested by previous U.S. intelligence estimates.

Then–House Speaker Newt Gingrich jumped on the report's findings, loudly proclaiming that they represented "the greatest warning for U.S. security since the end of the Cold War."[23]

Upon closer examination, the Rumsfeld Commission looked less like an objective assessment and more like a slightly more nuanced replay of the tactics used by the famous "Team B" panel of the 1970s—a team of conservative experts brought in to second-guess the CIA's official estimates of Soviet military strength. The Rumsfeld Commission members looked at essentially the same intelligence data used in the 1995 National Intelligence Estimate (NIE) and a subsequent independent review convened by former CIA Director Robert Gates. The fact that two analyses had already found no imminent missile threat from North Korea or Iraq did not deter the Rumsfeld group from crying wolf.[24]

The problem was not that the Rumsfeld Commission manufactured data or openly lied, but that it gave an alarmist slant to the information that the U.S. intelligence community had collected on emerging ballistic missile threats. For example, rather than looking at the realistic economic, political, and technical impediments facing so-called rogue states in developing long-range ballistic missiles, the commission focused on speculative questions like: "What if China *gave* North Korea advanced missile technology (or even a completed missile)?"[25]

No evidence was given as to why China would do such a thing, since Beijing itself was becoming increasingly concerned about the unstable behavior of North Korean dictator Kim Jong Il and was therefore extremely unlikely to want to help him develop dangerous missiles that could just as easily be used in Asia as against targets in the United States.

The Rumsfeld Commission also focused, not on what it would take for a "rogue nation" to build an amply tested, seemingly reliable missile, but rather on how one could be cobbled together with minimal testing and still be "good enough" to threaten the United States. It was at this point that the fingerprints of Lockheed Martin became discernible. According to *Washington Post* reporter Bradley Graham's account in his book *Hit to Kill*, the testimony of Lockheed Martin engineers was central to the Rumsfeld Commission's finding that a nation with "Scud-based" technology—that is, based on the short-to medium-range missiles possessed by both Iraq and North Korea—could achieve "first flight" of a long-range ballistic missile within five years of a decision to do so. According to Graham's account, "Rumsfeld scribbled a sentence on a piece of paper" during the engineers' briefing, then said, "Let me read something to you and see if this is what you're saying: using Scud technology, a country could test-fly a long-range missile within about five years. Is that what you're saying?" When the Lockheed engineers agreed with Rumsfeld's summary of their remarks, the commission proceeded to use a modified version of it as the central finding of their report. As a result, the opinions of employees of a company that stood to benefit from the perception of a greater missile threat were allowed to overrule the consensus of the U.S. intelligence community.[26]

Rumsfeld's bona fides as an objective analyst of missile trends were also in doubt. The missile defense lobby certainly didn't view him as neutral. In the fall of 1998, after the report was issued, Rumsfeld was the recipient of the Center for Security Policy's "Keeper of the Flame" award at a gala dinner attended by retired military officers, conservative political and foundation leaders, and representatives of major defense contractors, including Lockheed Martin. In addition to serving as CSP's largest annual fund-raiser, the event was regularly used to honor pro–missile defense ideologues ranging from Ronald Reagan to Curt Weldon to Newt Gingrich. Rumsfeld's other ties to the missile defense lobby included his service on the board of Empower America, the organization founded by former Reagan administration cabinet officials Jack Kemp and Bill Bennett. During the 1998 election cycle, just a few months after Rumsfeld's allegedly nonpartisan assessment of the missile threat was released, Empower America ran a series of misleading radio ads against members of Congress like Senator Harry Reid (D-NV) suggesting that they weren't interested in protecting "American families" because they neither shared Republican views of the severity of the missile threat nor supported the kind of system the missile defense advocates saw as necessary to address that threat.[27]

The Rumsfeld Commission report helped move Congress toward its spring 1999 votes calling for the deployment of a missile defense system "as soon as technologically possible." The push for missile defense was aided by an August 1998 ballistic missile test by North Korea. The test demonstrated no great capability, but it did show an intention on North Korea's part to seek long-range missiles. As noted earlier, the vote came with some qualifications with respect to costs and consequences for arms control, but there is no question that it pushed missile defense higher up on the policy and budgetary agenda.

Although all this lobbying activity didn't result in the deployment of a missile defense system, it did press the Clinton administration and the Congress to dramatically step up missile defense funding from about $3 billion per year when the Clinton administration took office to over $5 billion per year at the end of its second term. This increase led to well over $1 billion in missile defense contracts for Lockheed Martin. The company had a piece of every aspect of missile defense: short-, medium-, and long-range; in space, in the air, on the ground, and at sea; and detecting, targeting, and hitting incoming missiles. Lockheed Martin had contracts for systems that included the payload launch vehicle for the ground-based element of the missile defense program; the Space-Based Infrared Sensor (SBIRS)-High, a system designed to provide early warning of a ballistic missile attack; the Theater High-Altitude Area Defense (THAAD) system, a medium-range system designed to protect U.S. troops and military facilities as well as allied nations; the Airborne Laser (ABL) system, in partnership with Boeing and TRW; targeting components for the Space-Based Laser (SBL) system; the Patriot Advanced Capabilities-3 (PAC-3), a longer-range version of the Patriot missile system that had performed with decidedly mixed results in the 1991 Persian Gulf war; and the Aegis sea-based missile defense system. Lockheed Martin's diversification within the missile defense arena was to serve the company well as ideas about which aspect of the system to focus on shifted over time and from one administration to the next. The cumulative projected costs of the missile defense–related programs have reached over *$100 billion*. As of 2008, there was still at least $63 billion planned to be spent, including over $23 billion for the company's SBIRS satellite program.[28]

The contractor-conservative alliance that Jackson and his Lock-heed Martin colleagues helped build was active not only in promoting defenses against other countries' nuclear weapons—real or imagined—but also in helping to craft a more aggressive strategy for the deployment and potential uses of U.S. nuclear weapons. The clearest link between the neoconservative movement and the incoming Bush administration with respect to nuclear policy was the blandly named National Institute for Public Policy (NIPP). It was headed up by Dr. Keith Payne, a controversial figure who had co-authored a 1980 *Foreign Policy* article on nuclear war entitled "Victory Is Possible." NIPP board members included Kathleen Bailey, a former analyst at the Lawrence Livermore National Laboratory (LLNL); Robert Barker, a thirty-year veteran of Lawrence Livermore and a long-standing opponent of the Comprehensive Test Ban Treaty; retired military officers such as General George Blanchard and Admiral Harry D. Train II; and veteran conservative ideologues like Colin Gray (Payne's co-author in his 1980 article on nuclear warfighting) and Eugene Rostow, a former Reagan administration official who asserted early in Reagan's first term that the last international arms agreement worth supporting was the U.S.-Canada accord of the late 1800s that demilitarized the Great Lakes.

Jackson's Lockheed Martin colleague Charles Kupperman was also a member of NIPP's board. Although the institute was careful not to reveal too much about its funding sources, it did acknowledge that it received corporate contributions; given Kupperman's role, it is likely that Lockheed Martin was one of these donors.

In January 2001, just a few weeks before George W. Bush took office, NIPP released a report entitled "Rationale and Requirements for U.S. Nuclear Forces and Arms Control" that set the tone for the Bush administration's Nuclear Posture Review—the most important expression of the nation's nuclear weapons policy. The preface to the NIPP report made it clear that an important part of its agenda was to counter "public proposals for 'nuclear abolition' and deep reductions" in nuclear weapons. The Bush policy itself—substantial parts of which were leaked to the press—was an aggressive assertion of the value of nuclear weapons as a tool of U.S. national security policy.[29]

The Bush administration's stated nuclear doctrine was an abrupt departure from the policies of prior administrations, Democratic and Republican alike. Far from representing "new thinking," as some observers have suggested, the proposed Bush nuclear policy represented the triumph of a small circle of conservative theorists who had long pressed for expanding the role of nuclear weapons as a guarantor of U.S. military superiority and a tool for exerting political and strategic influence. Although President Bush pledged to substantially reduce the numbers of nuclear warheads deployed by the United States, his proposed policy dramatically *expanded* the role of nuclear weapons in U.S. strategy. If one looks beyond the numbers to the philosophy motivating the Bush administration's new approach to nuclear doctrine, its resemblance to pre-Reaganite, anti–arms control views of the role of nuclear weapons becomes clear.

In contrast to Ronald Reagan, who came to believe that the elimination of nuclear weapons should be the ultimate goal of U.S. policy, the Bush administration's Nuclear Posture Review gave nuclear weapons a new lease on life by pressing for the development of a flexible nuclear warfighting capability grounded in a reinvigorated nuclear weapons complex. Unlike his father, George Herbert Walker Bush, who removed tactical nuclear weapons from U.S. ground and naval units as a way of lessening the risk of a nuclear confrontation, George W. Bush's approach called for developing, testing, and deploying a new generation of low-yield nuclear weapons. And unlike the Clinton administration, which tried to pursue changes in U.S. nuclear policy without abandoning international arms control treaties, the Bush administration announced its intention to withdraw from one major agreement, the Anti-Ballistic Missile Treaty of 1972. Beyond that, its nuclear plans threatened to undermine the other major pillars of the global arms control regime.

The Bush approach was heavily influenced by the NIPP report cited earlier. This should not be entirely surprising given that key participants in the task force that produced the NIPP report went into policymaking positions in the Bush administration, including Stephen Cambone, who became a special assistant to Bush Secretary of Defense Donald Rumsfeld; Stephen Hadley, the Deputy National

Security Adviser in the Bush White House; and Robert Joseph, who went on to deal with counterproliferation issues at the National Security Council. NIPP study director Keith Payne also secured a relevant post when he was appointed chairman of the Pentagon's Deterrence Concepts Advisory Panel, which played a role in determining how the guidance supplied by the Nuclear Posture Review should be implemented.[30]

The NIPP report set the tone for the more aggressive Bush policy in its call for more "possible current/future deterrence and *wartime roles* for nuclear weapons [emphasis added]."[31] The reference to possible wartime uses of nuclear weapons was particularly disturbing. If Payne and his co-authors had had their way, nuclear weapons might have been used against Iraq to take out its relatively crude, non-nuclear-armed Scud missiles: "If the locations of dispersed mobile launchers cannot be determined with enough precision to permit pinpoint strikes, suspected deployment areas might be subjected to multiple nuclear strikes."[32]

The NIPP report also influenced each of the three key pillars of the new Bush nuclear doctrine. The first change implemented by Bush was to expand the nuclear hit list. The Pentagon was directed to develop "contingency plans" for using nuclear weapons against a wide range of potential adversaries, whether or not those nations possessed nuclear weapons. The list included traditional targets like China and Russia as well as new targets like Iran, Iraq, Libya, North Korea, and Syria. The NIPP report's recommendation for using nuclear weapons for "deterring weapons of mass destruction (WMD) use by regional powers" provided a partial rationale for this shift, as it covered cases like Iran, Iraq, and North Korea. And since the term WMD includes not only nuclear weapons but chemical and biological ones as well, NIPP was advocating the potential use of nuclear weapons against a non-nuclear-armed nation.

Second, the Bush plan mirrored the NIPP report in lowering the threshold on the use of nuclear weapons. The circumstances under which the use of nuclear weapons would be considered was expanded beyond situations threatening the national survival of the United States to include retaliation for the use of chemical or biological weapons, for an attack by Iraq on Israel or one of its neighbors, for a military conflict over the status of Taiwan, for a North Korean attack on South Korea, or simply as a response to "surprising military developments." Some of these scenarios had been implicit in prior U.S. policy, but never before had so expansive a set of situations been cited in which nuclear weapons might be used. This did not mean that nuclear weapons would automatically be used in any of these scenarios, but the existence of contingency plans for doing so was frightening enough.

Finally, Bush's policy endorsed the development of new, lower-yield nuclear weapons for use against "targets capable of withstanding non-nuclear attack," such as hardened underground bunkers. This point had been emphasized in the NIPP report, which called for "providing unique targeting capabilities" by fielding "simple, low-yield, precision-guided nuclear weapons for possible use against select hardened targets such as underground biological weapons facilities." After the review was released, the Pentagon's Defense Science Board announced that it would be looking at yet another potential use of nuclear weapons by studying the possibility of developing missile defense interceptors armed with nuclear warheads.

Defense expert William M. Arkin summed up the new Bush policy as follows: By elaborating "an integrated, significantly expanded planning doctrine for nuclear wars," it "reverses an almost two-decades-long trend of relegating nuclear weapons to the category of weapons of last resort."[33]

The new posture had financial implications for Lockheed Martin. To implement Bush administration policies, the Nuclear Posture Review called for a "New Triad" involving "offensive strike systems (both nuclear and non-nuclear)," "defenses (both active and passive)," and "a revitalized defense infrastructure that will provide new capabilities in a timely fashion to meet emerging threats."[34] Each element of the New Triad offered business opportunities to Lockheed Martin for expanding production of systems like the Trident missile (which was now under consideration as a launcher for nuclear as well as non-nuclear warheads); its wide range of missile defense projects, cited earlier; and the Sandia National Laboratories, a complex operated by

Lockheed Martin that was likely to be a beneficiary of any invest-ment in modernized "defense infrastructure."

Many of the same players who lobbied for a larger missile defense program and a more aggressive nuclear policy joined the chorus call-ing for U.S. intervention in Iraq. Bruce Jackson was at the center of the action. He was so wired that his extensive connections with hawkish think tanks led one prominent neoconservative to describe him as "the nexus between the defense industry and the neo-conservatives. He translates them to us, and us to them."[35]

Jackson's job was made easier by the fact that key members of the Project for the New American Century were appointed to the top pol-icymaking posts of the Bush administration, from Defense Secretary Donald Rumsfeld to Deputy Defense Secretary Paul Wolfowitz to perhaps the most influential figure of all, Vice President Dick Cheney. All were early advocates of the Iraq war, and all played a role in mis-leading the American public to justify U.S. intervention.

Although PNAC was primarily a networking and strategy group, it did produce a few substantive reports, most notably "Rebuilding America's Defenses," which came out in September 2000, just three months before George W. Bush was selected as the forty-third Presi-dent of the United States. It was the product of a study group that in-cluded familiar neoconservatives such as Stephen Cambone, Eliot Cohen, Frederic and Robert Kagan, William Kristol, I. Lewis Libby, Gary Schmitt, and Paul Wolfowitz.[36] The report was written by Thomas Donnelly, a former House Armed Services Committee staffer and defense journalist who went on to work as a vice president for Lockheed Martin in 2002 after his stint at PNAC ended.

Not surprisingly given the composition of the group, the report called for substantial increases in military spending—by a total of $75 billion to $100 billion over a five-year period. Much to Lockheed Martin's potential benefit, the project strongly endorsed spending more on its troubled, overpriced F-22 combat aircraft. To its credit, however, the PNAC report didn't take a "buy everything" approach: The recommended increase in F-22 funding was offset in the study's recommendations by a plea to eliminate the F-35 Joint Strike Fighter, another Lockheed Martin program. The result would be a net gain to the company in the short term, but hardly the bonanza it could have been if both planes were pushed simultaneously. In the end the company had little to worry about: The post-9/11 surge in military spending gave the Pentagon the go-ahead to keep funding the F-22 and the F-35 simultaneously for another decade.

The heart of the PNAC report wasn't about how much to spend on U.S. forces, but about how they should be used. It called for a capability to fight *at least* two large wars plus "constabulary" operations like the wars in Bosnia and Kosovo, all at the same time. This was an expansion of the Pentagon's already ambitious plans and may well have ended up costing even more than the report suggested in its budgetary recommendations.

Most important of all was the ideology embraced by the PNAC task force, which called for unquestionable American military dominance into the indefinite future. PNAC suggested that far from seeking a post–Cold War peace dividend, the United States should capitalize on the weakness of its potential rivals to "run up the score," as Secretary of Defense Robert Gates later put it in the context of the F-22 debate of 2009. In the words of the report, "At present America faces no global rival. America's grand strategy should aim to extend this advantageous position into the future as far as possible." To do so, said PNAC, "requires a globally predominant military capacity now and in the future."[37] There was no suggestion that U.S. security might be better served by diplomacy, arms control, economic integration, or other potential tools of conflict resolution.

In addition to building off PNAC's advocacy of a bigger, costlier, and more interventionary U.S. military, Jackson's efforts to promote regime change in Iraq were specifically aided by the work of the Committee for the Liberation of Iraq (CLI), a network he helped to found. His role even extended to helping to provide initial funding for the operation, along with longtime Republican donor Julie Finley, who had also worked with Jackson on the U.S. Committee to Expand NATO. The initial amount was small—$25,000, according to one account— but it was indicative of Jackson's commitment to the cause.[38]

Another key player in CLI was Randy Scheunemann, a former foreign policy adviser to Senators Trent Lott and Bob Dole. Scheunemann went on to serve as John McCain's head foreign policy adviser in the run-up to the 2004 presidential campaign. Scheunemann—joined by former PNAC members Donald Rumsfeld, Paul Wolfowitz, and Richard Perle—was a key supporter of Ahmad Chalabi, an Iraqi exile with a checkered past that included charges of bank fraud and a record of providing the CIA with questionable intelligence on Iraq's weapons of mass destruction program. Chalabi was such a controversial figure that both the CIA and the State Department had decided that he was too untrustworthy to use as a source of information on what was happening in Iraq, much less to be groomed as the post-Saddam leader of the country. But Rumsfeld and Wolfowitz held firm, even going so far as to parachute Chalabi and some of his supporters into Iraq during the 2003 U.S. invasion in hopes that he might go on to establish himself as the leader of Iraq in the post-Saddam era. But Iraqis showed little enthusiasm for Chalabi, and he was embroiled in yet another controversy when it was indicated that he had been sharing sensitive information with Iran after his return to Iraq. The preferred leader of key PNAC and CLI members didn't make it into power, but their efforts to promote the war itself were successful, with all the consequences that flowed from that decision.[39]

One of the most effective CLI members was retired General Barry McCaffrey, the former head of the U.S. Southern Command and the nation's drug czar during the Clinton administration. McCaffrey worked as a consultant to NBC News in the months prior to the intervention in Iraq and continued to do so after the war had begun. McCaffrey was a ubiquitous presence on the Iraq issue, appearing more than one thousand times on NBC and its cable counterparts and being quoted in literally thousands of news articles on the topic. Simultaneously, due to his close ties to the defense industry, he earned hundreds of thousands of dollars working as a lobbyist for a number of firms seeking to profit from contracts relating to the Iraq war. As a *New York Times* analysis put it:

> General McCaffrey has consistently advocated wartime policies and spending priorities in line with his corporate interests. But those interests are not described to NBC's viewers. He is held out to be a

dispassionate expert, not someone who helps companies get contracts related to the wars he discusses on television.[40]

An exhaustive *New York Times* investigation put McCaffrey at the center of a Pentagon-orchestrated plan to get retired military officials—many with ties to the defense industry—to use their numerous appearances on television to promote the Bush administration line on the war. McCaffrey appeared to cross the line in mid-2007 when he signed a contract with a company named Defense Solutions to help it lobby for a contract to deliver used armored vehicles from eastern Europe to military forces in Iraq. Among other activities on the company's behalf, he wrote to the head commander in Iraq, General David Petraeus, suggesting that "no other proposal is quicker, less costly, or more certain to succeed" than the one being put forward by Defense Solutions.[41]

McCaffrey was also a central player in a formal Pentagon public relations campaign that sought to use retired military officers as "surrogates" and "message force multipliers" in making the Bush administration's case for the Iraq war. Among other elements of the plan, McCaffrey and his cohorts received special Pentagon briefings that were meant to inform their media commentary.

PNAC and CLI members were particularly active in the months leading up to the U.S. intervention in Iraq, helping make the case whenever and wherever possible. The twin pillars of the Bush administration's argument for overthrowing the regime of Saddam Hussein were, first, that he was rapidly developing nuclear, chemical, and biological weapons, and second, that he might share whatever Iraq developed with Al Qaeda. Despite Herculean efforts on its part, the Bush administration was never able to make the Iraq–Al Qaeda connection. In fact, as a secular nationalist, Saddam Hussein was inclined to keep his distance from Al Qaeda, whose ideology was grounded in religious extremism. One of the more comical efforts to establish the Al Qaeda link was a trip to Europe by R. James Woolsey in the fall of 2002 that left European officials scratching their heads and brought back no evidence of any Saddam–Al Qaeda connection.

Given the weakness of the Al Qaeda argument, the administration turned next to the argument about weapons of mass destruction. Paul

Wolfowitz told *Vanity Fair* magazine that the WMD argument was basically settled upon because it was considered to be the best way to sell the war to the American people.[42] The Bush administration was so intent on using this rationale that it started the war before United Nations inspectors were able to finish their assessment of whether Iraq had nuclear, chemical, or biological weapons or the technology needed to build them. Once the war was finished and Saddam's regime had been driven from power, two exhaustive surveys—one done under UN auspices and one paid for by the United States known as the Iraq Survey Group—found that not only did Iraq lack nuclear, chemical, or biological weapons, but it lacked active programs to produce them. Even after this definitive proof, PNAC clung to the WMD argument, publishing an April 2005 report entitled "Iraq: Setting the Record Straight." The gist of the report was that there might still be weapons of mass destruction in Iraq, since the conclusions otherwise were "based principally on interviews with former officials of the Saddam regime involved in the programs."[43] In addition to the fact that any credible investigation would have to involve interviewing these individuals, the PNAC assertion conveniently ignored the extensive physical inspections of alleged weapons sites that were carried out by both UN and U.S. inspectors. The PNAC report's fallback position was that even if the reports of no weapons of mass destruction in Iraq were true, prior to the war everyone thought they were there, even Clinton administration officials. This line of argument ignored a significant body of critical analysis provided before the war by everyone from State Department and Department of Energy intelligence specialists to the UN inspectors themselves, who had found no weapons or weapons programs prior to the March 2003 U.S. intervention.

The attempts by PNAC and the Bush administration to rewrite history with respect to Iraq's weapons programs were ultimately unsuccessful. The administration took a major public relations hit when the evidence regarding Iraq's nonexistent weapons programs emerged. But it didn't prevent George W. Bush from being reelected in 2004, and it didn't change the fact that the war continued. According to an estimate developed by Nobel Prize–winning economist Joseph Stiglitz and his colleague Linda Bilmes, the full economic costs of the Iraq war have exceeded $3 trillion.[44] The human costs are even higher: thousands of U.S. soldiers killed or injured, along with tens of thousands of Iraqis.

While others suffered from the war, Lockheed Martin benefited. As a manufacturer of the Multiple-Launch Rocket System (MLRS), the company supplied an artillery piece that was used to launch cluster bombs against Iraqi opponents, leaving behind deadly fragments of unexploded bomblets that killed or injured both Iraqis and U.S. soldiers. The company's F-16 combat aircraft figured prominently in the bombing campaign that was central to the initial defeat of Iraq's armed forces. Lockheed Martin's Hellfire air-to-ground missiles were used to take out Iraqi armored vehicles. As the war ground on, Lockheed Martin's contracts diversified to include the supply of communications systems for U.S. military bases in Iraq. Along with Halliburton, Lockheed Martin was one of the biggest beneficiaries of the war.

While its connections to the Bush administration and the Iraq war lobby have paid off handsomely for the company, it has also tried to cultivate contacts among Democratic officials. One key connection comes via the Center for a New American Security (CNAS), formed in 2007 by Michele Fluornoy and Kurt Campbell, former Clinton administration officials who have since gone on to take top national security positions in the Obama administration. Fluornoy now serves as Undersecretary of Defense for Policy, the third-ranking position in the Pentagon. Campbell was confirmed in June 2009 as the Assistant Secretary of State for East Asian and Pacific Affairs.

Lockheed Martin is one of a dozen major defense contractors that fund CNAS. (To its credit, CNAS lists these and other major donors on its website.) This flow of funding from weapons makers prompted Senator James Webb (D-VA) to quiz Kurt Campbell about potential conflicts of interest during Campbell's confirmation hearing before the Senate Foreign Relations Committee. Campbell argued that there was no problem with CNAS's defense contractor funding:

> I think our reports have won extraordinary critical acclaim. You will note, Senator, you should look at all of them, we never talk about weapons systems. We do not talk about defense systems. . . . It is

true that a number of firms, both commercial firms and defense firms, have supported CNAS, but not nearly at the level they have supported other institutions around Washington. The truth is, I think even if—those institutions can also be interested in a strong defense and want to work closely with people who care about it. So I'm very comfortable with this.[45]

But Campbell's assertion that CNAS never talks about weapons systems hasn't held true. In a February 2010 report, "Arsenal's End: American Power and the Global Defense Industry," author Ethan Kapstein advocates for high Pentagon weapons budgets for items like the Lockheed Martin F-35, even as it absolves the company of any responsibility for cost overruns on the system. It is hard to imagine a better analysis from Lockheed's point of view. And while the report came out after Campbell left CNAS, it represents the kind of analysis that he implied would never be done by the organization.

This is not to suggest that officials like Fluornoy or Campbell are somehow captive to Lockheed Martin or other weapons manufacturers. But the funding of their former think tank by these firms does create the appearance of a conflict of interest. At a minimum, one can say that when it comes to courting influential think tanks, Lockheed Martin and its cohorts are strictly nonpartisan.

Chapter 10

GLOBAL DOMINATION

While contracts for supplying weapons for the wars in Iraq and Afghanistan are a significant part of Lockheed Martin's business, the new company that has taken form since the merger boom of the 1990s has a far wider reach. These activities include everything from involvement in interrogation and police training to profiting from the new post-9/11 wave of domestic surveillance activities.

Of all the new ventures that Lockheed Martin has undertaken, the least well known may be its role in interrogating prisoners at U.S. facilities in Iraq and at Guantanamo Bay, Cuba.

The fact that employees of private companies are even allowed to interrogate terror suspects came as a surprise to most Americans when it was revealed in the wake of the Abu Ghraib scandal. The revelations of the use of "enhanced interrogation techniques"—many of which were viewed by human rights analysts as torture plain and simple—rocked the world as pictures of naked inmates threatened by dogs and subjected to other serious abuses were disseminated in print and electronic media. The damage to the reputation of the United States as a country governed by the rule of law is still being felt, even as accountability has been limited to the low-level military personnel involved directly in the abuses.

As the scandal unfolded, it was revealed that employees of two private contractors—CACI and the Titan Corporation—were present when inhumane techniques were being used. According to a U.S. Army report compiled under the direction of Major General Antonio Taguba, Steven Stefanowicz, an interrogator employed by CACI, lied about his knowledge of abusive activities and told military police to engage in practices that he "clearly knew . . . equated to physical abuse."[1] No charges were filed against Stefanowicz as a result of these findings. Another civilian was accused of raping an Iraqi inmate. In all, six contractor employees were referred to the Justice Department for prosecution, but no charges have been filed against any of them. In a separate case resolved in 2007, a CIA contract employee named David Passaro was sentenced to eight and a half years in prison for beating a prisoner to death in Afghanistan.[2]

An analysis conducted by Osha Gray Davidson for *Salon* determined that private contractors were the rule, not the exception, at Abu Ghraib. All twenty of the translators working there were from Titan, and almost half of the analysts and interrogators were from CACI.[3]

Eugene Fidell, the President of the National Institute for Military Justice, has expressed particular concern about the Pentagon's use of private contractor employees to interrogate terror suspects. "That's really playing with fire," says Fidell. "That kind of activity, which so closely entails the national interest and exposes the country to terrible opprobrium, is something that ought to be done by people who are government employees."[4] This logic did not prevent Lockheed Martin from getting into the interrogation business.

The company's first brush with the issue of private interrogations came with its effort to buy the Titan Corporation. Unbeknownst to its management, Lockheed Martin's September 2003 bid for Titan almost placed it in the center of the Abu Ghraib torture scandal: It came more than six months before the Abu Ghraib photos were released and the allegations of abuses by Titan employees were made public.[5]

The Titan deal started to unravel in early 2004 when it was revealed that the company was being investigated by the Justice Department for overseas bribery. As a result, Lockheed Martin announced that it was extending the timeline within which the deal would be considered so that it could see how Titan dealt with the bribery investigations. At this point, the alleged interrogation abuses by Titan employees had yet to be revealed. Even after the allegations did come out in May, they did not appear to play a role in Lockheed Martin's decision about whether to buy Titan. The bribery charges were still the main issue.

By the time Lockheed Martin's self-imposed deadline for considering the deal came in June, the bribery case against Titan had yet to be resolved. Given its own past problems with bribery, Lockheed was reluctant to take on a company with the same issues.[6] So Lockheed withdrew its bid for Titan, a move that it did not "take lightly," in the words of company spokesperson Tom Jurkowsky. "We did not want the uncertainty that surrounded the transaction to continue indefinitely," Jurkowsky said. Lockheed Martin's concerns were justified. In March 2005, Titan paid $28.5 million in fines for giving $2 million to the reelection campaign of Mathieu Kerekou, the President of the African nation of Benin. At that point, it was the largest fine ever imposed under the Foreign Corrupt Practices Act.[7]

Despite the collapse of the Titan deal, Lockheed Martin became involved in the supply of both interrogators and translators to the U.S. government via two other routes. In March 2005, it bought the Sytex Corporation.[8] Sytex provided interrogators and translators for employment in Iraq at the prisons at Abu Ghraib, Camp Cropper, and Camp Whitehorse. The exact number of personnel supplied by Sytex is not known, but a sense of the scale of the effort can be gleaned from the fact that in one post-9/11 ad alone the company sought 120 "intelligence analysts," many of whom would have the skills needed to serve as translators and/or interrogators in Iraq.[9]

A serious issue regarding Sytex's military interrogation work came up in a report by the Army Inspector General. The report found that two of the four Sytex interrogators working at Camp Bagram in Afghanistan had not received training in military interrogation techniques that would have included instruction in the Geneva Conventions requirements on the treatment of prisoners of war.[10]

Sytex was not Lockheed Martin's only link to interrogation work. In early 2003, it acquired the federal government information technology unit of Affiliated Computer Services (ACS), a company that held a contract to supply up to fifty interrogators and intelligence analysts at Guantanamo Bay, Cuba.[11] FBI documents released in January

2007 indicated that ACS interrogators were involved in supervising U.S. government personnel—a practice that is prohibited. At least one private contractor employee engaged directly in abusive behavior, including wrapping duct tape around the head of a detainee. FBI personnel alleged that another civilian contract employee frequently "lost it" when interviewing prisoners.[12]

The incidents cited in the FBI reports predated Lockheed Martin's purchase of ACS. Lockheed spokesperson Tom Jurkowsky asserted that since its takeover of ACS, the company "did not direct the actions of any military member, active or reserve."[13] To date, there is no evidence to contradict Jurkowsky's claim.

There is one direct allegation of abusive behavior by a Lockheed Martin contract employee: the case of Mamdough Habib, a former taxi driver in Sydney, Australia, who spent over three years at Guantanamo before being released in January 2005. According to a May 2008 report by the Department of Justice's Office of the Inspector General, "Habib alleged that 'Mike,' a private contract interrogator with Lockheed Martin, had hit him during an interrogation."[14] The FBI agent whom Habib told about the incident suggested that it was highly unlikely that the interrogator in question would have hit a suspect. However, she was not present when the reported events occurred. The Naval Criminal Investigative Service (NCIS) has since launched an investigation into Habib's charges, but as of this writing the Pentagon has reported no results from the probe.

Tim Shorrock, a journalist whose book *Spies for Hire* offers the most comprehensive assessment yet made of the outsourcing of intelligence activities, has described Lockheed Martin as "a major force in military interrogations," but the most recent evidence of these activities ends in 2007. At that point the company was still actively recruiting interrogators. But according to Lockheed Martin spokesperson Matt Kramer, the company is no longer involved in "hiring, recruiting or providing interrogators."

Lockheed Martin's involvement in the interrogation of suspects in the "war on terror" is just a small part of the work it has performed for the CIA, the National Security Agency (NSA), the Defense Intelligence Agency (DIA), and other U.S. government intelligence and surveillance bodies. According to *Spies for Hire*, nearly three-quarters of the budget of the U.S. intelligence community goes to private contractors. This amounts to a market of $50 billion, the largest source of government funding for goods and services outside of the Pentagon. Retired Vice Admiral Herbert A. Browne, former head of a major intelligence contractor trade group, calls it the "Intelligence Industrial Complex." Tim Shorrock has identified Lockheed Martin as the largest contractor:

> The bulk of this $50 billion market is serviced by 100 companies. . . .
> At one end of the scale is Lockheed Martin, whose $40 billion in revenue and 52,000 cleared IT personnel [employees with high-level security clearances] make it the largest defense contractor and private intelligence force in the world.[15]

Lockheed Martin executives have acknowledged their central role. At a 2005 meeting, Ron Romero—the company's Director of Intelligence and Homeland Security Programs—noted that although "everyone talks about the Intelligence Community as 'these guys in government,'" in fact "you [the contractors] are all part of the Intelligence Community. *In fact, you probably make up the largest part of it* [emphasis added]."[16]

Among the activities cited by Shorrock that are now carried out by private companies are "running spy networks out of embassies, signals intelligence (SIGINT) collection, covert operations, and the interrogation of enemy prisoners."[17] In many cases the contractors doing this work are supervised not by government employees but by other contractors. And often even the budgets designed to pay for all of these activities are drafted by contractor employees.

One of the most important projects Lockheed Martin is involved in developing is the Distributed Common Ground System (DCGS), which will link everyone from fighter pilots to commanders on the ground to intelligence analysts to a common Internet-based data set. Steven Zenishek, an Air Force lieutenant involved in overseeing development of DCGS, is enthusiastic about its prospects: "For the first time, on a simple workstation, we'll be able to guide all our ISR [intelligence, surveillance, and reconnaissance] products . . . making sure

role in running a private, U.S. Army–financed intelligence network in Pakistan and Afghanistan. In mid-May 2010, the *New York Times* revealed that a network of companies coordinated by Lockheed Martin was gathering information in those two countries that was "used to track and kill people accused of being militants." The operation was an end run around rules limiting the presence of U.S. military personnel in Pakistan and prohibiting the Army from hiring contractors to engage in spying.

The companies working as subcontractors to Lockheed Martin as part of a $22 million contract included Strategic Influence Alternatives, American International Security Corporation, and International Media Ventures. A major player in the operation was Duane "Dewey" Clarridge, a former CIA employee who was involved in the Iran-Contra scandal—an illegal Reagan-era operation that sold weapons to Ayatollah Khomeini's Iran and used the proceeds to buy arms for the antigovernment Contra rebels in Nicaragua. Lockheed Martin's government partner in the spying venture—which the Pentagon claims was abandoned in mid-2010—was the Army's Special Operations Command (SOCOM). Dell Dailey, who took a major position at Lockheed Martin in late 2009, served a stint as a board member of International Media Ventures, and was a former head of SOCOM, may have played a role in putting the Lockheed-SOCOM deal together.

While interrogation, intelligence-gathering, and surveillance have been among the most controversial activities carried out by the "new Lockheed Martin," they are only one element of a large roster of activities that the company has engaged in that are not normally associated with a weapons manufacturer. These include the export of services like training police and peacekeepers, recruiting election monitors for the Balkans and the Ukraine, building overseas military facilities, firefighting at military bases, and even helping to write the Afghan constitution.

In April 2009, these new lines of business were highlighted by an extraordinary act of philanthropy: a donation of $1 million to the United States Institute of Peace (USIP). The company's rationale for the gift was to highlight the aspects of its work that it believes to be consistent with USIP's mission.

The USIP was created by Congress during the Reagan administration to "prevent and resolve violent international conflicts," "promote post-conflict stability and development," and "increase conflict management capacity, tools, and intellectual capital worldwide"—in short, to promote peace.

According to USIP, Lockheed Martin's donation will underwrite the annual Dean Acheson Lecture—named after the Truman administration's Secretary of State, who was involved in promoting the Marshall Plan and NATO. USIP's official announcement says that the company will be "prominently" recognized as a sponsor in all lecture-related educational materials, as well as being "included as a Founding Corporate Partner for the Institute's new National Mall headquarters and public education center campaign."[28]

So far there is no evidence that Lockheed Martin's sponsorship is influencing the content of the lecture series. The first speaker since the company's contribution was Secretary of State Hillary Rodham Clinton, who used the occasion to give a talk on the Obama administration's commitment to nuclear arms control.

Its close connection with the USIP is clearly a public relations coup for Lockheed Martin, helping rebut any stereotypes of the company as a greedy "merchant of death." But does it make sense to have a company involved in designing and producing advanced fighter planes, artillery, and even nuclear weapons so enthusiastically embraced by a peace research and advocacy organization?

In announcing the grant, Lockheed Martin CEO Robert J. Stevens cited the company's "thousands of employees supporting peacekeeping, stability operations and capacity building efforts around the world" as evidence that "Lockheed Martin understands the importance of working to prevent conflict and promote peace as vital components of global security."[29]

What on earth was Stevens talking about? Plenty, it ends up. From recruiting volunteers to monitor elections in Bosnia to building camps for peacekeepers in the Sudan, Lockheed Martin is profiting rather nicely from the projection of soft power—diplomacy, humanitarian relief, peacekeeping, reconstruction, and development activities aimed at curbing or preventing conflict. Lockheed Martin even has a section of its website headlined "Soft Power" that touts these activities.

Lockheed Martin is not the only major defense contractor to seek profits in what are traditionally referred to as "peace and stability operations." August Cole, a reporter for the *Wall Street Journal* who closely followed this evolution in the market for soft power–related activities, has described it as a logical response to the current budgetary realities: "Many of the companies that the United States has had in the defense industry know that their traditional business of building ships and planes is fading. And this is their latest push into the services market, which many of them think is the future."[30]

This may seem like an extraordinary statement at a time when U.S. military spending is at its post–World War II high. But the Pentagon budget is expected to level off in coming years, even as its composition shifts toward services at the expense of spending on traditional weapons platforms. Add to this the Obama administration's goal of doubling U.S. foreign aid to up to $50 billion per year by the middle of this decade, and the contours of a new growth area become clearer. Initially, Lockheed Martin was quite bullish on this approach: "When you think about the engagements we have today, winning the war is just one aspect," said Lockheed Martin Vice President Linda Gooden. "There's considerably more resources attached to winning the peace."[31] As noted later, this initial enthusiasm was to wane in mid-2010 when the company rethought its engagement in this area. But it was a fascinating experiment in expanding the business base of a major defense contractor into unlikely areas of work.

This aspect of Lockheed Martin's work was primarily conducted through PAE Worldwide Services, a Lockheed Martin subsidiary that engages in an impressive array of military and nonmilitary support services in current and former areas of conflict. Until Lockheed Martin bought it in September 2006, PAE was known as Pacific Architects and Engineers and had a long history of activities involving the construction and support of military bases. It received a major boost to its business during the Vietnam War, when it ran military construction projects and operated military facilities throughout Indochina, with over thirty thousand employees based in the region. At the time of its acquisition by Lockheed Martin, PAE had contracts to run facilities for the Departments of State and Defense, the Air Force and Navy, the governments of Canada and New Zealand, and the United Nations.

The *Wall Street Journal* has described PAE as "the logistics backbone of the 7,700-strong African Union troops in Darfur."[32] The work was done at first under a State Department contract. In the fall of 2007, the management of Darfur operations was taken over by a joint African Union/United Nations "hybrid force," and PAE then became a contractor to the UN rather than to the State Department. Under the terms of the successive contracts, PAE runs thirty-four base camps in Darfur while also providing vehicle maintenance and telecommunications services. The UN contract called for the following: "the establishment of new camps in El Fasher, Nyala, El Geneina, Zalingei in Darfur and El Obeid . . . and the provision of camp services including catering, medical, janitorial, welfare, and upkeep."[33]

Separate from its other Darfur contracts, in 2002 (prior to PAE's acquisition by Lockheed Martin) the State Department contracted with PAE to provide staff for the Civilian Protection Monitoring Team (CPMT), which tracks human rights abuses in Sudan. Their job is to investigate complaints from the local community and issue independent reports on their findings.

Georgette Gagnon, now Director of the Africa Division of Human Rights Watch, has questioned the concept of using companies like PAE for human rights monitoring: "There is not a lot of transparency about these contracts; we don't know how they vet recruits or what kind of training they get." Nor is it easy to find out, since unlike government agencies, which are covered by freedom of information laws, private companies generally claim "business confidentiality" as a reason to deny public access to detailed information about their activities in places like the Sudan.[34]

Lockheed Martin's work in support of United Nations peacekeeping efforts in Darfur sparked criticism in late 2007 on the grounds that the proposed $250 million deal was given to PAE on a no-bid basis. In a memorandum to UN-based journalist Matthew Lee, a UN spokesperson cited the "exigency" of the task as a reason to forgo the normal competitive bidding process. The memo asserts that "the nature and complexity of the requirement, coupled with the challenging timeline mandated by the Security Council, have made [it] so that PAE was the only contractor which could be selected."[35]

The concerns over Lockheed Martin's no-bid contract led to an audit by the UN's Office of Internal Oversight Services. The audit, released in January 2009, found that "the extraordinary measures [sought by the Secretary General] were not effective in facilitating the deployment of the African Union–United Nations Hybrid Operation in Darfur and exposed the United Nations to high financial and reputation risks."[36] In the specialized language of the United Nations, this qualifies as extremely harsh criticism.

The audit's main finding was that, in its rush to conclude the contract without competition, the UN overpaid PAE. Excess charges included costs for catering services that were never delivered; $4.3 million in charges for overseeing construction during a period in which no construction was taking place; and charging more than twice what the UN would normally pay for major items of equipment, including "rock crushers" at a cost of $1.1 million each.[37]

The UN's official position on the contract for PAE was that there wasn't time to hire anybody else and that one company was far more qualified than others to do the job. This argument mirrors the rationale given by the Bush administration when it awarded a no-bid, open-ended contract to Halliburton's Kellogg, Brown and Root division in advance of the 2003 U.S. intervention in Iraq. UN member states paid a substantial price for a similarly flawed approach.

Along with its work in the Sudan, PAE's most extensive involvement in Africa is in Liberia, where it builds and maintains military bases and does specialized training for the Armed Forces of Liberia (AFL). A January 2009 report by the International Crisis Group describes PAE's work in Liberia as including everything from helping to create a 40-member military band to training and recruiting 19 medics and 105 military police to helping found a 162-member military engineering brigade. As in the Sudan, PAE's work in Liberia is done alongside DynCorp, which is responsible for vetting recruits and providing basic training to the new, 2000-member AFL.

While DynCorp and PAE have generally received high marks for their vetting and training activities in Liberia, the International Crisis Group (ICG) and other independent analysts have raised a number of concerns. The biggest question, in the eyes of the ICG, is "whether democratic institutions responsive to civilian oversight can be built by private contractors in an atmosphere of at least partial secrecy."[38] For example, the report notes that information on "the training, its costs, or its implementation" was frequently denied on the grounds that it was "proprietary." Liberian President Ellen Johnson-Sirleaf has criticized this process: "A lot of money has been spent. We do not know what on. There's simply not enough transparency and accountability in the way this money is spent."[39]

PAE's State Department–funded work in Sudan and Liberia is part of a larger contract known as AFRICAP, an arrangement that puts the company on retainer for anything the department wants done on the continent. The first AFRICAP contract ran five years with a ceiling of $500 million and was one of two such contracts awarded (the second went to DynCorp). In September 2009, PAE won a second five-year AFRICAP contract valued at $375 million, one of four awarded at that time.[40] The ICG has criticized AFRICAP as essentially a "five year monopoly contract." The AFRICAP contracts are similar to the ones used to pay Halliburton for its worldwide work for the U.S. military—a contract whose open-ended nature and lack of oversight led to disastrous cost overruns and shoddy work. It remains to be seen whether AFRICAP will foster similar abuses.

Daniel Volman of the Africa Security Research Project raises a larger concern—the inability to control the use of the skills imparted under these programs: "If you look at the record for these programs in terms of teaching respect for human rights, professionalizing militaries, and preparing African armies for peacekeeping operations— all of which are perfectly laudable goals—the end result of the programs doesn't contribute very much to those," says Volman. "It's much more likely to be used for purposes not intended by the U.S. government: counter-insurgency warfare, terrorizing populations, and repressing internal dissent."[41] A March 2008 study by the U.S. Army's Strategic Studies Institute makes a similar point when it notes that "the image of DynCorp [and PAE] creating an armed elite is disconcerting to many Liberians," because "every armed group that has plundered Liberia over the past 25 years has its core in . . . U.S.-trained soldiers."[42]

An even more unconventional task taken on by PAE in Liberia was its attempt to create a new, more accountable justice system in the country. In conjunction with its partner HSC (the Homeland Security Corporation), PAE has put out a regular call for applicants to carry out similar projects around the world. For instance, an employment ad on PAE-HSC's website reads: "PAE, HSC and the U.S. Department of State are seeking qualified Civilian Police, Attorneys, Judges, Legal Professionals, Corrections Officers and others to assist in the establishment and maintenance of contemporary law and order techniques in priority areas around the globe. . . . PAE-HSC works to provide solutions at all levels of the justice process." An ambitious goal, to be sure, especially in a country like Liberia with a history of chaos and corruption. But according to an employee of a rival firm who saw PAE's operations up close, PAE didn't try very hard. He described the company's early work in this area as "a kind of meager little program" involving just a few lawyers, deriding it as "a little bit laughable." He further asked, "What does a recent law graduate from Tallahassee know about creating a justice system in Liberia?" But apparently PAE's work has improved over time, according to Liberia's Justice Minister Christiana Tah: "They've come in to really strengthen the system. . . . We can see the difference in the performance of the prosecutors, which was terrible."[43]

Mike McGovern, the principal author of the International Crisis Group report cited earlier, questions whether PAE would even have taken on this kind of work without a firm push from its new parent company, Lockheed Martin. McGovern describes the difference between pre– and post–Lockheed Martin PAE as follows: "My contacts back then when they were just a little logistics company were very positive . . . but the only connection between that PAE and the PAE owned by Lockheed Martin is the name. . . . They [PAE] used to maintain warehouses [or] keep a tractor running [and] suddenly they were doing judicial reform work." He further noted that the staff for the judicial reform project in Liberia "didn't know the first thing about the country, its culture, or its history."[44]

PAE's work is done under the umbrella of Lockheed Martin's Readiness and Stability Operations (RSO) division; "strategic planning" for the group is handled by Tom Callahan, who spent five and a half years at the State Department as Deputy Assistant Secretary of Legislative Affairs and as a senior adviser for the Bureau of Diplomatic Security. As further evidence of Lockheed Martin's interest in growing its business in Africa, in July 2009 Lockheed Martin RSO President Michael Dignam was appointed President of the Corporate Council on Africa, a trade association composed of U.S.-based companies doing business there. Its roster of members includes major firms like Chevron Oil and the minerals extraction firm Freeport McMoran.

PAE's most recent executive hire is Dell Dailey, appointed as company president in November 2009. Dailey has credentials on the "hard power" side of U.S. government activities. Prior to serving as Coordinator of Counterterrorism at the U.S. State Department, Dailey served as commander of the Joint Special Operations Command (JSOC), the body that coordinates missions undertaken by U.S. Special Forces in eighty countries.[45]

Lockheed Martin acknowledges that its efforts in these nontraditional areas are by no means altruistic. When it comes down to it, it's all about business, including the business of selling weapons. In *LM Today*, a company newsletter, it asserts that, "aside from representing a growing line of business, PAE's capacity building efforts benefit Lockheed Martin in another significant way: They introduce the company in a positive light to regions that might someday develop into markets for customers for information technology, infrastructure and defense systems." It was this question of whether PAE's activities could be leveraged to generate additional markets that was to determine Lockheed Martin's decision about whether to keep it as an integral part of the company for the long term.

Lockheed Martin's base construction, police and firefighter training, refugee operations, and peacekeeping support put the company in competition with companies that are better known for their work in these areas, such as Kellogg, Brown and Root, which specializes in reconstruction, base operations, and troop support work, and MPRI and DynCorp, which have been central actors in performing police and military training in Iraq and Afghanistan. One thing PAE's leadership avoids is direct security operations, such as the guarding of embassies or critical infrastructure. A company executive who spoke on condition of anonymity explained that PAE did not want to be seen as a "gun-toting" organization akin to Blackwater (now named Xe), the company responsible for shooting civilians in Iraq in the infamous Nisoor Square incident.

But Lockheed does one thing that other private military companies don't. For all of its talk of "soft power," the most important element of Lockheed Martin's global reach remains the fact that it is the world's top weapons-exporting company.

The last two years of the Bush administration and the first year of the Obama administration were good times for arms-exporting companies. Major foreign arms deals by U.S. companies more than doubled from 2001 to 2008, reaching a total of over $28 billion. The U.S. lead in the overall global weapons market increased dramatically as well. In 2008 more than *two-thirds* of all new arms sales agreements worldwide went to U.S. companies.[46]

Lockheed Martin is the biggest beneficiary of this trend, and one of its biggest export items is the F-16 fighter plane. Since 2006, the company has entered into agreements to sell nearly $13 billion worth of F-16s to Romania, Morocco, Pakistan, and Turkey. A relatively new, even more lucrative development is the large-scale export of current-generation Lockheed Martin missile defense systems like the PAC-3 (Patriot Advanced Capability) and the Theater High-Altitude Area Defense (THAAD) system. During 2007 and 2008, the company made agreements to sell one or more of these systems to the United Arab Emirates, Turkey, Germany, and Japan for a total of over $24 billion in business. Its C-130J military transport planes are destined for Israel, Iraq, India, and Norway in deals worth nearly $5 billion. Additional sales of Hellfire missiles, Apache helicopters, and various bombs and guidance systems are earning the company billions more.[47]

One of the most controversial recent sales of Lockheed Martin equipment was a $6 billion U.S. deal with Taiwan that included 114 of the company's PAC-3 missiles at a cost of $2.8 billion. (Raytheon is a partner of Lockheed in the PAC-3 program.) The deal sparked an angry response from China, which threatened to cut off military-to-military cooperation with the United States and impose sanctions on U.S. firms whose equipment was part of the deal. As of this writing, the threatened sanctions had not been imposed.[48]

Lockheed Martin would argue that its weapons exports provide stability by deterring war, but critics would suggest that weapons exports fuel arms races and make war more likely. In many cases, there is no clear answer to these questions: Does Romania need $4.5 billion worth of F-16s? Isn't Pakistan more likely to use its F-16s against India than against Al Qaeda or the Taliban? Does buying over $15 billion in missile defense technology protect the United Arab Emirates, or is it just making this purchase to curry favor with Washington?

These questions may seem academic—unless and until the weapons are used. In Turkey, for example, Lockheed Martin–supplied F-16s didn't just sit on a runway: They were used in a brutal fifteen-year war against Kurdish separatists affiliated with the Kurdish Workers' Party (the Turkish initials are PKK) that left thousands of villages bombed, burned, and abandoned and tens of thousands of people dead. Over 375,000 of the people driven from their homes during the conflict have yet to return.[49]

Both sides of the conflict engaged in serious human rights abuses. The Turkish military undertook a systematic scorched-earth policy in the southeastern provinces, attempting to eliminate support for the PKK by attacking entire areas alleged to be inhabited by at least some PKK sympathizers. For its part, the PKK engaged in assassinations, kidnapping, extortion, and destruction of property, including violence against anyone believed to be "cooperating with the Kurdish state," from civil servants and teachers to families of members of the "village guards," a militia armed and paid for by the Turkish military.[50]

Although the F-16 was far from the only weapon used in suppressing the Kurds, it was featured in air strikes—both within Turkey and in raids against alleged PKK sanctuaries in Iran and northern Iraq—that helped set the stage for more intensive raids using attack helicopters, armored personnel carriers, rifles, and anti-tank weapons.

Joel Johnson, then a lobbyist for the Aerospace Industries Association—of which Lockheed Martin is an active, dues-paying member—tried to justify Turkish bombing of Kurdish areas by essentially saying that everybody does it:

> It must be acknowledged that the Turks have not invented Rolling Thunder. We used B-52s to solve our guerrilla problem [in Vietnam]. The Russians used very large weapons platforms [in Afghanistan]. And Israelis get irritated on a reasonably consistent basis and use F-16s in Southern Lebanon. One wishes it didn't happen. Sitting in the comfort of one's office, one might tell all four countries that they're wrong. It's a lot easier to say that here than when you're there and it's your military guys getting chewed up.[51]

By the late 1990s and early 2000s, the war against the PKK had mostly been wrapped up. The dismantling of the PKK by force may have diminished levels of violence, but it has not solved the Kurdish problem by any means. Perhaps most tragically of all, a relaxation of tensions and an end to PKK violence might have been achieved without the needless deaths and displacement caused by the war in the southeast, if only the Turkish government had been willing to be more flexible in granting basic rights to Kurds living in Turkey.

Israel has been another major user of Lockheed Martin products, most notably in its summer 2006 intervention in Lebanon, where the company's F-16 fighters were used to bomb Lebanese targets, while its Multiple-Launch Rocket System (MLRS) was used to spray cluster bombs across the countryside. A cluster bomb is essentially a large canister—as long as thirteen feet and weighing up to two thousand pounds—packed with hundreds of "bomblets" that can have an explosive impact on an area the size of three football fields, spreading shrapnel along the way.

Although it is important to note that Hezbollah forces also fired missiles into northern Israel, including one hundred or more Chinese-made rockets packed with cluster munitions, the issue has been the extent to which Israel's attack was disproportionate, and whether it put civilians at risk unnecessarily. The attacks were devastating and indiscriminate enough to elicit Amnesty International's assertion that "war crimes" had been committed, and UN Undersecretary General for Humanitarian Affairs and Emergency Relief Jan Egeland called them "a violation of international humanitarian law."[52]

The use of cluster bombs was an important aspect of the war, but the larger attack of which they formed a part drew intense criticism as well. The Israeli Air Force launched more than seven thousand air strikes during the conflict, many of them with Lockheed Martin–supplied F-16s. The bombs hit roads, bridges, airports, factories, and power plants, killing over one thousand people and driving nearly one million more from their homes.[53] In Israel's 2008–2009 intervention in the Gaza strip, which by one account killed over fourteen hundred civilians, F-16s were used to run bombing raids as part of the overall military operation, known as Operation Cast Lead.[54]

As devastating as the aerial attacks in Lebanon and Gaza were, it has been the use of U.S.-supplied cluster bombs that has drawn the most international attention. Their military uses include attempting to slow down advancing troops, destroying airfields, and taking out surface-to-air missile sites. Because cluster bombs can kill or wound anything in a large area, there is a high risk of hitting civilians as "collateral damage" in the initial attack. They can also leave large numbers of unexploded bomblets on the ground that blow up later on impact—when stepped on inadvertently, or picked up by a child, or run over by a plow. After Israel dropped millions of cluster bomblets during its thirty-four-day war in Lebanon, hundreds of thousands were left unexploded. Within a few months of the war's end, these bomblets had killed nearly two dozen Lebanese civilians and wounded over 120 more. The bomblets can be as small as a soda can or a flashlight battery, and they don't look particularly menacing to someone unfamiliar with what they are. The results of this confusion can be devastating. To cite just one example, eleven-year-old Ramy Shibleh lost his right arm when he picked up a cluster bomblet that had gotten in the way of a cart that he and his brother were using to carry the pine cones they were collecting.[55] The bombing also had a crippling effect on agricultural production in southern Lebanon, where unexploded cluster munitions rendered fields and orchards unusable, making them the equivalent of mine fields. A commander of an Israeli rocket unit told the Israeli daily *Haaretz* that the saturation bombing of Lebanon was "monstrous; we covered entire towns in cluster bombs."[56]

The Lockheed Martin MLRS played a central role in the cluster-bombing of Lebanon. Researchers who went to Lebanon after the war found large numbers of M-26 rockets that had been fired from Israeli-owned, U.S.-supplied MLRS systems. Each MLRS can fire 12 rockets, and each rocket contains 644 M-77 submunitions. This means that each time the MLRS was used, it spread over 7,700 cluster bomblets over the Lebanese landscape.[57]

The Israeli case is a good example of how hard it is to control the use of exported weaponry once it is delivered, even when the recipient is a close ally like Israel. The nongovernmental advocacy group Landmine Action uncovered a secret U.S.-Israeli agreement governing the use of U.S.-supplied cluster bombs that indicated that they should be used "only for defensive purposes, against fortified targets, and only if attacked by two or more 'Arab states.'" It also limited them to being used only against "regular forces of a sovereign nation." A preliminary State Department investigation found "likely violations," but the ultimate findings of the review have been classified.

Cluster bombs were also used extensively by U.S. forces in Iraq. In the 1991 Persian Gulf War, more than 13 million bomblets rained down on Iraqi targets. The bomblets fell so thickly that the MLRS attacks were referred to in the combat zones as "steel rain." And a Government Accountability Office (GAO) report found that U.S. cluster bombs killed 22 U.S. soldiers and wounded 58 during the war as U.S. troops moved through desert areas littered with cluster munitions that had not exploded upon first impact.

While far fewer cluster bombs were used in the 2003 U.S. invasion of Iraq, just one attack on the village of al-Hilla killed 33 people and injured another 109. There are also reports that U.S. soldiers have been killed or wounded by unexploded cluster bomblets dropped by their own forces. One documented case is that of Travis Bradach-Nall, whose mother Lynn learned from friends in his unit that he was killed in July 2003 by a cluster submunition that exploded when a fellow Marine picked it up while clearing a field in Karbala, Iraq. While cluster munitions were used far less frequently in the 2003 Iraq war than in the 1991 conflict, an investigation by *USA* Today revealed that 10,782 cluster weapons were used, more than six times the number acknowledged by Richard Myers, the head of the U.S. Joint Chiefs of Staff. The newspaper report also found that at least eight U.S. soldiers were killed or wounded as a result.[58] After learning of the dangers of cluster munitions—which cost the life of her son—Lynn Bradach said, "I have learned enough to know that I don't want these weapons to protect me—or our soldiers."[59]

The impact of cluster bombs in conflicts well beyond Lebanon and Iraq has spurred international action, including a treaty banning the export and use of these systems that has been signed by over one hundred nations. The United States has yet to sign, in deference not so much to producers of bomblets and their delivery systems as to the Pentagon's desire to have them available for specific military scenarios. The U.S. Congress has instituted a de facto ban on exports of U.S. cluster bombs, a step in the right direction. A full ban on the production, use, and export of cluster bombs endorsed and promoted vigorously by the United States would save thousands of innocent lives. And it wouldn't put a dent in the fortunes of Lockheed Martin and other major defense contractors, who make the bulk of their revenues from big-ticket items like fighter planes, tanks, combat ships, and anti-missile missiles.

Another major source of ongoing revenue for the company is its role in missile defense and space programs. From ground-, sea-, air-, and space-based missile defense interceptors and targeting systems to launching the space shuttle to providing vehicles for the exploration of Mars and the moon, Lockheed Martin has been present in all major aspects of the military and civilian uses of space.

The company's involvement in virtually every facet of missile defense was underscored by President Obama's September 2009 decision to scrap a Bush administration plan to place missile defense components in Poland and the Czech Republic. Although companies like Boeing—which is responsible for the radar system that would have been deployed in the Czech Republic under the Bush plan— stood to lose from President Obama's change in course, at first blush it appeared that Lockheed Martin might actually come out ahead.

This unexpected outcome is tied to the fact that the Obama administration did not abandon missile defenses in Europe—it just restructured them. The Bush plan would have entailed putting a radar system in the Czech Republic and (initially) ten long-range interceptors in Poland; the Obama plan would rely on the sea-based Aegis missile defense system supplemented by medium-range missiles based in numerous European countries. Leaked Pentagon documents indicate that the number of Lockheed Martin interceptor rockets deployed in Europe could quadruple under the Obama plan.[60] And in January 2010, just three months after Obama announced the restructuring, plans for the deployment in Poland of Lockheed Martin–made PAC-3 missiles (an update of the Patriot missile that featured so prominently in the 1991 Persian Gulf War) were announced.[61] Then, in early February 2010, Romanian President Traian Basescu announced that his country was entering talks with the Obama administration to place Lockheed Martin–built PAC-3 missile interceptors there. The deal—which was announced by the Romanian leader before U.S. officials told Russia about it—sparked protests in Moscow. Russian Foreign Ministry spokesperson Andrei Nesterenko questioned the lack of consultation, noting in addition that "Russia has serious questions regarding the true purpose of U.S. missile defense in Romania. That is why we will consistently oppose any . . . unilateral actions in the missile defense field that could have a negative impact on the international security."[62]

The fact that Lockheed Martin should benefit from a change in missile defense policy is not so surprising if one looks at its current role in the roughly $10 billion per year missile defense program. In addition to the Aegis sea-based and the land-based PAC-3 intermediate range interceptor, Lockheed Martin builds the payload launcher for the Ground-Based Midcourse Defense System (GBMDS), a missile designed to intercept incoming nuclear warheads in outer space as they descend toward targets in the United States; the Medium Extended Air Defense System (MEADS), which is being developed as part of a consortium with European allies; the Theater High-Altitude Area Defense (THAAD) system; the Space-Based Infrared Sensor (SBIRS), a developing constellation of satellites designed to detect enemy ballistic missile launches; and the Airborne Laser (ABL), a system meant to use a laser-equipped Boeing 747 to hit long- and medium-range missiles as they are first taking off, in their "boost phase."[63]

Lockheed's role in the Airborne Laser project was carried out as part of a Boeing-led consortium known as "Team ABL." The Airborne Laser is one of the systems targeted for cuts by Secretary of Defense Robert Gates. He defunded a second prototype of the plane in early 2009, and current reports suggest that he is hoping to kill the program, which is eight years behind schedule and $4 billion over budget.[64] As a secondary supplier to the ABL program, Lockheed Martin will suffer less loss of business than the lead contractor, Boeing. Lockheed has plenty of larger missile defense contracts to replace its ABL funding, not just from interceptor missiles in Europe but also from sales of the PAC-3 and THAAD systems in the Middle East. As with the termination of the F-22 program, Lockheed Martin is big enough, and diversified enough, to weather the cut in the ABL program. For Lockheed Martin, what the Pentagon takes away with one hand it usually gives back with the other (and then some).

The focus on Lockheed Martin as a missile defense contractor has largely obscured its role in every facet of the civilian space program. The company partners with Boeing in the United Launch Alliance, the only source in the United States for launching Atlas and Delta rockets, which are central to putting commercial and military satellites into orbit. And as half-partner in the United Space Alliance, Lockheed Martin does all of the work needed to prepare the space shuttle for launch.

The company was also the prime contractor for the Orion crew exploration vehicle (CEV), which was part of the Constellation system slated to replace the space shuttle in getting cargo and astronauts to the International Space Station. According to the company's website, the Orion will also be capable of "safely transferring astronauts to and from . . . the Moon, Mars, and destinations beyond low earth orbit (LEO)."[65] But the Obama administration has decided to cancel the Constellation and radically decrease government funding for the Orion project as part of a new initiative to encourage the use of commercial providers to get personnel and material to and from the space shuttle. A scaled-back version of the Orion may be developed for use as a "lifeboat" capable of rescuing astronauts in the event of a problem with the Space Station.[66] This could represent a few billion dollars of additional spending on the Orion, but it is not necessarily the most efficient use of taxpayer funds. As former NASA administrator Michael D. Griffin put it, "This seems like an expensive proposition that makes simply continuing to use the Russians for crew rescue look like a bargain."[67] The congressional delegation from Colorado—where the Orion is built—has vowed to fight the Obama administration's plan to eliminate the Constellation project.

In the meantime, the company is building eight solar array panels that will generate all of the electricity needed to operate the International Space Station in orbit. When finished, the panels will cover twenty-six thousand square feet, the largest structure ever deployed in space.

The company's work in support of the space station is just the first stop for Lockheed Martin–built space systems. It built the Phoenix Mars lander, which landed on Mars on May 25, 2008, to take soil samples and look for water and carbon-containing compounds "by heating soil samples in tiny ovens and examining the vapors that are given off." The ultimate goal of the Phoenix was to help determine whether Mars can support life. Two years later, NASA determined that the lander had not survived the minus-195-degree winter at its landing site near Mars's north pole. In its life span on Mars, the explorer located significant sources of underground water.[68]

Lockheed also built the Mars Global Surveyor (MGS) and the Mars exploration rovers, named "Spirit" and "Opportunity." The MGS orbits the pole of Mars to study the planet's topography, mineral composition, and atmosphere. The rovers, which landed on Mars in January 2004, send back continuous data via the Odyssey satellite system, another Lockheed Martin product.[69]

Last but not least, Lockheed Martin was involved in the production of the "Stardust" vehicle, the first vehicle to gather dust from a comet for examination on earth. It is believed that comet dust may be the key to understanding the original cloud of dust and gas from which the sun and the planets were formed.[70]

While Lockheed Martin's work for the Pentagon, NASA, and for-eign governments continues to thrive, its biggest source of future growth may be on the home front. The company's efforts to benefit, however, from contracts for everything from homeland security to helping execute the 2010 census have run into some serious difficulties. Lockheed's rapid move into the homeland security market, for in-stance, led to the company's biggest fiasco in recent years—its mis-handling of an initiative aimed at preventing terrorist attacks on the United States by rebuilding the Coast Guard.

In the weeks and months after 9/11, the executive branch and the Congress were scrambling to get ahead of the curve in developing policies and practices that could fend off any future effort to attack the United States. One element of this new approach was a call to upgrade the Coast Guard, which for years had been neglected in favor of buying big-ticket systems for the Navy, Army, and Air Force. Un-like the invasion of Iraq—which was based on false allegations that Saddam Hussein's regime possessed or would soon possess nuclear, chemical, and biological weapons—building a more effective Coast Guard made good sense. Numerous experts on antiterrorism and homeland security agreed that there was a significant risk that a fu-ture attack might come from the sea, up to and including the possi-bility of a terrorist group bringing a nuclear weapon, a so-called "dirty bomb," or a biological or chemical weapon close enough to hit a major city. (A dirty bomb is a conventional bomb surrounded by ra-dioactive materials, as distinct from a nuclear bomb with massive ex-plosive power.)

The response to the demand for a better Coast Guard was a mas-sive program known as Deepwater, a proposed $17 billion effort that would build the equivalent of a small navy, with over 90 new ships, 124 small boats, nearly 200 new or refurbished helicopters and air-planes, over four dozen Unmanned Aerial Vehicles (UAVs), and an integrated surveillance and communications system that would allow all of these components to share critical information in real time. A *New York Times* summary of the capabilities sought by the Coast Guard gives some sense of Deepwater's ambitious goals: "The new fleet and equipment will allow the Coast Guard to stop ships away

from the coast line; instantly run lists of crew members and cargo ship-
ments through intelligence data bases; and check for biological, chemical, or radiological materials."[71] Unfortunately, the first round of
Deepwater development and procurement efforts failed on virtually
all of these fronts, leaving the Coast Guard weaker and less capable as
a result.

The winners of the Deepwater competition were Lockheed Martin and Northrop Grumman. The companies were to work in partnership not only to build their own pieces of the Deepwater but to
supervise the work of every other company involved in the program.
This "innovative" approach was touted as a way to reduce bureaucracy and increase efficiency compared with a system in which the
Coast Guard itself would retain primary control. What it ended up
proving was that contractors can be far *less* efficient than the government at running a major program like Deepwater. The problems
entailed in letting contractors run the show soon became apparent.
Anthony D'Armiento, an engineer who worked for both the Coast
Guard and Northrop Grumman on the project, called it "the fleec-
ing of America. It's the worst contract I've seen in my 20-plus years
in naval engineering."[72]

The original decision to give major contractors like Northrop
Grumman and Lockheed Martin the lead roles in Deepwater—and to
bundle the Coast Guard's diverse needs into one giant package—was
political. The Coast Guard leadership calculated from the beginning
that having two major weapons contractors on their side would be a
good way to extract major funding from Congress. As former Coast
Guard budget analyst Jim McEntire put it, "They have armies of lobbyists, and they can help get dollars to get the job done. The White
House and Congress listen to big industrial concerns."

So when Lockheed Martin and Northrop Grumman received
the Deepwater contract in June 2002—nine months after the 9/11
attacks—there was intense pressure to get new ships and planes deployed as soon as possible. But problems emerged almost immediately. The first major piece of the project—an effort to extend the
Coast Guard's main patrol boats from 110 to 123 feet long—resulted
in the production of eight ships that were unusable, at a cost of $100

million. The hulls cracked when the boats went to sea, and the engines didn't work properly. Coast Guard engineers rang the alarm bells about what they saw as a faulty design for the modified ships, but to no avail. Coast Guard engineer Chris Cleary pointed out at the time that "you could have buckling of the structure of the ship" under the planned approach. But Bollinger Shipyards, the contractor chosen by Lockheed Martin and Northrop Grumman to do the renovations, claimed otherwise.

As the development of the modified boats moved forward, each step could have been seen as part of a rich comedy of errors, if so much had not been at stake. After cracks appeared in the hull of the first ship, Bollinger tried to make a quick fix by attaching what *New York Times* reporter Eric Lipton described as "giant steel straps that looked like Band-Aids" to the sides of the ship. This desperate effort to repair the damage didn't work, and when additional problems plagued each of the first eight boats, the project was scratched.

With the plan for modified patrol boats in tatters, the Coast Guard and the contractors decided to accelerate work on the next largest boat in the proposed new fleet, a 147-foot ship known as the Fast Response Cutter. As with the modification of the patrol boats, design problems and cost issues soon emerged. When the first boat couldn't even pass a simple test that involved placing it in a water tank, the project was put on hold. A major part of the problem appeared to be self-dealing on the part of Northrop Grumman. The company advocated for the use of hulls made from nonmetal, composite materials. This approach had never been tried before on a ship that large. A former Northrop Grumman executive claimed that part of the company's rationale for going that route was that it had just built a new, state-of-the-art composite manufacturing facility in Gulfport, Mississippi, and the company wanted to steer some business to it. A former Northrop Grumman official acknowledged as much, saying that "it was a pure business decision. . . . And it was the wrong one."

Finally, the project moved to the National Security Cutter, the largest ship ever developed by the Coast Guard. Although an initial boat was launched at a cost of $564 million, Coast Guard engineers again had serious concerns about everything from hull cracks to an actual collapse of the hull. These problems prompted a letter from Rear Admiral Errol Brown to the director of the Deepwater program in which he cited "problems with the structural design . . . [that] compromise the safety and viability of the hull."

In addition to signing off on the flawed design in the first place, Lockheed Martin compounded the problems with the National Security Cutter by attempting to insert computerized consoles that it had originally designed for a navy aircraft carrier. The consoles didn't fit and had to be ripped out, all at taxpayer expense.

All of these problems finally grabbed the attention of Congress, and in May 2005 the Deepwater program's budget was cut in half by the House Appropriations Committee. This was when the Coast Guard's "investment" in the lobbying power of Lockheed Martin and Northrop Grumman paid off. The companies put on a full-court press on behalf of increased Deepwater funding. The lobbying campaign was coordinated with members from key states where elements of the system were being built, including Senator Olympia Snowe (R-ME), Representative Frank Lobiondo (R-NJ), Representative Gene Taylor (D-MI), and Mississippi's two powerful senators, Thad Cochran and Trent Lott. All of these members of Congress were part of the seventy-five-strong Congressional Coast Guard Caucus. For their part, the companies ran ads in D.C. newspapers and helped spark a letter-writing and lobbying campaign by the Navy League—an association of retired Navy personnel funded in part by Lockheed Martin and Northrop Grumman. Campaign contributions also helped grease the wheels. For example, Representative Lobiondo of New Jersey had the National Coast Guard Training Center in his district and a Lockheed Martin testing center for Deepwater just outside of it. He was also among the largest recipients of campaign contributions from the company.[73]

In the end the lobbying campaign carried the day. Not only was Deepwater funding not cut, it was actually increased to about $1 billion per year. This was enough to pay for the escalation of total program costs from $17 billion to $24 billion. But the companies did receive an embarrassing setback in April 2007 when the Coast Guard took back management of Deepwater from Lockheed Martin and Northrop Grumman. While the companies would still play a "major role" in the program, according to Coast Guard commandant Admiral Thad W. Allen, they would no longer be involved in major decisions like choosing ship designs. As a result of this change, the Coast Guard sought out less exotic, already proven designs like the Dutch Damen 4708. The first boats are expected to be ready for launch by 2011, ten years after the 9/11 attacks that prompted the Coast Guard modernization effort in the first place. Deepwater was one of the greatest management failures in the history of the Lockheed Martin Corporation.[74]

Lockheed has a chance to redeem itself through another shipbuilding project, the Littoral Combat Ship (LCS), a vessel that will be designed to operate in offshore waters and to deal with "asymmetric threats" such as pirates, drug runners, terrorists, and small attack boats. After costs on early versions of the ship more than tripled, Secretary of Defense Robert Gates restructured the program to create a competition between Lockheed Martin and Northrop Grumman to win the rights to build the next ten ships. A decision could be made as early as July 2010, and the winning company could gain $7 billion to $10 billion in new revenue.[75]

Deepwater isn't Lockheed Martin's only project concerned with domestic security. As the eighth-largest contractor for the Department of Homeland Security, Lockheed Martin has a number of other key projects funded by the agency.

Some of Lockheed Martin's biggest awards from the Homeland Security Department have involved the provision of services for airport screening carried out by the Transportation Security Agency (TSA). The company has provided everything from devices to scan for explosives to training and recruitment of the screeners themselves, under a $1.2 billion, seven-year contract. The employee screening and recruitment contract drew fire from public employee unions—and even from presidential candidate Barack Obama—for being awarded without letting existing government employees compete for the work. But no one was suggesting that the contract be rescinded, and as of this writing Lockheed Martin's work on it continues.[76]

One of the most intrusive projects that the company has undertaken is its work for the FBI on biometric technology. This involves everything from scanning the iris of a target individual to using facial recognition software to employing advanced techniques for obtaining fingerprints and DNA samples. Company literature focuses on the positive aspects of using biometrics—quicker movement through airport lines, identifying perpetrators of crimes, facilitating background checks, and matching biometric information with intelligence databases to find potential terror suspects. The privacy implications of making everyone's personal data an "open book" is glossed over—in fact, it's not mentioned at all—in Lockheed Martin's public relations materials. The following passage from the company's website is indicative of that attitude: "Thanks to biometric technology, people don't have to worry about forgetting a password or carrying multiple forms of identification. Things just got a little bit easier." No fuss, no muss—but also little or no privacy.

As with its involvement in space technology and missile defense, Lockheed Martin has multiple projects in biometrics. For example, it is the lead systems integrator for the Transportation Worker Identification Credential (TWIC), which will "enroll and credential" maritime workers with regular access to seaports. The company is also the main contractor for the First Responder Authentication Credential (FRAC), which helps verify the identities of police, firefighters, and medical personnel and—if it works as advertised—"quickly route them to where they're most needed at an incident site." Lockheed Martin is also developing a Verified Identity Pass (VIP) that will give certain individuals special treatment in passing through airport screening processes. And last but not least is the Integrated Automated Fingerprint Identification System (IAFIS), which maintains a database of 55 million fingerprints for the FBI.

The same company that keeps track of your fingerprints is involved in processing your tax forms and counting you and your neighbors for the U.S. census. Lockheed Martin's IRS work includes developing an automated system for preparing and storing tax notices; creating a system that maintains comprehensive data on all taxpayer interactions with the IRS, from paper submissions to phone calls to face-to-face contacts; running the IRS's "e-Services" process that allows electronic tax filing, as well as helping to facilitate communications between tax preparers and accountants; helping produce tax forms and manuals; and providing "subject matter experts" to support IRS staff.[77] And in March 2009, the company won a contract for something called the Integrated Customer Communications Environment (ICCE), a fancy name for new Internet and voice-mail systems to "allow taxpayers to place toll free calls to the IRS . . . to resolve basic to complex IRS account information without human intervention." Or as one critic put it, Lockheed Martin is "maintaining the IRS's proud record of never having any sort of actual human interaction with taxpayers."

There's no question that the IRS's antiquated systems needed an upgrade. The question is whether one company should be entrusted with so much of that process, including the handling and processing of sensitive data on individual taxpayers.

How many people are there in the United States? Lockheed Martin is on the case. In addition to its technology support for the year 2000 census, the company has expanded its role via a six-year, $500 million contract with the Census Bureau that was awarded in 2005. Under the contract, the company will develop the Decennial Response Integration System (DRIS), a complex service that will allow people to answer census questions over the Internet. The system will also gather information that comes from traditional paper forms and telephone calls. "It's like a big catch net, capturing all the data coming in no matter where it comes from," according to Associate Director for the 2010 Census Preston J. Waite. The work is carried out at two Lockheed Martin facilities—one in Baltimore, Maryland, and one in Phoenix, Arizona—and at a Census Bureau–owned site in Jeffersonville, Indiana. At the height of the census, each center would receive about eighteen tractor-trailer loads of mail per day, according to Lockheed Martin program manager Julie Dunlap.[78]

This is the first time that one company has served as the one and only central contractor involved in all aspects of compiling and standardizing census data. Lockheed Martin has provided similar census data services to Canada and the United Kingdom.[79]

The company highlighted its role in the census in a short educational video designed to encourage participation in the survey. The video features Lockheed Martin employees in matching polo shirts doing everything from processing data at banks of computer terminals to overseeing the printing of census forms. The film stresses their efforts to produce an "accurate portrait of America" that will be used in "determining our Congressional representation and the allocation of federal funds to improve and secure our way of life." All of this will be done in a fashion that will "assure security and privacy," the video goes on to note. It ends with the slogan "Counting Everyone, Because Everyone Counts," then fades to the Lockheed Martin corporate logo with its motto, "We Never Forget Who We're Working For." Whether the world's largest defense contractor should be working on the census is a question that has yet to be asked in Congress or the executive branch.[80]

While they're at it, Lockheed Martin is helping to sort your mail. The company's Distribution Technologies Unit in Owego, New York, has provided automated handling technology to the U.S. Postal Service (USPS) since 1995, most recently under a 2006 contract to provide cameras that can read both bar codes and addresses on packages to help sort them "without human intervention," in the words of Lockheed Martin VP Bruce Tanton.

The company's biggest USPS contract of all—an effort worth as much as $3 billion to $6 billion over eighteen years to provide all of the data, voice, and wireless services for the agency—was canceled in mid-2006. The awarding of the contract to Lockheed Martin was a surprise in the first place, given that it had sold off its telecommunications company four years earlier. Although the postal service was fairly circumspect in its explanation of why it dropped Lockheed Martin from the most lucrative USPS contract ever, market research analyst Ray Bjorkland of Federal Services, Inc., noted that, while the company "has a great track record with USPS for its mail handling systems," it "obviously screwed up on the telecom stuff." The lost contract may be a case of overreach, a phenomenon to be watched for as Lockheed Martin pushes into almost every aspect of products and services for the U.S. government.[81]

Lockheed Martin also couldn't get the job done when it tried to put security cameras in the New York City subways. Under a $212 million contract, the company was supposed to install over one thousand security cameras and three thousand motion sensors in subway stations throughout the city. But after four years of work, the company had yet to finish installing the cameras, and none of them worked as planned. Among other things, the cameras could not perform the promised task of identifying suspicious packages sitting on subway platforms. The Metropolitan Transit Agency (MTA)—the body responsible for operating the New York subways—finally fired Lockheed Martin in June 2009. In the meantime, the company had sued the MTA for $137 million, claiming that it wasn't allowed access to key subway tunnels needed to finish the job. The MTA countersued, arguing that Lockheed Martin was responsible for any delays in the installation of the system. As of this writing, neither of the lawsuits had been resolved.

At least one MTA official suggested that it bore partial responsibility for Lockheed Martin's failure, noting that "any IT [information technology] person will tell you that a contract like this could not have been done in the time allotted. They couldn't do it in three years."[82]

A detailed accounting of all of Lockheed Martin's government contracts could fill several large volumes. Suffice it to say that they are involved at one level or another in nearly everything the federal government does, from providing instruments of death and destruction to collecting taxes and recruiting spies. Even listing the government and quasi-governmental agencies the company has contracts with is a daunting task: the Department of Agriculture, the Bureau of Land Management, the Census Bureau, the Centers for Disease Control, the Coast Guard, the Department of Defense (including the Army, Navy, Air Force, and Missile Defense Agency), the Department of Education, the Department of Energy, the Environmental Protection Agency, the Federal Aviation Administration, the Federal Bureau of Investigation, the Federal Technology Department, the Food and Drug Administration, the General Services Administration, the Geological Survey, the Department of Homeland Security, the Bureau of Indian Affairs, the Internal Revenue Service, the National Aeronautics and Space Administration, the National Institutes of Health, the Social Security Administration, the Department of State, the U.S. Customs Service, the U.S. Postal Service, the Transportation Security

Agency, and the Department of Veterans Affairs. With this impressive array of clients—not to mention state and local governments, scores of foreign governments, and even the United Nations—the loss of any one deal will have minimal impact on the company as a whole. In the context of its overall business, temporary setbacks or cancellations in programs like the F-22 combat aircraft, the Airborne Laser system, or the Orion space vehicle are minor glitches. The company is nothing if not resilient.[83]

Part of that resilience is the company's ability to make adjustments on the fly, subtracting as well as adding areas of business in line with its emerging strategy. In keeping with this approach, the company announced in June 2010 that it planned to divest itself of its PAE unit, the linchpin of its efforts to profit from "soft power" activities in Africa and elsewhere. The rationale, according to the company's announcement, was that PAE had failed to serve as an "entry point" into other types of business—most notably information technology and systems integration.[84] Central PAE activities such as building bases, training military forces, and helping to build civil justice systems were not seen as lucrative enough if the clients for those services did not also buy other products from Lockheed Martin.

Another rationale for the proposed PAE divestiture no doubt had to do with the company's need to put attention to shoring up its core businesses by mending fences with the Pentagon, which continues to raise questions about Lockheed Martin's handling of the F-35 combat aircraft program.

But this is not to suggest that Lockheed is going to return to the days when it was almost entirely a builder of fighter planes, transport aircraft, and long-range missiles. For example, shortly after the company revealed its plans to unload PAE, it was announced that it would be receiving a $5 billion contract to provide logistics services to the U.S. Special Forces in support of their deployment to Afghanistan and other areas of current or potential conflict. The new contract will more than offset any business forgone due to the sale of PAE. The company is also getting a foothold in the lucrative market for unmanned aerial vehicles (UAVs), first off with the Persistent Threat Detection System, a blimp loaded up with cameras and sensors that can hover over an area and do surveillance without putting a pilot at risk.[85] Lockheed Martin is also the producer of the RQ-170, an unmanned surveillance vehicle that has been dubbed "the beast of Kandahar" because it has been seen hovering over that region of Afghanistan.[86]

What does this all add up to? Well, for one, it raises the question of whether one company should be entrusted with all of the power and influence described in this book. That is a question for the public and the Congress to decide, but in doing so they should take into account a statement by Lockheed Martin CEO Robert Stevens in a 2004 interview with the *New York Times*. He was far from modest in his assessment. "I don't take this lightly," said Stevens. "Our industry has contributed to a change in humankind."[87] The balance between positive and negative change remains to be seen and requires close monitoring of the company's far-flung activities. As President Dwight D. Eisenhower said, the only way to ensure against abuses by the military-industrial complex is to have "an alert and engaged citizenry." This is even truer now that the military-industrial complex has made the leap into the information age—to the point where the defense industry may eventually make as much from surveillance and services as it does from weapons of war. As one veteran journalist put it, "If I had to choose a candidate for Big Brother, I would choose Lockheed Martin."

If there was ever a need for the engagement and awareness urged by President Eisenhower, the Lockheed Martin story makes it clear that the time is now.

Acknowledgments

This book is the product of years of work, much of which occurred well before I received a book contract and finally sat down to write it. For that reason, it is impossible to thank everyone who was of help along the way. My apologies to anyone I have overlooked.

First, I want to thank my agent, Anna Ghosh, for convincing me to do this book in the first place and for keeping me on track during my moments of doubt along the way. My editor, Carl Bromley at Nation Books, did an excellent job as usual and is a pleasure to work with.

My colleague Frida Berrigan at the New America Foundation was an invaluable source of support, from giving me feedback on the manuscript to being a generally positive force. And I would like to thank the New America Foundation for serving as my institutional home during the writing of this book. It is an inspiration to work at an organization with so many talented people who have written so many important books. Our President and CEO, Steve Coll, and the head of our American Strategy Program, Steve Clemons, have done a tremendous job of creating an environment that makes it possible to undertake this kind of project.

I started thinking about this book in earnest while working at the World Policy Institute at the New School and did some of the writing that found its way into the book in the *World Policy Journal*. I am thankful to the editors I worked with at the journal, including the late James Chace and Sherle Schwenninger. The prodigious research by my former institute colleague Michelle Ciarrocca on the politics of missile defense is reflected here.

I have also done a number of articles for *The Nation* magazine that served as building blocks for key sections of this book, and I would like to thank my editors there, particularly Karen Rothmyer and Katrina vanden Heuvel. Jennifer Washburn was my co-author on a cover story for the magazine on Lockheed Martin's foray into the field of social services, and I thank her for helping me to get a handle on that aspect of the company's operations.

I received invaluable help from research librarians at Columbia University and the Library of Congress, and I am in their debt.

Thanks to Danielle Brian, Scott Amey, and Peter Stockton at the Project on Government Oversight (POGO) for sharing their insights and their library. My friends Jim Cason and Lora Lumpe were extremely supportive, and my conversations with them about the book helped me focus on what was most important.

I especially want to thank David Gold and Gordon Adams for helping me get into this line of work in the first place by hiring me to do my first research job in this field more than a few years back.

Although the sole financing for this book has come from my publisher, Nation Books, I would also like to thank the foundations and individuals who have funded my broader work on nuclear policy and military spending over the years: the Colombe Foundation, the Educational Foundation of America, the Janelia Foundation, the Ploughshares Fund, the Samuel Rubin Foundation, the Stewart Mott Fund, Cynda Arsenault, Ben Cohen, Alan Kligerman, and Mary Van Evera.

Most of all, I could not have done this without the love and support of my wife, Audrey Waysse, and our daughter, Emma Waysse Hartung.

Notes

CHAPTER 1: THE RISE AND FALL OF THE RAPTOR

1. R. Jeffrey Smith, "Premier U.S. Fighter Jet Has Major Shortcomings," *Washington Post*, July 10, 2009.

2. F-22 Raptor Team Web Site, www.f22-raptor.com/technology/stealth.html.

3. The letters, dated February 20, 2009, were posted at the website www.preserve raptorjobs.com and have since been taken down (copies in possession of the author).

4. Jodi Rell et al., letter to President Barack Obama, February 20, 2009.

5. For a detailed analysis of the jobs generated by the F-22 program, see William D. Hartung, "Military Spending and Employment: The Case of the F-22," February 23, 2009, New America Foundation, http://www.newamerica.net/publications/policy/military_spending_and_employment_case_f_22.

6. Ken Dilanian and Tom Vanden Brook, "Raptor in Dogfight for Its Future," *USA Today*, February 25, 2009.

7. Lockheed Martin Corporation, 2008 annual report, form 10K, p. 4.

8. Robert Pollin and Heidi Garrett-Peltier, "The U.S. Employment Effects of Military and Domestic Spending Priorities" (October 2007), University of Massachusetts Political Economy Research Institute (PERI) and Institute for Policy Studies.

9. "Lockheed's F-22 at Center of Congress Battle; Funding for Advanced Fighter Faces Some Enemies in House," *Orlando Sentinel*, September 12, 1999.

10. Juliet Eilperin, "F-22's Future Stalls as Last-Minute Bartering Begins," *Washington Post*, September 23, 1999.

11. John Mintz, "After House Setback, Lockheed Scrambles to Save F-22," *Washington Post*, September 12, 1999.

12. Richard Whittle, "Fierce Lobbying Aims to Save F-22; Lockheed, Air Force Enlist Help to Try to Get Fighter's Funding Restored," *Dallas Morning News*, September 9, 1999.

13. Ibid.

14. Ibid.

15. Ibid.

16. Jerry Lewis and Jack Murtha, "Why the F-22 Fighter Plan Doesn't Fly," *Washington Post*, August 2, 1999.

17. Don Melvin, "F-22 a High-Tech—and Costly—Lethal Weapon," *Atlanta Journal-Constitution*, February 2, 1997.

18. Steven M. Kosiak, "Funding for Defense, Homeland Security, and Combating Terrorism Since 9/11: Where Has All the Money Gone?" in Security Policy Working Group, *Security After 9/11: Strategy Choices and Budget Tradeoffs* (January 2003), p. 10; and International Institute for Strategic Studies, *The Military Balance 2002–2003* (London: Oxford University Press, October 2002), pp. 332–337.

19. Anne Marie Squeo and Andy Pasztor, "Pentagon's Budget Becomes Bulletproof," *Wall Street Journal*, October 15, 2001.

20. Secretary of Defense Robert Gates, "DoD News Briefing with Secretary Gates from the Pentagon," April 6, 2009.

21. Ibid.

22. Elizabeth Bumiller and Christopher Drew, "Military Budget Reflects a Change in U.S. Strategy," *New York Times*, April 7, 2009; Bob Keefe and Dan Chapman, "F-22 Fight on Horizon: Administration Plan to End Production Has Georgia, Much of Congress Furious," *Atlanta Journal-Constitution*, April 12, 2009; Bob Keefe, "Georgia Lawmakers: Don't Waste Money on Swine Flu Vaccine," *Atlanta Journal-Constitution*, May 8, 2009.

23. Elizabeth Bumiller and Christopher Drew, "Gates's Cuts to an Array of Weapons Systems Brings a Fight," *New York Times*, April 7, 2009.

24. Bob Cox, "Lockheed Martin No Longer Lobbying Against Defense Secretary's Decision on F-22," *Fort Worth Star-Telegram*, April 22, 2009.

25. Dan Eggen, "Plan to Cut Weapons Programs Disputed; Defense Supporters Say 100,000 Jobs Are in Jeopardy," *Washington Post*, April 28, 2009.

26. Gates, "DoD News Briefing with Secretary Gates from the Pentagon," April 6, 2009.

27. Bryan Bender, "The Dogfight Obama Seems Bound to Lose; Congress Backs F-22 Fighter the Pentagon Doesn't Want," *Boston Globe*, July 12, 2009.

28. Thomas Burr, "Bishop Helps Keep F-22 Production Alive," *Salt Lake Tribune*, June 19, 2009.

29. David Berteau, interview with the author, November 24, 2009.

30. The author played a role in the anti-F-22 effort, mostly by writing articles critical of the aircraft.

31. Defense Secretary Robert Gates, speech to the Economic Club of Chicago, July 16, 2009.

32. Ibid.

33. Ibid.

34. *Congressional Record*, 111th Cong., 1st sess., p. S7724.

35. Ibid., p. S7726.

36. Ibid., p. S7728.

37. "Inouye Earmarks Beneficial to Hawaii," *Honolulu Advisor*, August 23, 2009.

38. "Inouye, Cochran Benefit from Earmark Recipients," Taxpayers for Common Sense, August 23, 2009.

39. Lockheed Martin, "Lockheed Looks to Ocean as Global Energy Source," *The Monitor* (Fall 2009), p. 1; Kate Galbraith, "Creating Energy from the Deep," *New York Times*, April 30, 2009; Lockheed Martin, "Lockheed Martin Creates 30 New Jobs in Hawaii to Support THAAD Missile Testing" (press release), April 20, 2006; "Lockheed Martin Opens Facility in Honolulu," *Reliable Plant Magazine* (May 6, 2006).

40. *Congressional Record*, 111th Cong., 1st sess., p. S7731.

41. Ibid., p. S7740.

42. Laura M. Holson, "U.S. Military Contractors Set to Begin Rare Experiment in Cooperation," *New York Times*, December 17, 2001.

43. Jerry Knight, "Sorting Out Winners in the War on Terrorism," *Washington Post*, October 29, 2001.

44. Leslie Wayne, "Painting a Rosy Picture of a Costly Fighter Jet," *New York Times*, June 22, 2007.

45. Philip Shenon, "Jet Makers Prepare Bids for a Rich Pentagon Prize," *New York Times*, March 12, 1996.

46. Leslie Wayne, "One Fighter, 11 Nations and Building Problems," *New York Times*, July 22, 2004.

47. Greg Schneider, "Lockheed Martin Beats Boeing for Fighter Contract," *Washington Post*, October 27, 2001.

48. Ibid.

49. Norman Augustine, *Augustine's Laws: An Irreverent Guide to Traps, Puzzles, and Quandaries of the Defense Business and Other Complex Undertakings* (New York: American Institute of Aeronautics and Astronomics, 1983), p. 55.

50. "British Aerospace Joins Lockheed in Plane Project," *New York Times*, June 19, 1997.

51. Ibid.

52. Schneider, "Lockheed Beats Boeing for Fighter Contract."

53. Laura M. Holson, "Winning Jet Contract Is a Boon to Lockheed," *New York Times*, October 28, 2001.

54. Schneider, "Lockheed Beats Boeing for Fighter Contract."

55. Leslie Wayne, "One Fighter, 11 Nations, and Building Problems," *New York Times*, July 22, 2004.

56. Leslie Wayne, "Painting a Rosy Picture of a Costly Fighter Jet," *New York Times*, June 22, 2007.

57. Christopher Drew, "U.S. May Add Money to Program for F-35 Jet," *New York Times*, November 21, 2009.

58. U.S. Government Accountability Office, "Joint Strike Fighter: Accelerating Procurement Before Completing Development Increases the Government's Financial Risk," GAO-09–303, executive summary.

59. Christopher Drew and Thom Shanker, "Gates Shakes Up Leadership for F-35," *New York Times*, February 2, 2010.

60. Loren B. Thompson, "The F-35 Will Cost About What an F-16 Costs," Lexington Institute, April 13, 2010.

61. Bob Keefe, "Lockheed Weathers F-22's Demise," *Atlanta Journal Constitution*, April 26, 2009.

62. "Inouye: F-22 Might Still Be Sold Abroad," September 17, 2009, The Cable, http://thecable.foreignpolicy.com; Andrea Shalal-Esa, "Cost of F-22 to Japan as Much as $250 Million," Reuters, June 5, 2009; Andrea Shalal-Esa, "U.S. Sees Big Obstacles to F-22 Exports," Reuters, June 11, 2009.

63. David Berteau, interview with the author, November 24, 2009.

64. Gates, speech to the Economic Club of Chicago, July 16, 2009.

65. Peter Baker, "Helicopter Plan Is Excessive, Obama and McCain Agree," *New York Times*, February 23, 2009.

66. Leslie Wayne, "The Other '04 Race: Building Copter for Presidents," *New York Times*, July 11, 2004.

67. Ibid.

68. Anthony Capaccio, "Presidential Helicopter Report Cites Miscommunication," Bloomberg.com, March 24, 2009.

69. Berteau, interview with the author, November 24, 2009.

70. Gates, speech to the Economic Club of Chicago, July 16, 2009.

71. Berteau, interview with the author, November 24, 2009.

72. Figures are as of fiscal year 2008, the most recent year for which full statistics are available. They are taken from FedSpending.org, a database maintained by OMB Watch.

CHAPTER 2: FROM LOUGHEAD TO LOCKHEED

1. "Allan Lockheed, Aviation Pioneer—Co-founder of Aerospace Giant Is Dead at 80," *New York Times*, May 28, 1969.

2. Wayne Biddle, *Barons of the Sky: From Early Flight to Strategic Warfare—The Story of the American Aerospace Industry* (New York: Simon & Schuster, 1981), pp. 327–328; see also biography of Allan Lockheed, National Aviation Hall of Fame, www.nationalaviation.com.

3. Biddle, *Barons of the Sky*, pp. 70–71.

4. Ibid.

5. Walter J. Boyne, *Beyond the Horizons: The Lockheed Story* (New York: St. Martin's Press, 1998), p. 7.

6. Ibid., pp. 9–10.

7. Biddle, *Barons of the Sky*, p. 73.

8. Ibid., p. 74; Boyne, *Beyond the Horizons*, p. 10.

9. Boyne, *Beyond the Horizons*, p. 10; Biddle, *Barons of the Sky*, p. 74.

10. Biddle, *Barons of the Sky*, p. 108.

11. Ibid.

12. Ibid., p. 112.

13. Ibid., p. 113.

14. Ibid., p. 114.

15. Boyne, *Beyond the Horizons*, pp. 15–16.

16. Biddle, *Barons of the Sky*, p. 149.

17. Boyne, *Beyond the Horizons*, p. 35; Biddle, *Barons of the Sky*, p. 155.

18. Boyne, *Beyond the Horizons*, pp. 39–41.

19. Biddle, *Barons of the Sky*, p. 154.

20. Ibid., p. 159.

21. Ibid., pp. 327–328.

22. Ibid., p. 167.

23. Ibid., p. 176.

24. Ibid., p. 177.

25. Robert E. Gross, letter to Courtlandt S. Gross, May 24, 1932.

26. Robert E. Gross, letter to Courtlandt S. Gross, May 12, 1932.

27. Lockheed Aircraft Corporation, listing of receipts between June 1, 1932, and July 31, 1932, from the papers of Robert E. Gross, Library of Congress.

28. Biddle, *Barons of the Sky*, p. 218.

29. Ibid., p. 230.

30. Ibid., p. 226.

31. Ibid., p. 259.

32. Ibid., pp. 258–259.

33. Boyne, *Beyond the Horizons*, p. 72.

34. Biddle, *Barons of the Sky*, p. 224.

35. Robert E. Gross, letter to Courtlandt S. Gross, January 18, 1933.

36. Biddle, *Barons of the Sky*, pp. 202, 224.

37. Ibid., pp. 218–219.

38. Ibid., p. 261.

39. Biddle, *Barons of the Sky*, p. 258.

40. Robert E. Gross, letter to Mr. S. Megata, Okura and Company, August 3, 1937.

41. Robert E. Gross, letter to Mr. Norman Ebin, August 24, 1937.

42. U.S. Senate, Special Committee to Investigate the Manufacture and Sale of Arms and Other War Munitions, Senate Report 994 (hereafter referred to as Nye Committee Report), part 3, February 24, 1936, p. 1.

43. Ibid., p. 3.

44. Ibid., p. 68.

45. Biddle, *Barons of the Sky*, p. 234.

46. Ibid.

47. Nye Committee Report, p. 5.

48. Ibid., p. 9.

49. Ibid., p. 239.

50. Biddle, *Barons of the Sky*, p. 263.

51. Ibid.

52. Anthony Sampson, *The Arms Bazaar: From Lebanon to Lockheed* (New York: Viking Press, 1977), p. 94.

53. George Swayne, letter to Robert E. Gross, March 17, 1939.

54. Ibid.

55. Robert E. Gross, letter to Mr. A. H. Self, Second Deputy Undersecretary of State, Air Ministry, London, March 22, 1939.

56. Ibid.

57. Robert E. Gross, letter to Frederick R. Warburg, Kuhn, Loeb and Company, December 24, 1941.

58. Robert E. Gross, letter to Lawrence C. Ames, March 28, 1939.

59. Biddle, *Barons of the Sky*, p. 260; employment figure from Boyne, *Beyond the Horizons*, p. 100.

60. Biddle, *Barons of the Sky*, p. 286.

61. Ibid.

CHAPTER 3: FROM WAR TO COLD WAR

1. Wayne Biddle, *Barons of the Sky* (New York: Simon & Schuster, 1991), pp. 270–271.

2. Ibid., p. 288.

3. Robert E. Gross, letter to Clayton Crane, November 1, 1946.

4. Robert E. Gross, letter to Edward Stettinius, March 14, 1947.

5. Biddle, *Barons of the Sky*, pp. 289–290.

6. Robert E. Gross, letter to Henry F. Atkinson, May 26, 1947.

7. Robert E. Gross, testimony before Senate Committee Investigating the National Defense Program, Aviation Subcommittee, on "Aircraft Reconversion and America's Airpower Policy," Seattle, Wash., August 24, 1945.

8. Ibid.

9. Ibid.

10. Ibid.

11. Biddle, *Barons of the Sky*, p. 290.

12. Ibid., p. 291.

13. Walter Boyne, *Beyond the Horizons: The Lockheed Story* (New York: St. Martin's Press, 1998), p. 141; "Constellation Flights to Resume in 3 Weeks, Says Gross of Lockheed," *Wall Street Journal*, August 5, 1946.

14. Boyne, *Beyond the Horizons*, p. 138.

15. "Lockheed Says Output of Super Constellations Set Record Last Year," *Wall Street Journal*, January 13, 1955.

16. Robert P. Brundage, "Planes for Peace: Aircraft Manufacturers Chart Service Programs to Entice New Business," *Wall Street Journal*, August 17, 1945.

17. Biddle, *Barons of the Sky*, p. 293.

18. Ibid., p. 295.

19. Ibid.

20. Ibid., pp. 295–296.

21. Ibid., p. 296.

22. "Survival in the Air Age: A Report by the President's Air Policy Commission," Washington, D.C., January 1, 1948, pp. 6–7.

23. Ibid., pp. 32–33.

24. Oliver P. Echols, testimony before Senate Subcommittee on Interstate and Foreign Commerce on the Air Policy Board, Washington, D.C., May 17, 1947, p. 4.

25. Ibid., pp. 4, 6.

26. Robert Gross, testimony before Senate Subcommittee on Interstate and Foreign Commerce on the Air Policy Board, Washington, D.C., May 17, 1947, p. 34.

27. Ibid.

28. Ibid., p. 35.

29. Ibid., p. 36.

30. Ibid.

31. Ibid., p. 38.

32. Ibid., p. 39.

33. Ibid., p. 40.

34. Ibid., p. 41.

35. Ibid., p. 44.

36. Robert E. Gross, "The Air Transport Plane in War and Peace," September 1950 (location and audience not specified).

37. Donald Patillo, *Pushing the Envelope: The American Aircraft Industry* (Ann Arbor: University of Michigan Press, 2001), pp. 151–154.

38. Ben R. Rich and Leo Janos, *Skunk Works* (Boston: Little, Brown and Co., 1994), p. 145.

39. Ibid., p. 111.

40. Boyne, *Beyond the Horizons*, p. 175.

41. Rich and Janos, *Skunk Works*, pp. 107–108.

42. Ibid., pp. 111–112.

43. Ibid., p. 144.

44. Ibid., p. 167.

45. Ibid., p. 164.

46. Ibid., p. 166.

47. Ibid., p. 167.

48. Rear Admiral W. F. Raborn, testimony before House Committee on Science and Astronautics, "Progress of Atlas and Polaris Missiles," Washington, D.C., July 28 and 29, 1959, pp. 153–154.

49. Harvey M. Sapolsky, *The Polaris System Development: Bureaucratic and Programmatic Success in Government* (Cambridge, Mass.: Harvard University Press, 1972), pp. 160–163.

50. Ibid., p. 18.

51. Ibid., pp. 46, 51–52.

52. Jack Raymond, "Undersea Firings of Polaris Missile Beset by Troubles," *New York Times*, April 15, 1961; "Polaris Missile Blown Up in Test," *New York Times*, August 2, 1960.

53. Hanson W. Baldwin, "Accuracy Hailed: Tests Are First Held Underseas—Message Sent to the President," *New York Times*, July 21, 1960.

54. Jack Gould, "TV: The Polaris Story—Step-by-Step History of Missile by Murrow and Friendly on CBS," *New York Times*, October 12, 1960.

55. "In One Big Gulp," *Time*, August 22, 1960.

56. "Lockheed Comes Back," *Time*, March 30, 1962.

57. Ibid.

CHAPTER 4: THE C-5A SCANDAL

1. Berkeley Rice, *The C-5A Scandal: A $5 Billion Boondoggle by the Military-Industrial Complex* (Boston: Houghton Mifflin, 1971), p. 1.

2. William Proxmire, *Report from Wasteland* (New York: Praeger, 1970), p. 49.

3. Rice, *The C-5A Scandal*, pp. 1–2.

4. Ibid., pp. 3–4.

5. Senator William Fulbright, hearings before Joint Economic Committee, Subcommittee on Economy in Government, on "The Military Budget and National Economic Priorities," pt. 1, p. 116, as cited in Rice, *The C-5A Scandal*, p. 4.

6. Hearings before Senate Armed Services Committee on "Military Procurement for Fiscal Year 1970," pt. 2, June 3, 1969, pp. 2007–2028, as cited in Rice, *The C-5A Scandal*, p. 16.

7. *Baltimore News American*, May 7, 1969, as cited in Rice, *The C-5A Scandal*, pp. 12–13.

8. *New York Times*, March 3, 1968, as cited in Rice, *The C-5A Scandal*, p. 14.

9. The company eventually set up a facility in Greenville, South Carolina, responsible for maintenance and modifications on the C-5A and other major Lockheed aircraft programs.

10. Rice, *The C-5A Scandal*, pp. 76–77.

11. Representative L. Mendel Rivers, hearings before House Armed Services Committee on "Military Procurement for Fiscal Year 1970," pt. 2, pp. 3101–3152, as cited in Rice, *The C-5A Scandal*, p. 86.

12. Ibid.

13. A. Ernest Fitzgerald, *The High Priests of Waste* (New York: W. W. Norton and Co., 1972), p. 3.

14. Ibid., pp. 54–55.

15. Rice, *The C-5A Scandal*, p. 25.

16. Ibid., p. 23; Fitzgerald, *The High Priests of Waste*, p. 49.

17. Rice, *The C-5A Scandal*, p. 26.

18. Fitzgerald, *The High Priests of Waste*, p. 3.

19. Ibid., p. 48.

20. Ibid., p. 217.

21. Ibid., pp. 220–221.

22. Ibid., p. 223.

23. Ibid.

24. Ibid., p. 224.

25. Ibid., p. 252.

26. Ibid., p. 256.

27. Ibid., pp. 274–275.

28. Ibid., pp. 230–231, 246.

29. Ibid., p. 273.

30. Ibid., p. 277; Rice, *The C-5A Scandal*, p. 102.

31. Fitzgerald, *The High Priests of Waste*, pp. 271–272; Rice, *The C-5A Scandal*, p. 101; Proxmire, *Report from Wasteland*, p. 47.

32. Hearing before House Committee on Energy and Commerce, Subcommittee on Oversight and Investigations, on "Harassment of Air Force Employees," 99th Cong., 1st sess., November 6, 1985, p. 13.

33. Ibid., p. 322.

34. A. Ernest Fitzgerald, *The Pentagonists: An Insider's View of Waste, Mismanagement, and Fraud in Defense Spending* (Boston: Houghton Mifflin, 1989), pp. 1–3.

35. Rice, *The C-5A Scandal*, p. 78.

36. Ibid., p. 83.

37. Ibid.

38. Hearings before House Government Operations Committee, Subcommittee on Military Operations, on "Government Procurement and Contracting," pt. 4, 91st Cong., 1st sess., p. 1179, as cited in Fitzgerald, *The High Priests of Waste*, p. 253; and Rice, *The C-5A Scandal*, pp. 163–164.

39. *Washington Post*, September 22, 1969, as cited in Rice, *The C-5A Scandal*, pp. 169–170.

40. U.S. Securities and Exchange Commission, *Report of Investigation in Re Lockheed Aircraft Corporation*, HO-423, May 25, 1970, pt. 2, pp. 57–58, as cited in Rice, *The C-5A Scandal*, p. 176.

41. *Washington Post*, August 31, 1969, as cited in Rice, *The C-5A Scandal*, p. 112.

42. U.S. General Accounting Office, *Staff Study on the C-5A Weapon System*, March 1971, p. 43, as cited in Fitzgerald, *The High Priests of Waste*, pp. 305–306.

43. Rice, *The C-5A Scandal*, p. 28.

44. Ibid., p. 155.

45. Fitzgerald, *The High Priests of Waste*, pp. 315–316.

46. Rice, *The C-5A Scandal*, p. 161.

47. Ibid., p. 162.

48. Hearings before the Subcommittee on Economy in Government, Joint Economic Committee on Acquisition of Weapons Systems, pt. 5, September 29, 1971, p. 1280; hereafter referred to as the Durham hearings.

49. Ibid.

50. Fitzgerald, *The High Priests of Waste*, pp. 321–322.

51. Durham hearings, p. 1337.

52. Ibid., pp. 1307–1324.

53. Ibid., pp. 1330–1331.

54. Rice, *The C-5A Scandal*, p. 49.

55. Ibid., p. 50.

56. Ibid., p. 56.

57. Ibid., p. 114.

58. Ibid.

59. Ibid., pp. 125–126.

60. Ibid., p. 134.

61. Ibid., pp. 140–142.

62. Fitzgerald, *The High Priests of Waste*, p. 293.

63. *Washington* Post, May 29, 1970, as cited in Rice, *The C-5A Scandal*, pp. 188–189.

64. Fitzgerald, *The High Priests of Waste*, p. 294.

65. Ibid., p. 295.

CHAPTER 5: BAILOUT: TOO BIG TO FAIL?

1. Richard Kaufman, interview with the author, April 2, 2009.

2. Steve Chapman, "A Cheapskate's Ample Legacy," December 18, 2005, Creator's Syndicate, available at Real Clear Politics, www.realclearpolitics.com.

3. Ibid.

4. Neil Sheehan, "Pentagon Offers Settlement to Lockheed in Money Dispute," *New York Times*, December 31, 1970.

5. A. Ernest Fitzgerald, *The High Priests of Waste* (New York: W. W. Norton and Co., 1972), p. 283.

6. "Lockheed Seeks Pentagon's Help," *New York Times*, March 6, 1970.

7. Neil Sheehan, "Impasse Reported on Lockheed Cost," *New York Times*, January 27, 1971.

8. Richard F. Kaufman, *The War Profiteers* (New York: Bobbs-Merrill, 1970), p. 225.

9. Neil Sheehan, "Pentagon Offers a Settlement to Lockheed in Money Dispute," *New York Times*, December 31, 1970.

10. Hearings before Senate Committee on Banking and Urban Affairs on "Emergency Loan Guarantee Legislation," pt. 1, Washington, D.C., June 7–16, 1971, p. 31.

11. Ibid., p. 35.

12. Peter Stockton, interview with the author, March 10, 2009; A. Ernest Fitzgerald, *The Pentagonists: An Insider's View of Mismanagement and Fraud in Defense Spending* (Boston: Houghton Mifflin, 1989), p. 8.

13. Robert B. Semple Jr., "Future Defense Contracts to Be Awarded in Stages," *New York Times*, July 28, 1970.

14. Gene Smith, "Lockheed Shows 'a New Kind' of Combat Aircraft; Decision Pending Intricate Turns," *New York Times*, December 13, 1967.

15. Kaufman, *The War Profiteers*, p. 71.

16. Robert H. Phelps, "Ex-Military Men Gain in Industry," *New York Times*, March 23, 1969.

17. Berkeley Rice, "C-5A + L-1011 = Lockheed's Financial Crisis: What Price Lockheed," *New York Times,* May 9, 1971.

18. Ibid.

19. Ibid.

20. Ibid.

21. Richard Severo, "John Connally of Texas, a Power in 2 Political Parties, Dies at 76," *New York Times*, June 16, 1993.

22. Ibid.

23. Ibid.

24. Richard Witkin, "Lockheed's Need of Loans Is Cited," *New York Times,* April 28, 1971.

25. Richard Witkin, "Humphrey Backs Loan to Lockheed," *New York Times,* April 24, 1971.

26. Eileen Shanahan, "Haughton Defends Role at Lockheed," *New York Times*, June 12, 1971.

27. Hearings before Senate Committee on Banking and Urban Affairs on "Emergency Loan Guarantee Legislation," pt. 1, Washington, D.C., June 7–16, 1971, p. 22.

28. Ibid., p. 24.

29. John W. Finney, "President Urges Prompt Passage of Lockheed Aid," *New York Times*, July 25, 1971.

30. *Congressional Record–Senate*, August 2, 1971, p. 28743.

31. Ibid., pp. 28743–28744.

32. Ibid., p. 28745.

33. Ibid.

34. Ibid., pp. 28759–28760.

35. Ibid., p. 28760.

36. Ibid., pp. 28761–28762.

37. David E. Rosenbaum, "Lockheed Vote Was the Center of Battle of Lobbyists," *New York Times*, August 8, 1971.

38. University of Virginia, Miller Center, Presidential Recordings Program, Conversation 007–046, August 2, 1971, 12:04–12:09 P.M.

39. *Congressional Record–Senate*, August 2, 1971, p. 28767.

40. Ibid., p. 28774.

41. Ibid., p. 28781.

42. Rosenbaum, "Lockheed Vote Was the Center of Battle of Lobbyists."

43. *Congressional Record–Senate*, August 2, 1971, p. 28782.

CHAPTER 6: BRIBERY

1. Hearings before Senate Subcommittee on Multinational Corporations on "Multinational Corporations and U.S. Foreign Policy—Lockheed Aircraft Corporation," pt. 14, February 4, 1976, pp. 1, 1–14.

2. Anthony Sampson, *The Arms Bazaar: From Lebanon to Lockheed* (New York: Viking Press, 1977), pp. 231–233.

3. Ibid., p. 226.

4. Ibid., pp. 226–228.

5. "The Widow Maker," *Time*, November 10, 1975.

6. Sampson, *The Arms Bazaar*, pp. 232–233.

7. Ibid., p. 233.

8. Hearings before Senate Committee on Banking, Housing, and Urban Affairs, on "Lockheed Bribery," August 25, 1975, pp. 29–30.

9. Sampson, *The Arms Bazaar*, p. 236.

10. Ibid., pp. 236–237.

11. Robert Lindsey, "Kotchian Calls Himself the Scapegoat," *New York Times*, July 3, 1977.

12. Sampson, *The Arms Bazaar*, p. 127.

13. Ibid., p. 130.

14. Ibid., p. 129.

15. Ibid., p. 120.

16. Ibid.

17. Hearings before Senate Subcommittee on Multinational Corporations on "Multinational Corporations and U.S. Foreign Policy—Lockheed Aircraft Corporation," pt. 14, February 4, 1976, p. 349; "Dutch Officials Name Bernhard in Bribery Case," *New York Times*, February 9, 1976; Sampson, *The Arms Bazaar*, p. 139.

18. Sampson, *The Arms Bazaar*, pp. 138–139.

19. Ibid.

20. Ibid., p. 144.

21. Hearings before Senate Subcommittee on Multinational Corporations on "Multinational Corporations and U.S. Foreign Policy—Lockheed Aircraft Corporation," pt. 14, p. 23; Sampson, *The Arms Bazaar*, p. 136.

22. Hearings before Senate Subcommittee on Multinational Corporations on "Multinational Corporations and U.S. Foreign Policy—Lockheed Aircraft Corporation," pt. 14, pp. 23–24.

23. Ibid., pp. 29–31.

24. Sampson, *The Arms Bazaar*, p. 136; hearings before Senate Subcommittee on Multinational Corporations on "Multinational Corporations and U.S. Foreign Policy—Lockheed Aircraft Corporation," pt. 14, p. 26.

25. Hearings before Senate Subcommittee on Multinational Corporations on "Multinational Corporations and U.S. Foreign Policy—Lockheed Aircraft Corporation," pt. 14, p. 25.

26. W. G. Myers, memo for file, June 8, 1965, reproduced in ibid., pt. 12, p. 938.

27. D. D. Stone, memo for file, November 15, 1965; P. F. Dobbins and T. J. Cleland, Lockheed-Georgia, memo to R. I. Mitchell, May 14, 1971; both in ibid., pp. 954, 984.

28. P. F. Dobbins and T. J. Cleland, memo to R. I. Mitchell, May 14, 1971; R. I. Mitchell, memo to P. F. Dobbins and T. J. Cleland, May 26, 1971; both in ibid., pp. 984, 986.

29. Sampson, *The Arms Bazaar*, p. 190.

30. Ibid., pp. 194–195.

31. Robert M. Smith, "Lockheed Documents Disclose a $106 Million Payout," *New York Times*, September 13, 1975; "Businessman Adnan Khashoggi's High-Flying Realm," *Time*, January 19, 1987.

32. "Businessman Adnan Khashoggi's High-Flying Realm."

33. Hearings before Senate Committee on Banking, Housing, and Urban Affairs, on "Lockheed Bribery," August 25, 1975, pp. 28–29; hearings before Senate Subcommittee on Multinational Corporations on "Multinational Corporations and U.S. Foreign Policy—Lockheed Aircraft Corporation," pt. 12, p. 1088.

34. A. H. Kaplan, memo for file, August 15, 1968, in hearings before Senate Subcommittee on Multinational Corporations on "Multinational Corporations and U.S. Foreign Policy—Lockheed Aircraft Corporation," pt. 12, p. 1024.

35. Sampson, *The Arms Bazaar*, pp. 195–197.

36. Ibid., p. 200.

37. Ibid., pp. 200–201.

38. Robert M. Smith, "Simon Criticizes Lockheed for Obscurity on Bribery," *New York Times*, August 26, 1975.

39. Sampson, *The Arms Bazaar*, p. 276.

40. Richard Halloran, "Japanese Raid Lockheed and Others in Bribe Case," *New York Times*, February 24, 1976.

41. Ibid.

42. "Tanaka Indicted on Bribe Charge in Lockheed Case," *New York Times*, August 17, 1976.

43. Steve Lohr, "Tanaka Is Guilty in Bribery Trial," *New York Times*, October 12, 1983.

44. Paul Kemezis, "'No Problems,' Bernhard Says of Bribery Case," *New York Times*, February 15, 1976; Bernard Weinraub, "Dutch Prince Quits Posts as Inquiry Board Assails His Links with Lockheed," *New York Times*, August 27, 1976.

45. Richard Witkin, "Lockheed Heads Expected to Quit in Bribe Scandal," *New York Times*, February 12, 1976.

46. Robert Lindsey, "Kotchian Calls Himself the Scapegoat," *New York Times*, July 3, 1977.

47. Ibid.

CHAPTER 7: REAGAN TO THE RESCUE

1. U.S. Department of Defense, *National Defense Budget Estimates for FY 2010*, June 2009, pp. 185–186.

2. Anne Hessing Cahn, *Killing Détente: The Right Attacks the CIA* (University Park: Pennsylvania State University Press, 1998), p. 28.

3. Frances Fitzgerald, *Way Out There in the Blue: Reagan, Star Wars, and the End of the Cold War* (New York: Simon & Schuster, 2000), pp. 83–84.

4. Ibid., pp. 50–51.

5. Arthur Macy Cox, "Why the U.S., Since 1977, Has Been Misperceiving Soviet Military Strength," *New York Times*, October 20, 1980; Cahn, *Killing Détente*, pp. 132–137.

6. U.S. Department of Defense, *National Defense Budget Estimates for FY 2010*, p. 185.

7. U.S. Department of Defense, "100 Companies Receiving the Largest Dollar Volume of Prime Contract Awards (Top 100)," FY 1980–FY 1984 editions.

8. Dina Rasor, *The Pentagon Underground: Hidden Patriots Fighting Against Deceit and Fraud in America's Defense Program* (New York: Times Books, 1985), p. 160.

9. Ibid., p. 161.

10. Ibid., p. 162.

11. Ibid., pp. 163–164.

12. Ibid., pp. 164–165.

13. Ibid., pp. 148–149.

14. Ibid., pp. 149–150.

15. Ibid., p. 150.

16. Hearing before House Committee on Energy and Commerce, Subcommittee on Oversight and Investigations, on "Harassment of Air Force Employees," November 6, 1985, p. 304.

17. Ibid., p. 159.

18. Ibid., p. 170.

19. Wayne Biddle, "Price of Toilet Seat Is Cut for Navy," *New York Times*, February 6, 1985.

20. Richard C. Gross, "Head Covering Drops $540 in Cost," United Press International, February 5, 1985.

21. Biddle, "Price of Toilet Seat Is Cut for Navy," n. 17.

22. Ibid.

23. Michael Weisskopf, "Firm Backs $544 Price on Toilet Seat Covers; No Outside Bids Received," *Washington Post*, November 27, 1985.

24. Gregory Gordon, "Lockheed Overstated Effort to Cut Toilet Assembly Costs," United Press International, February 18, 1986.

25. Timothy Bannon, "Air Force Can Make Own Toilet Pans, but Pays $300 Instead," United Press International, February 2, 1986.

26. A. Ernest Fitzgerald, *The Pentagonists: An Insider's View of Waste, Mismanagement, and Fraud in Defense Spending* (Boston: Houghton Mifflin, 1989), p. 218.

27. Bannon, "Air Force Can Make Own Toilet Pans, but Pays $300 Instead."

28. "Lockheed President Responds to Parts Controversy," *Aviation Week and Space Technology*, May 26, 1986.

29. Ibid.

30. Ibid.

31. Rasor, *The Pentagon Underground*, pp. 62–63.

32. Ibid., pp. 67–69.

33. Ibid., p. 69.

34. Ibid., pp. 76–77.

35. Ibid., p. 70.

36. Ibid., p. 67.

37. Ibid., p. 68.

38. Ibid., pp. 80–81.

39. Ibid.

40. Ibid., p. 81.

41. Ibid.

42. Ibid., p. 233.

43. Ibid., p. 234.

44. Ibid., p. 236.

45. The following information on the Lockheed–Air Force lobbying campaign for the C-5B is from Rasor, *Pentagon Underground*, pp. 237–252.

46. GAO report quoted in a September 30, 1982, article by Bob Adams of the *St. Louis Post-Dispatch*, cited by Rasor, *Pentagon Underground*, pp. 258–259.

47. Rasor, *Pentagon Underground*, p. 259.

48. Ibid., p. 260.

49. Ibid., p. 261.

50. For more, see Gordon Adams, *The Iron Triangle: The Politics of Defense Contracting* (New York: Council on Economic Priorities, 1981).

51. Fitzgerald, *Way Out There in the Blue*, pp. 205–206.

52. Judith Miller, "Nuclear Freeze Vote: Both Sides Call It a Victory," *New York Times*, August 7, 1982.

53. Fitzgerald, *Way Out There in the Blue*, p. 181.

54. Ibid., pp. 181–182.

55. Ibid., p. 187.

56. Ibid., p. 191.

57. Ibid., pp. 194–206.

58. Ibid., p. 195.

59. Ibid., pp. 205–206.

60. Ibid., pp. 244–245.

61. Tim Weiner, "Inquiry Finds 'Star Wars' Tried Plan to Exaggerate Test Results," *New York Times*, July 23, 1994.

62. Ibid.

CHAPTER 8: SAINT AUGUSTINE'S LAWS

1. Much of the first portion of this chapter draws from William D. Hartung, "Saint Augustine's Rules: Norman Augustine and the Future of the American Defense Industry," *World Policy Journal* 13, no. 2 (Summer 1996): 65–74.

2. Center for Responsive Politics, "Defense Aerospace," database available at OpenSecrets.org, http://www.opensecrets.org/pacs/industry.php?txt=D01&cycle =1998.

3. David Usborne and Michael Harrison, "Boeing Ousts Condit as Chairman," *The Independent*, December 2, 2003.

4. Kenneth Adelman, "Commentary: Argument for a Military Strike on Iraq Using Shakespeare's 'Othello,'" National Public Radio, *All Things Considered,* August 26, 2002.

5. Caroline Adenberger, "Spotlight: An Interview with Norman R. Augustine," *bridges* 22 (July 2009).

6. Ken Adelman, "Out to Launch," *The Washingtonian* (December 1994): 35–41.

7. Norman R. Augustine, *Augustine's Laws* (New York: Viking/Penguin, 1987), p. vi.

8. Dov Zakheim and Ronald Kadish, "One-Stop Defense Shopping," *Washington Post*, April 28, 2008; John Mintz, "Going Great Guns," *Washington Post*, October 22, 1995.

9. Charles Sennott, "Conversion: High-Stakes Gambling," *Boston Globe*, February 11, 1996.

10. Barbara Starr, "Augustine Bids for Super-Status," *Jane's Defence Weekly*, July 16, 1994, p. 28; Kenneth Adelman and Norman R. Augustine, *The Defense Revolution* (San Francisco: ICS Press), pp. 217–223.

11. Robert A. Rosenblatt and Ralph Vartabedian, "GE Sale to Create Aerospace Giant," *Los Angeles Times*, November 24, 1992.

12. Floyd Norris, "A 'Merger of Equals' with Martin Marietta Most Equal," *New York Times*, August 31, 1994.

13. Amy Borrus, "This Is Going to Be the Biggest Kahuna Around," *Business Week*, September 12, 1994.

14. Hartung, "Saint Augustine's Rules."

15. Among other places, the information in this paragraph can be found in Norman Augustine's official bio at http://www.wsu.edu/augustine/biography.html.

16. Hartung, "Saint Augustine's Rules."

17. William D. Hartung, "The Speaker from Lockheed," *The Nation*, January 16, 1995.

18. Details of the merger deal are contained in a series of articles by Patrick J. Sloyan, most notably "Sweet Deal from the Pentagon: Top Brass OK $60 Million Break to Ex-Employer," *Newsday*, June 30, 1994; see also hearing before House Armed Services, Committee, Investigation and Oversight Subcommittee, on "DoD Policy on Defense Industry Mergers, Acquisitions, and Restructuring," July 27, 1994.

19. Lawrence J. Korb, "Merger Mania: Should the Pentagon Pay for Defense Industry Restructuring?" *Brookings Review* 14 (Summer 1996).

20. William D. Hartung, "Welfare Kings," *The Nation*, June 19, 1995; Project on Government Oversight, "Payoffs for Layoffs: Much More Than a Sound Bite," March 11, 1997; Bernie Sanders, "Payoffs for Layoffs Have to Stop," *Los Angeles Times*, January 11, 1996.

21. Andrew Pollack, "Antitrust Concerns May Scuttle Merger of 2 Arms Makers," *New York Times*, March 10, 1998.

22. Leslie Wayne, "For Lockheed, a Showdown over a Merger," *New York Times*, March 23, 1998.

23. Tim Smart, "Justice Dept. Resisting Lockheed-Northrop Deal," *Washington Post*, March 10, 1998.

24. Leslie Wayne, "U.S. Moves to Block Deal for Northrop," *New York Times*, March 24, 1998.

25. Greg Schneider, "U.S. Denies Blindsiding Lockheed—Justice Says 'Concerns' About Deal Were Known," *Baltimore Sun*, April 15, 1998.

26. Thomas E. Ricks and Jeff Cole, "Lockheed Caught Napping in Policy Shift; Antitrust Move Came as Contractor Missed Signs of Change," *Wall Street Journal*, June 28, 1998.

27. Leslie Wayne, "U.S. Moves to Block Deal for Northrop," *New York Times*, March 24, 1998.

28. Lawrence J. Korb, "Defense Mega-Mergers Weaken the Nation," *Newsday*, May 6, 1998.

29. Greg Schneider, "Giant Merger Now in Doubt," *Baltimore Sun*, March 25, 1998.

30. Greg Schneider, "No Hard Feelings at Lockheed Martin; Company to Put Aside Battle with Government," *Baltimore Sun*, July 18, 1998.

31. Jacques Gansler, interview with the author, November 20, 2009.

32. For details on arms export subsidies, see William D. Hartung, "Corporate Welfare for Weapons Makers: The Hidden Costs of Spending on Defense and Foreign Aid" (policy analysis), Cato Institute, August 12, 1999.

33. On Lockheed Martin and NATO expansion, see William D. Hartung, "Welfare for Weapons Dealers 1998: The Hidden Costs of NATO Expansion," World Policy Institute Special Report (March 1998).

34. The bulk of the material in this section is drawn from William D. Hartung and Jennifer Washburn, "Lockheed Martin: From Warfare to Welfare," *The Nation*, March 2, 1998.

35. For an early view of Lockheed's foray into social services, see Jennifer Caspar, "A Former Parking Czar's New Target: Now with Lockheed, John Brophy to Hunt Child Support Deadbeats," *Washington Post*, July 1, 1991.

36. Steven Thomma, "States Explore Privatizing Government Functions," Knight Ridder/Tribune News Service, March 1997.

37. Martha M. Hamilton, "Texas Poor Constitute Rich Prize; Three Contenders Aim for Billion-Dollar Welfare Services Contract," *Washington Post*, November 12, 1996.

38. "Probe Sought into Possibility That Ex-Employees of State Broke Law by Working for Private Firms," *Dallas Morning News*, October 10, 1996; John Moritz, "Union Says Former State Officials Have Conflicts of Interest," *Fort Worth Star-Telegram*, October 10, 1996; Wayne Slater, "Bush Denies He's Swayed by Ex-Aides; Negative Perception Troubles Governor," *Dallas Morning News*, July 19, 1996.

39. Data from Center for Responsive Politics, "Defense Aerospace," database available at OpenSecrets.org, http://www.opensecrets.org/pacs/industry.php?txt =D01&cycle=1998.

40. Hartung and Washburn, "Lockheed Martin: From Warfare to Welfare."

41. For a discussion of the kinds of problems Lockheed encountered in attempting to collect child support payments, see Ed Mendel, "Computer Fiasco Costs State Dearly; $1.2 Billion in Fines over Child Support System," *San Diego Union-Tribune*, March 28, 2007.

42. Anitha Reddy, "Lockheed Finishes Reorganization; Firm Sells IMS to Dallas Company," *Washington Post*, July 20, 2001.

43. Ibid.

44. Toyota Company, "Toyota's New Safety and Quality Panel Gets First Assignment" (press release), April 30, 2010.

45. Bob Keefe, "CIA-Funded Venture Firm Seeks High-Tech Aid for U.S. Spies," Cox News Service, October 7, 2004.

46. Tim Shorrock, *Spies for Hire: The Secret World of Intelligence Outsourcing* (New York: Simon & Schuster, 2008), pp. 143–149.

47. "Panel Wants Redesign of V-22 Osprey," Associated Press, April 19, 2001; "Osprey Update," *Newshour with Jim Lehrer*, April 18, 2001.

48. "Provost Announces Government Inquiry into Lincoln Lab Misconduct Charges," *MIT Faculty Newsletter* (March–April 2006); Angeline Wang, "Lincoln Lab Not Guilty of Fraud, DoD Says," *The Tech* (MIT), April 3, 2007.

CHAPTER 9: THE ADVOCATE

1. Project for the New American Century, "Statement of Principles," June 3, 1997.

2. Project for the New American Century, letter to Trent Lott and Newt Gingrich, May 29, 1998.

3. William D. Hartung and Jonathan Reingold, "About Face: The Role of the Arms Lobby in the Bush Administration's Radical Reversal of Two Decades of U.S. Nuclear Policy," World Policy Institute Special Report (May 2002).

4. Ibid., appendix A.

5. Elizabeth Newell, "DHS Deputy's Departure Adds to Leadership Gap," *Government Executive*, September 24, 2007.

6. Figures calculated by the author, based on data at OMB Watch's Fedspending .org website, www.fedspending.org.

7. William D. Hartung, *How Much Are You Making on the War, Daddy? A Quick and Dirty Guide to War Profiteering in the Bush Administration* (New York: Nation Books, 2003), p. 17; William D. Hartung, *Welfare for Weapons Dealers 1998: The Hidden Costs of NATO Expansion* (New York: World Policy Institute, March 1998);

Jeff Gerth and Tim Weiner, "Arms Makers See Bonanza in Selling NATO Expansion," *New York Times*, June 29, 1997; Bill Mesler, "NATO's New Arms Bazaar," *The Nation*, July 21, 1997.

8. Gerth and Weiner, "Arms Makers See Bonanza in Selling NATO Expansion."

9. Leon V. Sigal, *Hang Separately: Cooperative Security Between the United States and Russia, 1985–1994* (New York: Century Foundation Press, 2000), p. 81.

10. Gerth and Weiner, "Arms Makers See Bonanza in Selling NATO Expansion."

11. Ibid.

12. David Ruppe, "Lockheed Tutored NATO Prospects on Acquisition," *Defense Week*, August 18, 1997.

13. Ibid.; Lockheed Martin, "Defense Planning Seminar—For Poland," outline of seminar held October 29–30, 1996, Sheraton Towers and Hotel, Warsaw, Poland; "Lockheed Martin Hosts Industrial Cooperation Conferences in Central Europe" (company press release), September 26, 1996.

14. "Lockheed Martin Hosts Industrial Cooperation Conferences in Central Europe"; "Hungarian Officials Get Flight Demonstrations in Lockheed Martin F-16s" (company press release), October 29, 1996.

15. Leslie Wayne, "Polish Pride, American Profits," *New York Times*, January 12, 2003.

16. Data from Center for Responsive Politics, "Defense Aerospace," database available at OpenSecrets.org, http://www.opensecrets.org/pacs/industry.php?txt=D01&cycle=1998.

17. John Judis, "Minister Without Portfolio," *The American Prospect*, April 30, 2003.

18. "Statement of the Vilnius Group Countries," February 5, 2003.

19. Information from Center for Security Policy's 1998 annual report and from the CSP website.

20. Hartung and Reingold, "About Face"; William D. Hartung, "Rumsfeld II," *Wall Street Journal*, January 12, 2001.

21. Hartung and Reingold, "About Face," pp. 16–17.

22. Bradley Graham, *Hit to Kill: The New Battle over Shielding America from Missile Attack* (New York: Public Affairs Press, 2001), pp. 101–102, 109–111.

23. William D. Hartung and Michelle Ciarrocca, "Tangled Web: The Marketing of Missile Defense 1994–2000," Arms Trade Resource Center, World Policy Institute (June 2000), p. 7.

24. For an analysis of the Rumsfeld panel, see Greg Thielmann, "Rumsfeld Reprise: The Missile Defense Report That Foretold the Iraq Intelligence," *Arms Control Today* (July–August 2003).

25. Quoted in Commission to Assess the Ballistic Missile Threat to the United States (the Rumsfeld Commission), executive summary, July 15, 1998, p. 20.

26. Graham, *Hit to Kill*, pp. 43–44.

27. Hartung and Ciarrocca, "Tangled Web," p. 8.

28. Hartung and Reingold, "About Face," pp. 8–10; U.S. Department of Defense, *Selected Acquisition Reports*, summary tables as of September 30, 2008.

29. Keith Payne (study director), "Rationale and Requirements for U.S. Nuclear Forces and Arms Control," National Institute for Public Policy, Washington, D.C. (January 2001).

30. Information on NIPP board members is available at www.nipp.org/board ofadvisors.php.

31. Payne, "Rationale and Requirements for U.S. Nuclear Forces and Arms Control," p. 6.

32. Ibid.

33. William M. Arkin, "Secret Plan Outlines the Unthinkable," *Los Angeles Times*, March 10, 2002.

34. Hartung and Reingold, "About Face," p. 4.

35. Judis, "Minister Without Portfolio."

36. Thomas Donnelly, "Rebuilding America's Defenses," Project for the New American Century, Washington, D.C. (2002).

37. Ibid.

38. Eric Schmitt, "Threats and Responses; Bipartisan Hawks: New Group Will Lobby for Change in Iraqi Rule," *New York Times*, November 15, 2002.

39. For a full treatment of Chalabi's role in the run-up to the Iraq war and his ties to U.S. neoconservatives, see Aram Roston, *The Man Who Pushed America Towards War: The Extraordinary Life, Adventures, and Obsessions of Ahmad Chalabi* (New York: Nation Books, 2008).

40. David Barstow, "One Man's Military-Industrial Media Complex," *New York Times*, November 29, 2008.

41. Ibid.

42. "Wolfowitz Comments Revive Doubts About Iraq's WMD," *USA Today*, May 30, 2003.

43. Project for the New American Century, "Iraq: Setting the Record Straight" (April 2005).

44. Joseph Stiglitz and Linda Bilmes, "The Three Trillion Dollar War," *Financial Times*, February 23, 2008.

45. Nathan Hodge, "Why Does Lockheed Spend Money on Think Tanks," December 4, 2009, The Danger Room, available at: http://www.wired.com/danger room/2009/12/why-does-lockheed-spend-money-on-think-tanks/.

CHAPTER 10: GLOBAL DOMINATION

1. Pratap Chatterjee and A. C. Thompson, "Private Contractors and Torture at Abu Ghraib," CorpWatch, May 7, 2004. The relevant section of the Taguba report is available at: http://www.dod.gov/pubs/foi/detainees/taguba/.

2. Tim Weiner, *Legacy of Ashes: The History of the CIA* (New York: Doubleday, 2007), p. 509.

3. Osha Gray Davidson, "Contract to Torture," *Salon*, August 9, 2004.

4. Tim Shorrock, *Spies for Hire: The Secret World of Intelligence Outsourcing* (New York: Simon & Schuster, 2008), p. 13.

5. Al Lewis, *CBS Market Watch*, September 16, 2003.

6. Project on Government Oversight, "Federal Contractor Misconduct Data Base," http://www.contractormisconduct.org/.

7. Renae Merle, "Lockheed Martin Scuttles Titan Acquisition," *Washington Post*, June 27, 2004; Tim Weiner, "Titan Corp. to Pay $28.5 Million in Fines for Foreign Bribery," *New York Times*, March 2, 2005.

8. "Lockheed Martin Agrees to Purchase Sytex Group, Inc." (company press release), February 18, 2005.

9. Pratap Chatterjee, "Meet the New Interrogators: Lockheed Martin," Corp-Watch, November 4, 2005.

10. Ibid..

11. Ibid.

12. Griff Witte and Renae Merle, "Contractors Are Cited in Abuses at Guantanamo; Reports Indicate Interrogation Role," *Washington Post*, January 7, 2007.

13. Ibid.

14. "Habib Sick After Grilling at Gitmo," *The Australian*, May 22, 2008.

15. Shorrock, *Spies for Hire*, p. 12.

16. Ibid., p. 24.

17. Ibid., p. 12.

18. Ibid., p. 155.

19. Ibid., p. 156.

20. Tim Shorrock, interview with the author, January 28, 2010.

21. Shorrock, *Spies for Hire*, pp. 221–227.

22. William Arkin, "Domestic Military Intelligence Is Back," *Washington Post* (online), October 29, 2005.

23. Shorrock, *Spies for Hire*, pp. 177–178.

24. Ibid., p. 178.

25. Ibid., p. 205.

26. R. James Woolsey, "Why We Spy on Our Allies," *Wall Street Journal*, March 17, 2000.

27. Ibid.

28. United States Institute of Peace, "Lockheed Martin Contributes $1 Million to Endowment of the United States Institute of Peace," April 24, 2009.

29. Ibid.

30. August Cole, "Lockheed Looks Beyond Weapons: Contractor Targets Growth with Services in Strife-Torn Areas," *Wall Street Journal*, September 24, 2007.

31. Ibid.

32. Ibid.

33. United Nations press release, October 15, 2007.

34. Pratap Chatterjee, "Darfur Diplomacy: Enter the Contractors," CorpWatch, September 21, 2004.

35. Matthew Russell Lee, "For Darfur, Lockheed Martin Gets UN Sole Source Contract, Questions Raised," *Inner City Press*, October 15, 2007.

36. United Nations General Assembly, "Audit of the Use of Extraordinary Measures for the African Union–United Nations Hybrid Operations in Darfu" (report of the Office of Internal Oversight Services), January 2, 2009.

37. Ibid.

38. International Crisis Group, "Liberia: Uneven Progress in Security Sector Reform," Africa Report 148, January 13, 2009.

39. Ibid.

40. "African Peacekeeping Efforts to Be Supported by PAE—Company to Continue Role Under State Department AFRICAP Contract," PR Newswire, September 29, 2009.

41. Lawrence Delevingne, "Defense Contractors Growing African Business," *Business Week*, October 23, 2008.

42. David Isenberg, "Dogs of War: Back to Africa," United Press International, May 30, 2008.

43. August Cole, "Defense Industry Pursues Gold in 'Smart Power' Deals," *Wall Street Journal*, March 23, 2010.

44. Mike McGovern, interview with the author, January 14, 2010.

45. "Dell Dailey Named President of PAE," PR Newswire, November 17, 2009.

46. Richard F. Grimmett, "Conventional Arms Transfers to the Developing World 2001–2008," Congressional Research Service, September 4, 2009, p. 24.

47. Data in this section are from the website of the Department of Defense, Defense Security Cooperation Agency.

48. Helene Cooper, "U.S. Approval of Taiwan Arms Sales Angers China," *New York Times*, January 30, 2010; V. Phani Kumar, "China Takes Tough Stance on U.S. Arms Sales to Taiwan: Boeing, Lockheed, Raytheon Could Face Sanctions," *MarketWatch*, January 31, 2010.

49. On the internal displacement of the Kurdish population, see Human Rights Watch, *World Report 2006* (New York: Seven Stories Press, 2006), p. 408.

50. Tamar Gabelnick, William D. Hartung, and Jennifer Washburn, *Arming Repression: U.S. Arms Sales to Turkey During the Clinton Administration* (New York: World Policy Institute, October 1999), p. 19.

51. David Morrison, "Turkish War Concern for America," *National Journal*, April 15, 1995.

52. Amnesty International, "Israel/Lebanon: Evidence Indicates Deliberate Destruction of Civilian Infrastructure," August 23, 2006; BBC News, "UN Denounces Israel Cluster Bombs," August 30, 2006.

53. Amnesty International, "Israel/Lebanon," pp. 1–3.

54. United Nations Fact-Finding Mission on the Gaza Conflict, "Head of UN Fact-Finding Mission on Gaza Conflict Urges Accountability for War Crimes; Insists Impunity Undermines Peace Process and Encourages Violence," September 29, 2010.

55. Frida Berrigan, "What We Leave Behind: From Kosovo to Lebanon, Cluster Bomb Casualties Continue to Mount," *In These Times*, December 11, 2006.

56. Meron Rappaport, "IDF Commander: We Fired More Than a Million Cluster Bombs in Lebanon," *Haaretz*, December 19, 2006.

57. Human Rights Watch, "Flooding South Lebanon: Israel's Use of Cluster Munitions in Lebanon in July and August of 2006," February 16, 2008, pp. 29–36.

58. Paul Wiseman, "Cluster Bombs Kill in Iraq, Even After Shooting Ends," *USA Today*, December 11, 2003.

59. Lynn Bradach, "Ban the Cluster Bomb," *Los Angeles Times*, December 2, 2008.

60. Tony Capaccio, "Lockheed, Raytheon Gain in Gates's European Missile Defense Plan," *Bloomberg News*, January 14, 2010.

61. Judy Dempsey, "Poles Accept U.S. Missiles Close to Land Held by Russia," *New York Times*, January 22, 2010.

62. "Russia Fumes at U.S. Defense Plan," Associated Press, February 26, 2010.

63. For more details on Lockheed Martin's missile defense programs, see William D. Hartung and Jonathan Reingold, "About Face: The Role of the Arms Lobby in the Bush Administration's Radical Reversal of Two Decades of U.S. Nuclear Policy," World Policy Institute Special Report (May 2002).

64. "Gates: Scrap 2nd ABL," Photonics.com, April 6, 2009, available at: http://www.photonics.com/Article.aspx?AID = 37010.

65. For an account of challenges in the Orion program, see Fred Guterl, "A Private Space Shuttle," *Newsweek*, October 9, 2009.

66. Kenneth Chang, "Obama Vows Renewed Space Program," *New York Times*, April 15, 2010; Jeremy Hsu, "NASA's Orion Capsule to Be Reborn as Escape Pod for Space Station," *Popular Science*, April 14, 2010.

67. Kenneth Chang, "Obama Vows Renewed Space Program," *New York Times*, April 15, 2010.

68. Greg Avery, "NASA Declares Mars Lander Phoenix Dead," *Denver Business Journal*, May 24, 2010; Lockheed Martin, "Lockheed Martin–Built Phoenix Spacecraft Successfully Lands on Mars" (press release), May 25, 2008.

69. For details, see the Lockheed Martin website.

70. As detailed in the "Space Exploration" section of the Lockheed Martin website.

71. "Company News: Lockheed and Northrop Win $17 Billion Military Job," *New York Times*, June 26, 2002.

72. Eric Lipton, "Failure to Navigate: Billions Later, Plan to Remake the Coast Guard Fleet Stumbles," *New York Times*, December 9, 2006. Unless otherwise noted, quotes in this section are from this article.

73. Ibid.

74. Christopher C. Cavas, "U.S. Coast Guard Chooses New Patrol Boat," *Defense News*, September 30, 2009.

75. Sydney J. Freedberg Jr., "Small Ships, Big Stakes," *The National Journal*, May 22, 2010.

76. "Lockheed Martin Wins Homeland Security Contract Worth $1.2B," *Homeland Security News*, July 7, 2008; Alice Lipowicz, "Obama Singles Out TSA Contract with Lockheed," *Washington Technology*, November 24, 2008. For an excellent synopsis of the breadth of Lockheed Martin's work, focusing in significant part on its domestic programs, see Tim Weiner, "Lockheed and the Future of Warfare," *New York Times*, November 28, 2004.

77. "Lockheed Martin Awarded $33 Million Contract to Support IRS" (company press release), January 22, 2008.

78. Marjorie Censer, "Lockheed Plays Key Role in Census," *Washington Post*, April 19, 2010.

79. Mary Mosquera, "Lockheed Gets Census Job," *Washington Post*, October 3, 2005.

80. Noah Shachtman, "Never Fear, Michele Bachmann!—Lockheed Martin Ensures Census Security," *The Danger Room*, July 8, 2009.

81. Carolyn Duffy Marsan, "USPS Quietly Cancels 18-Year Network Outsourcing Deal," *NetworkWorld*, December 15, 2006.

82. On Lockheed Martin's surveillance contract with the MTA, see Sewell Chan, "Lockheed Martin Is Hired to Bolster Transit Security in N.Y.," *New York Times*, August 23, 2005; William Neuman, "More Delays for Cameras in the Subways," *New York Times*, June 26, 2008; William Neuman, "Lockheed Sues to Pull Out of Security Contract with Transit Agency," *New York Times*, April 29, 2009; Tom Namako, "Tech Firm Booted," *New York Post*, June 25, 2009.

83. For information on Lockheed Martin's contracts and the agencies it works for, see OMB Watch's Fedspending.org website.

84. Marjorie Censer, "Lockheed Martin Retools to Meet New Pentagon Rules on Conflict of Interest," *Washington Post*, June 3, 2010; Lockheed Martin, "Lockheed Martin Announces Actions to Reshape Portfolio, Strengthen Performance" (press release), June 2, 2010.

NOTES TO CHAPTER 10

85. Jim Mackinnon, "Lockheed Martin Lands High-Tech Blimp Contract," *Akron Beacon-Journal*, October 14, 2009.

86. Michael Hoffman, "Unveiling the 'Beast of Kandahar,'" *Air Force Times*, December 23, 2009.

87. Tim Weiner, "Lockheed and the Future of Warfare," *New York Times*, November 28, 2004.

Index

Aboulafia, Richard, 27
Abu Ghraib scandal, 215–216, 217
Abuse, 215–219, 231–232, 249
Adams, Gordon, 155
Adelman, Kenneth, 165
Aegis missile defense project, 189, 198,
    203, 236
Aerojet General, 66
Aerospace industry, 60, 67–68, 75,
    165–166
Affiliated Computer Services Inc. (ACS),
    186, 217–218
Afghanistan, 8, 217, 222, 248, 249
Africa, 225–230
AFRICAP, 226
Agena rocket, 68
Agnew, Spiro, 79–80
Air Force
    bailout regarding C-5As, 89–94
    C-5A Galaxy and, 69–70, 73, 75–76, 82,
        87
    F-22 Raptor fighter plane and, 5, 6, 15
    Fitzgerald and, 79, 80–81
    jobs of whistle-blowers in, 139–140
    peacetime sales of Lockheed to, 54–55
    Pratt & Whitney scandal, 137–138
    wing fix issue in overpricing scandals,
        146–147, 149
Air Force, Office of Special Investigations
    (OSI), 78
Air Policy Commission, 55–56, 59
"Air Transport Plane in War and Peace,
    The" (address by Gross), 59–60
Airborne Laser (ABL), 237

Al Qaeda, 211, 220, 231
Alcor Aircraft Corporation, 37–38
Alexander, Lamar, 174
All Nippon Airlines (ANA), 116, 118–119,
    130
Allen, Thad W., 242–243
Alne, David, 127–128
Altus Air Force, 86
Ambrose, Stephen E., 105
American Airways, 40
American International Security
    Corporation, 222
Amnesty International, 232–233
Anderson, Glenn, 152
"Antelope Cobbler" (Italian prime
    minister), 123
Anti-Ballistic Missile (ABM) Treaty, 200,
    205
Arctic Circle, first flight over, 37
Arkin, William A., 207, 220–221
Armed Forces Journal International, 152
Armey, Dick, 185
Armrest, $670.06, 139, 140
Arms Bazaar, The (Sampson), 118–119
Army, 5, 6, 34, 102, 222
Army's Special Operations Command
    (SOCOM), 222
Arnold, Hap, 35
"Arsenal's End" (Kapstein), 215
Arthur Young and Company, 79–80
Aspin, Les, 171
Atherton, Howard, 71
Atkinson, Henry F., 52
Augusta-Westland, 26–27, 28

Augustine, Norm
  books written with Adelman, 165
  community organizations and
    connections of, 169–170
  efforts to buy Northrop Grumman,
    175–178
  F-35 project and, 20
  introduction to, 163–164
  lobbying and, 170, 174
  with Martin Marietta after Soviet
    Union collapse, 167–168
  merger of Martin Marietta with
    Lockheed, 168, 171–175
  NATO and, 180–181, 194
  outside roles and projects of, 187–189
  pinnacle of Aerospace industry and,
    165–166
  stepping down of, 164, 187
  on Toyota safety and quality panel 2010,
    187
  weapon exports and government
    subsidies, 178–180
  See also Welfare services, privatizing
Augustine's Laws (Augustine), 165, 166
Auto industry, 15, 36
AVCO, 71
Aviation Week and Space Technology
  (magazine), 143

B-1 long range bomber, 151
BAE Systems, 19
Bailout, Lockheed
  of C-5A Galaxy by Air Force and
    Pentagon, 89–94
  Cheyenne helicopter and, 101–104
  overpricing scandals and, 148, 149
  Proxmire and, 95–97
  Rolls-Royce Corporation, 104–105
  Senate debate regarding, 108–114
  struggle for loan guarantees in,
    105–108
  terms of, 98
  threat of bankruptcy, 97–98
  TPP approach and, 99–100
Baker, Howard, 150
Baker, James, 157, 193–194
Baldwin, Hanson, 67
Ballistic missiles. *See* Missiles, ballistic

Bankruptcy, 38–40, 68, 94, 97–98
  See also Bailout, Lockheed
Bannon, Timothy, 143
Basescu, Traian, 236
Beckman, Kenneth, 83
Beckner, Everet, 192
Bedell, Berkeley, 138
Belgium, King and Queen of, 35–36
Belli, Melvin, 117
Bellmon, Henry, 109
Bendix Corporation, 166
Benjamin, Bryce, 187
Berlin Wall, 193–194
Bernhard, Prince, 121–122, 131
Berteau, David, 12, 25, 28
Bethesda, MD, 166, 168
Biddle, Wayne, 31, 38, 47, 56
Biden, Joe, 12
Big Brother, 249
Bilmes, Linda, 212–213
Biometric technology, 243–244
Biplanes, 32, 36
Bishop, Rob, 12
"Bison" bombers, 63
Bissell, Richard, 63, 64
Bjorkland, Ray, 246
Blackwell, Mickey, 19
Blair, Tony, 26
Block, Herbert Lawrence (Herblock),
    136–137, 140
Boats. *See* Ships
Boeing, 7, 40
  C-5A Galaxy and, 70
  C-5B lobbying campaign and, 152
  F-22 Raptor fighter plane and Senate,
    2–3, 18
  foreign sales of, 43–44
  McDonnell Douglas purchase, 20–21, 70
  merger of Lockheed and Martin
    Marietta, 175
  scandals of, 164
  twin-engine fighters and, 48–49
  V-22 aircraft of, 188
Bolling, Richard, 114
Bollinger Shipyards, 241
Bolton, Claude, 5
Bombs
  cluster bombs, 232–235

dirty bombs, 239
nuclear, 24
See also Nuclear weapons; *specific types of jet bombers*
Bowen, Gordon, 15, 194–195
Boxer, Barbara, 16, 17–18, 140
Boyne, Walter, 61
Bradach, Lynn, 234, 235
Bradach-Nall, Travis, 234–235
Brazil, 42
Bresnen, Steve, 183
Brewster, Owen, 58
Bribery
  charges against Lockheed for, 128–129
  with Germany, 119–120
  with Holland, 121–122
  with Indonesia, 123–125
  with Italy, 122–123
  Japan and various other countries'
    responses to Lockheed's, 123–124,
    128–131
  with Japan for L-1011 airliners,
    117–119
  Kotchian and, 131–132
  in sale of munitions, 44–45
  with Saudi Arabia, 125–128
  in Titan Corporation, 216–217
Britain, 19, 21, 22, 26, 46–48
Brooks, Jack, 153
Brown, Alex, 175
Brown, Errol, 242
Browne, Herbert A., 219
Buckley, James, 108, 110
Buffenbarger, R. Thomas, 2–3
Bullock, Bob, 183
Bumpers, Dale, 5
Burbage, Tom, 21, 22
Burbank, CA, location, 47
Burbank Daily Record, 39–40
Burke, Kelly, 153
Burt, Richard, 157
Bush administration (George W.), 26
  F-22 Raptor fighter plane and, 7, 14
  marketing of Iraq war, 197–198, 211
  missile defense programs and, 235–236
  nuclear policies of, 204–207
  weapons of mass destruction and,
    212–213

Bush, George Herbert Walker, 134, 161,
  169, 205
Bush, George W. (as governor), 181, 183,
  184
Bush, Jeb, 191
Business Leaders for Sensible Priorities, 13
Bydgoszca Air Show, 196
Byrd, Robert, 113

C-130 Hercules cargo planes, 123,
  126–127
C-130 transport aircraft, 69, 135
C-130J and C-5 transport aircraft, 24
C-5A Galaxy, 68, 135
  actual operations failures of, 86
  bidders for, 70–73
  cost overrun of, 86
  genesis and size of, 69–70
  misgivings of costs and performance of,
    76–78, 99–100
  overpricing scandals involving, 137, 139
  Pentagon procurement problems,
    145–149
  safety problems and bailout regarding,
    89
  studies of deficiencies regarding,
    84–86
  toilet seat pans for, 143
  TPP for, 73–75
  See also Bailout, Lockheed; Fitzgerald,
    A. Ernest
C-5B transport plane lobbying scandal,
  149–151, 152–153, 154–155
CACI, 215–216
Callahan, Tom, 229
Callan, Byron, 19
Calles, Elias, 33
Cambone, Stephen, 205
Campaign contributions, 29, 185, 242
Campbell, Kurt, 213–214
Canada, transport of Hudson bombers
  through, 46–47
Capp, Al, 61–62
Carlucci, Frank, 149, 150, 153
Carter administration, 134
Carter, Jimmy, 133
Casablanca (film), 40
CBS Reports program, 67

Center for a New American Security
(CNAS), 213–214
Center for Security Policy (CSP),
198–199, 202
Central Intelligence Agency (CIA), 60, 62,
63, 219
Augustine and, 187
Chalabi and, 210
Rumsfeld Commission and, 201
Team B and, 134
Chaco War, 45
Chalabi, Ahmad, 209–210
Chambliss, Saxby, 9, 10, 11, 12, 15, 24
Chao, Pierre, 186
Charles, Robert, 73–75, 77, 90
Charleston, SC, 71–72, 86
Cheney, Dick, 102, 188, 191, 192, 208
Cheney, Lynne, 192
Cheyenne helicopter, 101–103
Chicago, 13–15, 25, 32
Chile and Peru, 45
China, 13, 14, 231
Church, Frank, 121–122, 127
CIA. *See* Central Intelligence Agency
(CIA)
Civil Aeronautics Board (CAB), 54, 104
Civilian Protection Monitoring Team
(CPMT), 225
Clarridge, Duane "Dewey," 222
Cleary, Chris, 241
Clinton administration
Augustine and, 170
military cuts and, 167
missile defense funding and, 203
nuclear policies of, 205
subsidies for exports, 180
welfare privatization and, 182–183,
185
Clinton, Bill, 164, 200
Clinton, Hillary Rodham, 26–27, 223
Cluster bombs, 232–235
Clutter, Jack, 119
Coast Guard, 239–243
Coffeemaker, $7662, 136–137, 139, 140
Coffman, Vance, 4–5, 177
Cohen, William, 142, 177, 178, 188
Cold War
military force of U.S., 67–68

post, 166–167, 180
weapons of, 13
Cole, August, 224
Coleman, Garnet, 184
Colombia, 123–124
Colonial Realty, 83
Colson, Charles, 80
Commercial planes, 54–55, 72
See also Constellation airliner; *specific
commercial planes by name*
Commission on the Ballistic Missile
Threat to the United States
(CABMTUS), 199, 200–201
Committee for the Liberation of Iraq
(CLI), 197, 209–210, 211
Committee on the Present Danger (CPD),
133–134
Communications, 221–222
Communism, 59, 135
Comprehensive Test Ban Treaty (CTBT),
199
Condit, Phil, 164
Congress, 3–4
C-5A Galaxy and, 75–77, 85
C-5A Galaxy bailout and, 92
cluster bombs and, 235
Coast Guard ships and, 242
F-22 Raptor fighter plane and, 14
Fitzgerald's firing by Air Force and, 79
legislation to curb excess profits, 49–50
and peacetime government subsidies
request, 55
and Polaris project, 66
Reagan military buildup and, 136
Congress of Industrial Organizations
(CIO), 41
Connally, John, 105–107, 111
Constellation airliner, 51–52, 54
Contractors
Lockheed Martin as nation's largest
military, 28–29
misconduct of, 29–30
Contractors for Peacekeeping activities,
223–230
Counterintelligence Field Activity (CIFA),
220–221
Cranston, Alan, 94, 107, 110, 111, 113, 155
Credit Suisse First Boston, 186–187

Crimes of C-5A Galaxy. *See* C-5A Galaxy;
    Fitzgerald, A. Ernest; Securities and
    Exchange Commission (SEC)
Curtiss Aircraft, 32, 33, 34
C-X transport plane (later C-17), 149
Czech Republic, 46, 235

Dailey, Dell, 222, 229
Darden, "Buddy," 4
Darfur, 225
D'Armiento, Anthony, 240
Dasaad, Isaak, 124–125
Davidson, Osha Gray, 216
Deepwater (Coast Guard program),
    239–243
Defense Appropriations Committees,
    154–155
Defense News, 195
Defense Policy Advisory Committee on
    Trade (DPACT), 168, 179
Defense Revolution, The (Augustine and
    Adelman), 165
DeLauer, Richard, 152
DeMint, Jim, 17
Demisch, Wolfgang, 175
Department of Defense, 75, 84, 97–98, 188
Department of Energy, 29
Department of Homeland Security
    (DHS), 192–193
Department of Justice, 29
Department of State, 29
Department of Transportation, 29
Detroit Aircraft Company, 37–38, 38–39
Deutch, John, 169, 171
Dick, William W. Jr., 102
Dignam, Michael, 229
Dingell, John, 143
Distributed Common Ground System
    (DCGS), 219–220
Dodd, Christopher, 9, 11, 15
Dole, Elizabeth and Bob, 169
Dominance, 209, 247–249
Douglas Aircraft Corporation
    air transport market and, 40
    Augustine and, 166
    C-5A Galaxy and, 70
    eventual merger with Boeing, 70
    foreign sales of, 43–44

Jack Northrop and, 36
legislation to curb excess profits and, 49
presentation of company's profits, 50
twin-engine fighters and, 48–49
WWI, 34
See also McDonnell Douglas
Douglas DC-1, 40
Douglas, Donald, 54
Dow Jones industrial, 18, 54, 68
Dunlap, Julie, 245
Dunn, Michael, 9
DuPont Corporation, 44
Durham, Henry, 86–88, 88–89, 145–146
Dyment, John, 79–80
DynCorp, 226–228, 230

Earhart, Amelia, 38, 40
Echelon, 221
Echols, Oliver P., 56–57
Economic Club of Chicago, 13–15, 25
EDS, 182, 183, 185
Egeland, Jan, 232–233
Eggers, Bill, 186
Ehrlichman, John, 80
Eisenhower, Dwight D., 17, 26, 60, 62–65,
    249
Electra transport plane, 40, 41, 43, 45, 46,
    67–68
Electric Boat Company (later General
    Dynamics), 45
Electronics Industries Association, 128
Emanuel, Rahm, 12
Employment. *See* Jobs
Empower America, 202
England. *See* Britain
Ensign, John, 17
Ervin, Clark Kent, 192–193
Evans, Richard, 183
Exports, military, 42–48, 178–180, 230,
    232–235

F-1 ("flying boats"), 33, 34
F-104 Starfighter, 116–117, 119–120, 121
F-16 combat aircraft, 178–180, 213
    as Lockheed Martin's biggest export, 230
    Poland and surrounding countries,
        194–197
    used by Israel in bombings, 233

F-18 fighter jet (McDonnell Douglas), 155

F-1A plane, 34–35

F-22 Raptor fighter plane
advertising and costs of, 1–3, 5–6, 11
approval of funding for, 6
greatest rival of, 24
jobs and, 2–5, 10–11, 24
Lockheed Martin's increased military contracts and, 28–29
ongoing support for, 24–25
peacetime aviation funding talks and, 58
PNAC requests for increased spending on, 208–209
resilience of Lockheed Martin and, 248
Senate debate regarding, 11–18
September 11 funding and, 7–9

F-35 Joint Strike Fighter (JSF), 8, 13, 15, 248
customers and production of, 19–20
difficulties regarding, 22–24
instead of F-22 Raptor planes, 13, 14
jobs and, 10–11
Lockheed Martin's victory over Boeing regarding, 18–19, 20–21

F-5 Tiger aircraft, 127

Fahd, Prince, 126

Fast Response Cutter (ship), 241

FBI, 217–218, 243–244

Federal Register, 171

Feinstein, Diane, 17–18

Fidell, Eugene, 216

Film industry, 40

Finances. *See* Military spending; Money; Tax money

Finletter, Thomas, 55–56, 59

Finley, Julie, 209

First Responder Authentication Credential (FRAC), 244

Fitzgerald, A. Ernest, 80–81, 93, 99
C-5B lobbying campaign and, 154
career tenure threats and firing of, 78–79, 90, 91
hearings with House Armed Services Committee, 81–82
iced out of weapons cost assessment work, 78
Lockheed bailout and, 97

overpricing scandals and, 139, 144, 146, 149
overview of initial involvement with C-5A Scandal, 75–76
Pratt & Whitney scandal, 137–138
requested to testify about problems in military procurement, 77
and whistle-blower Henry Durham, 86–87

Fitzgerald, Frances, 157

Fluornoy, Michele, 213, 214

"Flying boats" (F-1), 33, 34

Fokker, Anthony, 46

Fokker (Dutch aircraft maker), 122

Ford, Gerald, 133

Ford Motor Company, 37, 73

Foreign clients, exports to, 42–48, 178–180, 230, 232–235

Foreign Corrupt Practices Act, 217

Fort Worth, TX, 21

Foster, John, 64

Frech, W.P., 87

Friendly, Fred, 67

Fukuda, Taro, 116

Fulbright, William, 70, 84

Funding. *See* Military spending; Money; Tax money

Gaffney, Frank, 198

Gagnon, Georgette, 225

Galbraith, Peter, 197

Gansler, Jacques, 178

GAO, 84–86

Gates, Robert, 1, 201, 209, 237
Economic Club of Chicago speech, 13–15, 25
F-35 Joint Strike Fighter plane problems and, 22–23, 24
funding for F-22 Raptor fighter plane, 7–11, 12–13
presidential helicopters and, 28

Gaza, 233

General Accounting Office (GAO) studies, 145–146, 147, 149
C-5B lobbying campaign and, 153–154
HOE program and, 160

General Dynamics (GD), 152

General Electric, 66, 135
  C-5A Galaxy and, 71
  C-5B lobbying campaign and, 152
  Lockheed bailout and, 111
  presidential helicopters and, 27
  purchase by Martin Marietta, 167–168
General Motors, 37
Gentry, Renee, 177–178
Georgia. *See* Marietta, Georgia
German Air Force, 117
Germany, 45, 46, 120
Gerritsen, Teengs, 120–121
Gerth, Jeff, 194
Gingrey, Phil, 9
Gingrich, Newt, 151, 170, 179, 191, 201
Glenn L. Martin Company, 43–44
Global Domination, 209, 247–249
Goen, Jeff, 10
Goldwater, Barry, 111–112
Goldwater, Barry Jr., 102
Gooden, Linda, 224
Gorbachev, Mikhail, 193–194
Gould Corporation, 138
Government
  Lockheed Martin's revenues and profits
    from, 3
  money flowing from to military
    manufacturers in WWII, 49
  peacetime subsidies from, 52–54, 55–56,
    57–59
  subsidies for exports, 178–180
  subsidized loans for Lockheed Martin
    from, 196
  subsidizing of Lockheed–Martin
    Marietta merger, 171–175
Government Accountability Office
  (GAO), 23, 234
Government loans for Lockheed. *See*
  Bailout, Lockheed
Graham, Bradley, 201–202
Graham, Daniel O., 134
Gramm, Phil, 185
Grassley, Charles, 140
Great Britain, 21, 22, 46–48
Great Depression, 38–42
Greenstreet, Bob, 138, 139–140
Gregg, Judd, 17
Griffin, Michael D., 238

Gross, Courtlandt, 39, 42, 46
Gross, Robert, 39, 40–42
  bribery with Holland and, 121
  early Lockheed foreign military
    contracts via, 42–48
  Korean War and, 59–60
  legislation to curb excess profits and,
    49–50
  Lockheed's deal with Great Britain,
    47–48
  Lockheed's financial losses in first
    quarter of 1960, 68
  and peacetime government subsidies
    request, 52–54, 55–56
  post WWII reflection, 51–52
  speech to Senate Subcommittee,
    57–59
Ground-Based Midcourse Defense System
  (GBMDS), 236
Guantanamo Bay, Cuba, 215, 217–218
Gui, Luigi, 130
Gund, Edward, 185–186

Habib, Mamdough, 218
Hadley, Stephen, 192, 205–206
Hal Roach Studios, 40
Halliburton, 102, 192, 213, 226, 227
Hancock, Dain, 195–196
Hancock, Robert, 137–138
Harassment of Air Force Employees
  (congressional inquiry), 139–140
Haughton, Daniel, 71, 87–88, 96, 129
  bribery scandals and, 128, 129–130, 131
  Hawkins and, 103
  Indonesian bribery and, 124
  L-1011 airliners and bribery with Japan,
    118
  loan guarantees for Lockheed bailout
    and, 107–108
  Lockheed bailout and, 99, 109–110
  Saudi Arabian bribery and, 127
Hauser, Ernest, 120
Hawaii, 16–17
Hawkins, Willis, 102, 103
Hearst, William Randolph, 37
Heath, Edward, 117
Helicopters, 25–28, 101–103
Helzel, Max, 126

Herblock (*Washington Post* cartoonist), 136–137, 140
Herrera, Linda, 186
Hill Air Force Base, Utah, 12
Hinchey, Maurice, 27–28
Hit to Kill (Graham), 201–202
Hitler, Adolf, 46, 47–48
  See also Nazi Germany
Hiyama, Hiro, 116, 117–118
Hoenig, Joe, 128
Hollifield, Chet, 82, 83
Hollywood, CA, 36
Homeland Security, 239–247
Homing Overlay Experiment (HOE), 155, 159–161
House Armed Services Committee, 12, 81, 86, 173
House Committee on Science and Astronautics, 67
Housing and Urban Development, 29
HS-2L plane (Curtiss Aircraft), 34
HSC (the Homeland Security Corporation), 228
Hudson bombers (military variation of Super Electra), 46–47, 61
Hull, Ken, 116
Humphrey, Hubert, 106, 108, 114
Hunsaker, Jerome, 34
Hussein, Saddam, 191, 197–198, 211–212
Hutchison, Kay Bailey, 185

Indonesia, 123–125
Information Management Services (IMS), 181–182, 186
Inouye, Daniel, 16–17, 24–25
In-Q-Tel (CIA venture capital company), 187
Integrated Automated Fingerprint Identification System (IAFIS), 244
Integrated Customer Communications Environment (ICCE), 245
Intelligence community, U.S., 219–223
  See also Central Intelligence Agency (CIA)
Intercontinental ballistic missiles (ICBMs), 64, 134, 156
Internal Revenue Service (IRS), 244–245

International Association of Machinists and Aerospace Workers (IAM), 2–3, 5, 10, 41, 111
International Crisis Group (ICG), 227, 228
International Media Ventures, 222
Interrogation of prisoners, 215–217
Investors, Lougheed Aircraft Manufacturing Company, 36, 37, 38–40
Iran-Contra scandal, 222
Iraq
  and Al Qaeda connection never able to be made, 211
  cluster bombs in, 234–235
  F-22 Raptor fighter plane and, 8
  interrogation and abuse of prisoners in, 215–216
  lies regarding missiles in, 200, 201–202
  "Iraq: Setting the Record Straight" (PNAC), 212
Iraq war
  advocates of, 165, 208–211
  costs of in financial and human terms, 212–213
  invasion and, 191
  marketing for, 197–198, 210–211, 212
"Iron Triangle," 155
Israel, 232–234
Italy, 22, 122–123, 130

J. P. Morgan Securities, 175
Jackson, Bruce, 180, 191–192
  connections of, 193
  marketing of Iraq war, 197–199, 204, 208
  military domination and, 209
  NATO and, 197
Jackson, Henry, 150
Jackson, Michael, 192–193
Jakarta, 124
Japan, 43, 45
  bribery scandals and, 129–130
  Electra transport planes from Lockheed, 42, 46
  F-22 Raptor fighter plane and, 24
  L-1011 airliners and, 115–116
JetStar transport plane, 68, 121

Jobs, 24, 26, 41
C-5A Galaxy bailout and, 94
F-22 Raptor fighter plane and, 1–4, 8–9, 10–11, 15–16, 17–18
F-35 Joint Strike Fighter plane and, 22
during Korean War, 60
in Lockheed bailout hearings, 107
at Lockheed during WWII boom, 49
performed by Lockheed Martin, overview, 29, 247–248
Johnson, Clarence "Kelly," 61–62
Johnson, Edwin, 58
Johnson, Joel, 232
Johnson, Lyndon, 71, 105
Johnson-Sirleaf, Ellen, 227
Johnstown, PA, symphony orchestra, 27
Joint Strike Fighter (JSF). *See* F-35 Joint Strike Fighter (JSF)
Jones, David C., 157
Jones, Tom, 122
Jong, Kim Il, 201
Jonsson, Thomas, 138–140
Joseph, Robert, 205–206
JSF. *See* F-35 Joint Strike Fighter (JSF)
Jupiter missile, 65
Jurkowsky, Tom, 217, 218
Justice Department, 176

Kaplan, A. H., 127
Kapstein, Ethan, 215
Kaufman, Richard, 95
Keating, Dave, 148
Kecskemet Air Base, Hungary, 196
Keeler, Fred (investor in Lougheed Aircraft Manufacturing Company), 36, 37–38
Kellogg, Brown and Root, 226, 229–230
Kelly Air Force Base, TX, 143
Kennan, George, 59
Kennedy administration, 63, 68
Kennedy, Edward, 155
Kennedy, John F., 65
Kennedy, Ted, 11
Kerekou, Mathieu, 217
Kerrey, Bob, 197
Kerry, John, 11, 18
Kettering, Charles, 37

Khashoggi, Adnan, 125–128, 131
Khrushchev, Nikita, 64
Kinsey, Marcia, 184
Kishi, Nobusuke, 116
Kissinger, Henry, 129–130
Kitchen, Lawrence O., 141, 152
Kitty Hawk, NC, 31
Klein, Joel, 178
Kodama, Yoshio, 115–116, 117, 118, 126, 129
Korb, Lawrence J., 173
Korean War, 59
Kotchian, A. Carl
bribery and, 115–116, 117, 118–119, 123, 128, 131–132
Cheyenne helicopter and, 101
Kramer, Matt, 218
Kupperman, Charles, 198, 204
Kutler, Jon, 21–22
Kyl, Jon, 199

L-1011 Tristar airliner, 92–93, 107
bribery scandals and, 130
for Japan after government loan guarantees, 115–117
Lockheed bailout and, 98–99, 104–106, 107–110, 114
Laird, Melvin, 81, 100
Landmine Action, 234
Language Weaver, Inc., 187
Larsen, Finn J., 101
Lebanon, 232–235
Lee, Matthew, 225–226
Lefebvre, Olvidio, 123
Leggett, Robert, 91
Lehman, John, 141
Levi, Edward, 129
Levin, Carl
C-5B lobbying campaign and, 152
F-22 Raptor fighter plane and, 11, 12, 13, 14–15
missile amendments and, 200
Levin-McCain amendment, 13, 14, 17
Levy, Richard, 184
Lewis, Jerry, 4–5, 6–7, 8, 14
Lexington Institute, 23
Liberia, 226–227, 228–229
Lieberman, Joseph, 9, 10

L'il Abner (comic strip), 61–62
Lindbergh, Charles, 36–37
Lipton, Eric, 241
Littoral combat ship program, 24
LM Today, 229
Loans, government. *See* Bailout, Lockheed
Lobbying
  Augustine and, 170
  campaign of C-5B, 150–155
  for Coast Guard ships, 242
  F-22 Raptor fighter plane and, 4–7,
    8–10
  money spent for, 29
  of Shelley for Lockheed, 182
Lockheed Aircraft Corporation
  bucking trend of military as biggest
    aviation client, 38
  out of business in 1930s, 38–39
  as takeover target, 37–38
Lockheed Martin
  biggest source of future growth for,
    239–249
  biometric technology and, 243–245
  Bush administration, Iraq war and now
    Democratic connections, 213–214
  Coast Guard ships and, 239–243
  entrusting power and influence to, 249
  F-16 combat aircraft sales to European
    countries, 195–196
  IMS, 181–182, 186
  interrogation business of, 215–217, 222
  Iraq war and, 213
  IRS and US Census data and, 245–246
  merger of Lockheed and Martin
    Marietta to become, 168, 171–175
  Northrop Grumman and, 175–178
  nuclear weapons and, 207
  other government contracts of, 246–249
  peacekeeping business or "soft power,"
    223–230
  personal data of U.S. citizens by,
    220–221
  privatization of welfare services,
    181–187
  role in missile defense and space
    programs, 235–238
  U.S. Intelligence community and,
    219–222

as world's largest weapons manufacturer,
    163–164
  as world's top exporter of weapons,
    232–235
Lockheed Sales Mission: 70 Days in Tokyo
    (Kotchian), 119
Loral Corporation, 168
Lott, Trent, 191
Loughead Aircraft Manufacturing
    Company, 31, 36
Loughead, Allan and Malcolm
  early years of aviation company and
    early life of, 31
  education of, 32
  Electra transport plane and, 40–42
  first crack at aviation business, 32–33
  incorporation of Lockheed Aircraft
    Corporation, 36–37
  Lockheed Aircraft Corporation's
    takeover, bankruptcy and rebuying of,
    37–40
  resignation with Lockheed Aircraft
    Corporation and restarting of other
    companies, 37–38
  Robert Gross investor and, 39
  WWI and, 33–35, 36
Loughead Brothers Aircraft, 37–38
Loughead, Flora (mother of Loughead
    brothers), 31, 32
Lougheed, Victor (older half-brother of
    Loughead brothers), 32

M-10 Electra, 40, 41
M-12 Electra, 41
Magnuson, Warren, 58
Manor, "Chip," 174
Marietta, Georgia, 10, 24, 71, 85, 87, 89,
    151
Marines, 19, 22, 188
Markey, Ed, 156
Mars Global Surveyor (MGS), 238
Martin, Glenn L., 163
Martin Marietta, 163, 166–167, 168,
    171–175
Marubeni trading company, 116, 119
Massachusetts Institute of Technology,
    188–189
Mattingly, Matt, 4

May Day, Soviet Union, 64
May, William, 37
MB-1 bomber (Douglas Aircraft
  Corporation), 34
McCaffrey, Barry, 210–211
McCain, John, 11, 12, 13, 17, 25–26
McCain-Levin amendment, 13, 14, 17
McCarthy, Joseph, 96
McCurdy, Dave, 151
McDonnell Douglas
  C-X transport plane winner, 149
  F-18 fighter jet of, 155
  F-35 Joint Strike Fighter plane and,
    20–21
  Lockheed bailout and, 109–110, 111
  merger with Boeing, 70
  See also Douglas Aircraft Corporation
McDonnell, John, 81
McEntire, Jim, 240
McFarlane, Robert, 158–159, 160–161
McGovern, Mike, 228–229
McKinney, Michael, 184
McNamara, Robert, 72–73, 75, 99–100
Medium Extended Air Defense System
  (MEADS), 236
Mergers, 20–21, 163
  of Douglas to Boeing, 70
  of Lockheed and Martin Marietta, 168,
    171–175
  Northrop Grumman and Lockheed
    Martin, 175–178
Metcalf, Lee, 113, 114
Metropolitan Transit Agency (MTA), 247
Meuser, Fred, 120, 121, 122
Michalski, Richard, 10
Michel, Robert, 150
Mideast War, 1973, 147
Miki, Takeo, 129
Military Procurement Project, 137
Military spending
  after Soviet Union collapse, 166–167
  Air Policy Commission and, 56
  Augustine and, 170
  F-22 Raptor fighter plane and, 4, 14
  F-35 Joint Strike Fighter plane and,
    23–24
  in Kennedy administration, 63
  Korean War and, 59–60

moving towards soft-power related
  activities, 224
  in Obama administration, 8, 10
  PNAC requests for, 208–209
  of Reagan, 135–137
  and September 11 terrorist attacks, 7–8,
    187
  VH-71 presidential helicopter and,
    25–26
  Vietnam war and, 133
  See also Overpricing of military parts;
    Tax money
Miller, Doug, 196
Miller, Gerald, 186
Mineta, Norman, 192
Mintz, Morton, 87
Misconduct of contractors, 29–30
  See also Project on Government
    Oversight (POGO)
Missiles, 16–17
  ballistic, 60, 64–65, 188–189, 200–203,
    205, 230–231, 235–236
  Intercontinental ballistic, 64, 134, 156
  in Iraq, 200, 201–202
  scud, 202, 206
  submarine launched ballistic, 65–68,
    134–136, 156
MLRS. See Multiple-Launch Rocket
  System (MLRS)
Model G plane (first plane of Loughead
  brothers), 33, 34
Mojave Desert, 21
Mollenhoff, Clark, 80–81
Money, 42, 45, 47, 203
  for C-5A Galaxy, 74, 76–77, 81–82, 86,
    89–94
  campaign donations, 29, 185, 242
  in Cold War era, 67–68
  for F-35 planes, 23
  for Iraq war, 212–213
  in Italian bribery, 123
  in Japan's bribery scandals with
    Lockheed, 130
  legislation to curb excess profits, 49–50
  of Lockheed Martin, overview, 29–30
  Lockheed–Martin Marietta merger
    subsidized by government and,
    173–174

Money (*continued*)
  peacetime government subsidies, 52–54,
    55–56, 57–59
  from Polaris project, 65–66
  of Saudi Arabian bribery, 126
  to U.S. Intelligence community, 219
  for VH-71 presidential helicopter,
    28–29
  See also Bailout; Military spending; Tax
    money
Montgomery, G. V. "Sonny," 4
Montgomery, John, 32
Montoya, Joseph, 106
Moorhead, William, 76, 80, 83, 85–86, 98,
  99
Moran, James, 4
Morrow Board, 55
Moscow, 63, 193–194, 236
Moss, Stephen, 26
Motion pictures, 40
Mott, Charles, 37
Mullen, Michael, 14
Multiple-Launch Rocket System (MLRS),
  213, 232, 234
Murray, Patty, 16, 17–18
Murray, Williamson, 5
Murrow, Edward R., 67
Murtha, John "Jack," 4–5, 6–7, 8, 14, 27–28
Myers, Richard, 235
Myers, W. G., 124

Naishtat, Elliott, 182
National Aeronautics and Space
    Administration (NASA), 29, 187,
    238
National Aviation Coordination Agency
    (NACA), 61
National Aviation Hall of Fame, 38
National Institute for Public Policy
    (NIPP), 204, 205–207
National Security Agency, 220, 221
National Security Cutter (ship), 241–242
National Taxpayers' Union, 137
NATO. *See* North Atlantic Treaty
    Organization (NATO)
Naval Criminal Investigative Service
    (NCIS), 218
Navy, 15, 33, 40, 54–55, 65–68, 138

Nazi Germany, 45, 46, 120–121
NBC News, 210
Nesterenko, Andrei, 236
Netherlands, 120, 131
Neutrality Act of 1935, 45–46, 46–47
Nevada, 36
New Deal, 40–41
New York Subway security cameras,
    246–247
New York Times, 67, 101, 105, 113–114
  bribery scandals and, 129, 131–132
  Coast Guard and, 239–240
  F-35 Joint Strike Fighter plane and, 24
  government subsidized loans and, 196
  McCaffrey and Iraq war, 210–211
  merger of Lockheed and Martin
    Marietta, 168
  NATO and, 194
  Robert Stevens in, 249
  spying and, 222
Newsham, Margaret, 221
Nitze, Paul, 134
Nixon, Richard
  A. Ernest Fitzgerald's firing by Air
    Force and, 79, 80–81
  Adnan Khashoggi and, 126
  government loans for Lockheed and,
    105–108
  Kotchian's bribery scandals and, 132
  L-1011 airliners and Japan, 118
  Lockheed bailout and, 111–112
  Proxmire and, 96
  swearing in as president and C-5A
    bailout, 90
North Atlantic Treaty Organization
    (NATO), 119–120, 180, 193–194,
    197
North Korea, 200, 201–202, 203
Northrop Grumman, 19, 21, 175–176
  Deepwater project and, 240–243
  presidential helicopters and, 27
Northrop, Jack, 34, 36–37, 54
Northrop (rival of Lockheed), 122, 127
Northwest Airlines, 40
Norway, 22
Nuclear age, 57, 60
Nuclear bombs, 24
Nuclear freeze campaign, 156–159

Nuclear Posture Review, 204–205, 207
Nuclear war, 136, 157–159, 204
Nuclear weapons, 60, 134–135, 199, 204–207, 236
Nye Committee, 43–46
Nye, Gerald, 44, 46

Obama administration, 10, 213–214
  budget battles during first year of, 25
  F-22 Raptor fighter plane and, 7
  foreign aid and, 224
  missile defense programs and, 235–236
  Predator aircraft in Pakistan during, 8
  predator strikes and locating people under, 220
Obama, Barack
  F-22 Raptor fighter plane and, 2–3
  pentagon budget of, 14
  veto of F-22 and, 12–13, 18
  VH-71 presidential helicopter and, 25–26
Ocean Thermal Energy Conversion (OTEC) facility, 16–17
Oden, Ken, 184
Office of Special Investigations (OSI), Air Force, 78
O'Neill, Tip, 152
OPEC (Organization of Petroleum-Exporting Countries), 125
Orion crew exploration vehicle (CEV), 237–238
Ormsby, Robert B., 143–145, 148
Orr, Verne, 80, 149, 150, 153
Osano, Kenji, 117
OSI. *See* Air Force, Office of Special Investigations (OSI)
Othello (Shakespeare), 165
Outsourcing, 29
Overpricing of military parts, 137–145, 145–149, 150–155

P-38 twin-engine fighters, 48–49
P-3C Orion antisubmarine warfare (ASW), 122, 135
P-80 fighter plane, 58, 61
PAC (Political Action Committee), 154–155

PAC-3 (Patriot Advanced Capability) missile, 230–231, 236
Pacific Missile Range Facility, Kauai, 16–17
Packard, David, 98, 104
PAE Worldwide Services, 224–225, 226, 227, 228–230, 248
Pakistan, 8, 220, 222, 230, 231
Palm Beach, CA, 38
Palmer, Carl, 154
Pan American, 40, 54
Panama-Pacific Exposition, 33
Pantchoulidzew, Colonel, 121
Paris Air Show, 22, 160
Paris, Paul, 146–147, 148
Passaro, David, 216
Paterson, David, 2–3
Patriot missile, 188–189
Payne, Keith, 204, 206
"Payoffs for layoffs" (in Lockheed–Martin Marietta merger), 174–175
Peace Action, 13
Peacekeeping activities, 223–230
Peacetime government subsidies, 52–54, 55–56, 57–59
Peacetime sales, 54–55
Pearl Harbor, 43
Pentagon, 12, 13, 22, 29, 213–214
  Augustine and, 188, 189
  bailout regarding C-5As, 89–90, 92, 96–97
  budget decline after Vietnam war, 133
  budget levels in Kennedy administration, 63
  C-5A Galaxy and, 73
  C-5B lobbying campaign and, 152
  F-22 Raptor fighter plane and, 6, 12
  F-35 Joint Strike Fighter plane and, 19, 20, 23
  Fitzgerald and, 75–76, 80, 137
  interrogation of terror suspects, 216
  Lockheed–Martin Marietta merger subsidized by government and, 172–175
  in Reagan era, 135
  Saudi Arabian bribery and, 127
  scandals with Boeing in, 164
  September 11 terrorist attacks and, 7
  spy planes for, 60–61

Pentagon Underground, The (Rasor), 137, 138

Percy, Charles, 124

Perle, Richard, 157, 210

Perot, Ross, 182

Perry, William, 167, 169, 171

Persistent Threat Detection System, 248–249

Personal data of U.S. citizens, 220–221

Personal Responsibility and Work Opportunity Reconciliation Act (PRWORA), 181

Peru and Chile, 45

Peshawar, Pakistan, 64

Petraeus, David, 211

Phoenix Mars lander, 238

Pike, Otis, 81–82, 102

Pino, Jeffrey, 26, 27

Pipes, Richard, 134

PKK, 231–232

Plew, James, 32

PNAC. *See* Project for the New American Century (PNAC)

POGO (Project on Government Oversight), 13, 29–30

Poland, 195–197, 235

Polaris project, 65–68

Polaris submarines, 60, 135–136

Poore, H. Lee, 89

Pork barrel politics, 21, 26, 27, 71, 146
C-5B lobbying campaign and, 151
defined, 14, 16
Lockheed bailout and, 114

Postal service, U.S., 42, 246

Postol, Theodore, 188–189

Powell, Colin, 166–167, 198

Power, 29–30, 223–230

Powers, Gary Francis, 64

Pratt & Whitney, 2–3, 10, 137–138

Predator strikes, 220

Predator (unmanned aircraft), 8

Presidential helicopters, 25–28

Price, Tom, 9

Princeton, 165–166, 187, 189

Project for the New American Century (PNAC), 191–192, 198, 208–210, 211, 212

"Project Groundbreaker," 221

Project on Government Oversight (POGO), 13, 29–30

Project on Military Procurement, 139, 142–143, 144

Proxmire, William
C-5A Galaxy and, 69, 76–77, 79, 88
death threats to, 87
L-1011 airliner and, 93, 118
Lockheed bailout and, 90, 91–92, 95–97, 111, 112–113
revolving door reports by, 102–103
Saudi Arabian bribery and, 127
wing fix issue in overpricing scandals, 147–149

Pryor, David, 160

Queen Juliana, 121

R&D contracts, 74

Raborn, W.F., 65, 66, 67

Radars, Soviet Union, 60–61, 63

Ragsdale, James, 141

Rape, 216

Raptor fighter plane. *See* F-22 Raptor fighter plane

Rasor, Dina, 137, 138, 144
C-5B lobbying campaign and, 150, 154
overpricing scandals and, 145–147, 148, 149
Project on Military Procurement, 139, 142–143

Raytheon, 11, 175

Reagan, Ronald
CPD involvement of, 134
CSP fund-raiser and, 202
lobbying campaign of C-5B and, 150
military buildup by and threat of nuclear war, 135–136, 155–159
programs where Lockheed pushed legal envelope in, 155–156
"Star Wars" project of, 155, 156, 157–161

"Rebuilding America's Defenses" (PNAC), 208–209

Recession, 15, 94
See also Great Depression

Reconstruction Finance Corporation (RFC), 40–41, 46

Reich, Otto, 192
Reid, Harry, 202
Reno, Janet, 176, 177
Revolving door, 102–103, 164, 183–184,
    193
Rice, Berkeley, 69, 85
Rich, Ben, 61, 62
Rivers, L. Mendel, 71–72, 76, 81–82
    C-5A Galaxy and, 86, 92
    Hawkins defense by, 103
Rodman, Burton, 34
Rogers, William P., 128–129
Rolls-Royce Corporation, 104–107,
    117–118
Romania, 180–181, 194, 236
Romero, Ron, 219
Roosevelt administration, 47
Roosevelt, Franklin Delano, 40–41
Roosevelt, Kermit, 127
Rossiter, Bernard, 84
Rostow, Eugene, 134, 156–157
Roth, William, 141, 142
Royal Air Force, 46–48
RQ-170 (unmanned surveillance vehicle),
    249
Rumor, Mariano, 130
Rumsfeld Commission, 200–203
Rumsfeld, Donald, 191, 199–202, 205, 208,
    210
Ruppe, David, 195
Russell, Richard, 71, 76
Russia, 193–194, 236
    See also Soviet Union

Salon, 216
Sampson, Anthony, 118–119, 120
San Francisco, CA, 31, 33
San Francisco Chronicle, 31
Sanders, Bernie, 173
Sandia National Laboratories, 24, 207–208
Sandoval, Jesse, 143
Santa Clara Valley, CA, 31
Sapolsky, Harvey, 66
Saud, Ibn, 126
Saudi Arabia, 123–124, 125–126
Scandals. *See specific scandals by name*
Schedler, Spencer, 79–80
Scheunemann, Randy, 209–210

Schlesinger, James, 134
Schweiker, Richard, 93
Scott, Hugh, 108–109
Scud missiles, 202, 206
SDI (Strategic Defense Initiative), 155,
    158–161
Securities and Exchange Commission
    (SEC), 83, 128
Senate Appropriations Committee, 71
Senate Armed Services Committee, 11–12,
    71
Senate Committee Investigating National
    Defense Programs, 52
Senate Debate, Lockheed bailout, 108–114
    See also Bailout, Lockheed
Senate, F-22 Raptor fighter plane and,
    2–3, 12–14
Senate Special Committee to Investigate
    the Manufacture and Sale of Arms
    and Other War Munitions (Nye
    Commission), 43–44
Senate Subcommittee on Interstate and
    Foreign Commerce, 56–57
September 11, 2001, terrorist attacks
    boom in military spending after, 187
    F-22 Raptor fighter plane and, 7–8, 18
    rebuilding of Coast Guard after,
    239–243
Shah of Iran, 135
Shaheen, Jeanne, 17–18
Shakespeare in Charge (Augustine and
    Adelman), 165
Shelley, Dan, 181–182, 183
Shibleh, Ramy, 233
Ships, 24, 68, 239–243
Shorrock, Tim, 218–219, 220
Shultz, George, 134, 156, 159
SIEP (Structural Information
    Enhancement Program), 146
Sikorsky Helicopter Company, 26–27, 28
Sirius plane (modified version of Vega), 37
Skoda Works, 46
"Skunk Works" (Lockheed division),
    61–62
Sloyan, Patrick, 171
Smith, Gene, 101
Smith, Margaret Chase, 92
Smith, Robert, 199

Smith, Roger, 121, 122, 123
Socialist Party, 130
Soft power, 223–230
Somali pirates, 15
Southern California Council of State
    Chambers of Commerce, 52–53
Soviet ICBM (intercontinental ballistic
    missile), 64
Soviet Union
    collapse of, 166–167
    CPD and, 133–135
    former satellite states of, 193–194
    Reagan's fears of being second to,
        154–155
    U-2 spy planes and, 60–61, 62–65
Space programs, 155, 156, 157–161, 235,
    237–238
Space-Based Infrared Sensor (SBIRS), 236
Spare parts scandals. *See* Overpricing of
    military parts
Special Projects Office (SPO), 66, 67
Spending. *See* Military spending; Money;
    Tax money
Spies for Hire (Shorrock), 218–219
"Sport Biplane" (S-1), 36
Sputnik satellite, 65, 166
Spy planes, 62–63
Spying with surveillance, 221–222
Squier, Carl B., 39–40
St. Louis Post-Dispatch, 154
St. Louis University, 146
Stadler, Rich, 142
"Star Wars" project, 155, 156, 157–161
"Stardust" vehicle, 238
Stearman-Varney, 38–39
Stefanowicz, Steven, 215
Stennis, John, 76, 91
Stevens, Robert, 9–10, 186, 249
Stevens, Robert J., 223
Stevenson, Adlai III, 109–110
Stiglitz, Joseph, 212–213
Stocks, Lockheed, 18, 54, 68, 83
Stockton, Peter, 76, 83, 99, 143
Stone, D. D., 124–125
Stonechipher, Harry, 7
Strategic Defense Initiative (SDI), 155,
    158–161
Strategic Influence Alternatives, 222

Strategic Studies Institute, 227–228
Strauss, Franz-Josef, 119–120
Strickland, Ted, 2–3
Structural Information Enhancement
    Program (SIEP), 146
Subcommittee on Economy and Efficiency
    in Government, 147–148
Subcommittee on Multinational
    Corporations, 121–122, 127
Submarine-launched ballistic missiles
    (SLBMs), 65–68, 134–136, 156
Subsidies, 52–54, 55–56, 57–59, 172–175
    See also Money
Sudan, 225
Sultan, Prince, 126
Super Electra plane, 43
    See also Electra transport plane; Hudson
    bombers
Supersonic transport plane (SST), 96
Surveillance projects, 221–222, 246–247,
    248–249
Swayne, George, 47–48
Swine flu vaccinations, 9
Switzerland, 120
Sytex Corporation, 217

Taft, Robert IV, 113
Taguba, Antonio, 215
Tah, Christiana, 228
Talmadge, Herman, 94, 113
TALON. *See* Threat and Local
    Observation Notice (TALON)
Tanaka, Kakuei, 116, 117–118, 130
Tanassi, Mario, 130
Tanner, Bruce L., 9
Tanton, Bruce, 246
Taiwan, 230–231
Tax money
    F-16 combat aircraft, 178–180
    Lockheed Martin and government, 3
    and Lockheed Martin as nation's largest
        military contractor, 28–29
    Lockheed–Martin Marietta merger
        subsidized by government and,
        173–174
    Lockheed's waste with, 88–89
    for Raptor fighter plane, 1–2, 5–6
    See also Military spending; Money

Taxpayers for Common Sense, 13, 16
Taylor, David W., 34
Teal Group, 177–178
Team B panel, 134
Technology Strategies Alliances (TSA), 171
Teets, Peter B., 192
Tellep, Daniel, 168
Teller, Edward, 157–158
Texas, privatizing of welfare services in, 181–187
Texas State Employees Union (TSEU), 183, 184, 184–185
Texas Workforce Commission, 183
Thailand, 78
Theater High-Altitude Area Defense (THAAD) antimissile system, 16–17, 236, 237
Thierot, Ferdinand, 33
Thompson, Loren, 23–24
Threat and Local Observation Notice (TALON), 220–221
Threlfal, Roger, 175
Thurmond, Strom, 221
TIES (Texas Integrated Enrollment System), 182, 183–184
Time magazine, 68, 129
Tinker Air Force Base, OK, 137
Titan Corporation, 215–217
Today Show (NBC), 140
Toilet pans, 143
Toilet seat, $600, 136–137, 140–142, 185
Tonight Show, The, 140
Top-secret departments. *See* "Skunk Works" (Lockheed division)
Torture, 215–216
Total Information Awareness (TIA), 220
Total package procurement (TPP), 73–75, 99–100
Transportation Security Agency (TSA), 243
Transportation Worker Identification Credential (TWIC), 244
Travis Air Force Base, CA, 138–139
Trident (SLBM), 135–136, 156, 181, 207
Tristar program. *See* L-1011 Tristar airliner
Truman Doctrine, 59
Truman, Harry, 55, 59

Turkey, 123–124, 230, 231
TWA, 54, 114
Twin-engine fighters, 48–49

U-2 spy plane, 60–61, 62–65, 67–68
U.N. Security Council, 197–198
United Auto Workers (UAW) union, 41, 111
United Kingdom, 19, 21, 22, 26, 46–48
United Nations (UN), 225–226
United States Institute of Peace (USIP), 222–223
United States Postal Service (USPS), 42, 246
United Technologies Corporation, 26
Unmanned aerial vehicles (UAVs), 8, 248–249
U.S. Air Force. *See* Air Force
U.S. Army, 5, 6, 34, 102, 222
U.S. census, 244, 245–246
U.S. Committee to Expand NATO, 197, 198
U.S. Marines, 19, 22, 188
U.S. Navy, 15, 33, 40, 54–55, 65–68, 138
U.S. soldiers, cluster bombs and, 234–235
USA Today, 3

V-22 aircraft (Boeing), 188
Vaccinations, swine flu, 9
Van Cleave, William, 134
Vanity Fair magazine, 211–212
Vega (first plane of Lockheed Aircraft Corporation), 36–37, 38–39
Vehicles of the Air (Loughead, Victor), 32
Verified Identity Pass (VIP), 244
VH-71 presidential helicopter, 25–28
"Victory Is Possible" (Payne), 204
Vietnam War
    decline in military spending after, 133
    PAE services during, 224–225
    Pentagon budget levels and, 63
    pressure on U.S. military transport systems by, 69, 70
    wing fix issue in overpricing scandals, 147
"Vilnius Ten," 197
Volman, Daniel, 227
VuGraph briefing, C-5A Galaxy, 75

Wages. *See* Jobs
Waite, Preston J., 245
Wall Street, 46, 54, 186
Wall Street Journal, 7, 55, 221, 224, 225
War Department, 49–50
Washington, D.C., elite of, 13, 14
Washington Post, 1, 84, 87, 140, 153, 201
Washington Post cartoons, 136–137, 140
Watergate scandal, 129, 132
Way Out There in the Blue (Fitzgerald), 157
Wayne, Leslie, 196–197
Weapons exports, 178–180, 230,
    232–235
Weapons of mass destruction, Saddam
    Hussein and, 191, 197–198, 206–207,
    210, 211–212
Webb, James, 213–214
Weber, Vin, 191
Weicker, Lowell, 109
Weinberger, Caspar, 135, 136–137, 139,
    157
Weiner, Tim, 194
Weisbrod, Hubert, 120, 121, 122
Weldon, Curt, 199, 200
Welfare services, privatizing, 181–187
Westinghouse, 66
Westmoreland, William, 102

Whistle-blowers, 86–87, 139, 221
    See also Fitzgerald, A. Ernest
"Whiz Kids, the," 73
"Why We Spy on Our Allies" (Woolsey),
    221
Wilkins, George, 37
Wilson, T., 152
Wilson, William R., 97–98
Wing fix issue, overpricing scandal,
    145–147
Wolfowitz, Paul, 134, 191, 208, 210,
    211–212
Woolsey, R. James, 211, 221
World War I, 33–36, 44
World War II, 38, 40, 49–50, 51–55, 55–56
World War III, 56
World Wildlife Fund, 122, 131
Wright, Orville and Wilbur, 31

X-32 (Boeing design), 21
X-35 (Lockheed Martin design), 21
XP-900 fighter plane, 38

Young, Andrew, 151

Zenishek, Steven, 219–220
"Zero Overpricing Program," 139